D1010774

Films *of*
Endearment

Films *of* Endearment

Films *of* Endearment

A Mother, a Son and the '80s Films That Defined Us

MICHAEL KORESKY

HANOVER
SQUARE
PRESS

HANOVER
SQUARE
PRESS™

Recycling programs
for this product may
not exist in your area.

ISBN-13: 978-1-335-77379-1

Films of Endearment: A Mother, a Son and the '80s Films That Defined Us

This edition published by arrangement with Harlequin Books S.A.

Library of Congress Cataloging-in-Publication Data has been applied for.

Hanover Square Press
22 Adelaide St. West, 40th Floor
Toronto, Ontario M5H 4E3, Canada
HanoverSqPress.com
BookClubbish.com

Printed in U.S.A.

For my dad

Films *of* Endearment

Introduction:
Home Movies

"You must be tired." It's the first thing she says when I get off the bus. Every time. It's usually quickly followed by another statement: "You must be hungry."

Parents have a lot of "musts" to give, a lot to project onto their children's moods, wants, and needs. My mother is not wrong: I'm usually both tired and hungry after the four-and-a-half-hour bus ride from New York to Newton, the Boston suburb where she picks me up. She then drives me to Chelmsford, the much smaller Massachusetts town where I grew up and where she still lives. My dad, who loved driving and adored cars with the fervency of a heartsick romantic, used to be the one to pick me up; this is never out of my mind as she and I ride back home.

We pull off the highway into Chelmsford, and a sense of calm washes over me. The anxiety and intensity of New York are gone for the moment; they belong to someone else, that adult who lives back in that big, ugly-beautiful city, who scoffed at endless subway delays, who rushed across sidewalks before the walk sign's timer runs out, who gritted his teeth in agony as the person next to him on public transportation played his music too loud.

It's been an extended period since I was last home, so my mom talks the whole ride, making up for lost time. The latest news about family and friends and neighbors, information about any upcoming singing gigs she has scheduled, what new TV shows she's watching, what she's recently rented from Netflix—yes, she still rents the discs. As do I.

As we drive on from the town's center, the neighborhoods grow denser, the houses get smaller, the trees more plentiful. We turn onto winding Walnut Road, with its forty-two houses, all built on suburban tracts in the fifties; our modest house sits in the middle, where the street crooks off at a ninety-degree angle—approaching first-time drivers wrongly assume it's a dead end. I still call it "our" house; it's the house I grew up in, the only house I've ever lived in. It's been painted sky blue for many years, but this surprises me every time. I always think of it as russet brown. The driveway is wide enough to welcome two cars, but there's only one car now.

We've made it inside. Safe. The house seems to live and breathe, a being unto itself. I notice little biological changes to its lifeblood with each visit: a recently added I HEART My Grand-Dogs magnet on the fridge, or a Life Is Short… Eat Cookies plaque on the wall, or a differently colored teakettle on the stove. This time, there's a plush new carpet running up the staircase that leads to the second floor, the site of my bedroom growing up, where I now dump my travel bags. Though it's technically been remade as a guest room, many of my childhood treasures line the shelves that are built into the walls: my *70 Years of the Oscar* and *The Films of the Eighties* coffee table tomes and Pauline Kael and Japanese cinema volumes; my Chris Van Allsburg picture books (my favorite was the rigorously ambiguous *The Mysteries of Harris Burdick*, each of its stories boiled down to one sentence and an unsettling illustration); my improbable

Bram Stoker's Dracula souvenir mug. Upon a recent trip I discover in my room a creaky wooden jewelry box full of movie-theater stubs from the nineties. I didn't realize my mother kept them for me; with dates, titles, and cinema names they provide a road map to my entire Massachusetts movie-going experience as a kid.

A light lunch has been prepared, probably a tuna salad or tabbouleh with pita bread. If it's fall or winter, we eat in the more formal dining room, as we do now; if spring or summer, hopefully on the screened-in porch, so we can feel the breeze and see the branches of the oak trees sway. It used to not have screens; it started out as a deck, which my dad built with his own two hands when I was almost five. The foundation has remained strong and has supported the family for decades.

It's usually a Saturday when I first get in to Chelmsford, so without too much work to do, I have time, even hours, to talk, to catch up with her. Lunch chatter is full of digressions: how my husband, Chris, is doing and how hard he's working running an arts nonprofit back in New York (*hard*); updates about our dog, Lucy, and my mom's cat, Daisy (both sweet, no surprises); if there's anything I need to know about my mom's health (broken wrist or a locked-up knee or her heart arrhythmia). We move on to more important topics, like what books we're reading or TV shows we're watching. Then the most important topic of all: What movie are we going to watch tonight?

Obsession is entirely the wrong word to describe the way Leslie and I talk about movies. Rather, they're a way of life, a totalizing force that informs our experiences and interactions. When you love movies so desperately, you see the world differently through them and because of them. And you return to them, because movies change as we change, grow as we grow, friends that reveal new facets with every viewing. And like friends, sometimes they can betray you, reveal themselves to be not as caring, not as sensitive, not as sophisticated, as you once thought—though this can never completely change the affection, the love, you once felt for them.

My mother instilled this love. My father, Bobby, enjoyed movies, too, as does my older brother, Jonathan, but not to the same level that my mother and I do, not as emotional, moral, and aesthetic inspiration. I was destined to take that love to yet another height. After I spent a childhood watching movies—and watching them, and watching them, and then watching them again—they would become my profession: writing about movies, talking about them, researching them, editing other people's writing about them, making them. Through my work at such institutions as Museum of the Moving Image, The Criterion Collection, Film at Lincoln Center, and the legendary-to-cinephiles *Film Comment* magazine, I have been privileged to get close to the world of movie love, to spread its gospel, and to learn more about film than I ever knew there was to learn.

It's difficult to imagine I would have had the same feeling of idolatry toward cinema if not for my mother, who taught me from an early age that movies were not just entertainment. We both view movies as an essential art form, and this is reflective of a rare emotional and intellectual symbiosis that can make our familial bond seem more like a friendship. Art can nourish one's soul, but it can also encourage shared values and mutual trust—and, perhaps most importantly, it can challenge us to think past our presumptions about what is right and what is wrong, what is good and what is bad. Art, even popular art like film, engenders the kind of nuance that is missing from our daily news briefings, our politics, our personal crusades. Art also creates a form of communication, gives us the chance to talk about things we may not be as open or willing to talk about as they apply to "real life."

I have long suspected that having this attachment with my mother made coming out of the closet in my early twenties easier than it might have been, and easier than it must be for many others—even though nothing so emotionally loaded as revealing one's true self can ever be easy. Without movies, who knows where or who I'd be.

Movies taught us both to look at the world with a humane curiosity. The emergence of my truer self seemed to converge rather than conflict with her needs as a parent. The relationship between a mother and her gay son comes with its own strange ligature, after all. The bond is strong, formed by millions of indefinable tiny molecular and cultural determinants. It's unbreakable, mysterious, bone-deep. It's also reliant on a kind of willful ignorance: a sense that we know each other so ineffably well that we have no need to dig deeper, to fully understand one another as individuals making their way through the world alone. In a way, queerness—which exists in interdependence and conflict with the long-held structures of the heteronormative world—necessarily keeps such a parent-child relationship at a remove. But that should never stop us from looking for and at one another.

So much of what I have long known about my mother is from anecdotes connected to movies. I know she busted open her mother's piggy bank in 1959 to steal enough pennies to go see *Ben-Hur* for the second time—and got caught. I know that on her first date with my father in 1968, while eating dinner before seeing Barbra Streisand's much-anticipated movie debut in *Funny Girl*, she spilled an entire plate of steak tips and gravy onto her pale pink dress—and proceeded to hide the dress in the closet from her mother. I know that in 1982, when I was three, she and my father went out with friends to see the horror movie *Poltergeist*—which features an infamous scene in which a man rips big fleshy chunks of skin off his own face—and made the near-fatal mistake of tucking into a big pepperoni pizza dinner beforehand.

It was only when my mother turned seventy, and I was on the cusp of forty, that I realized I wanted to know more.

Her husband of forty-one years, my father, had died seven years before. He had early-onset Alzheimer's, his mind first showing signs of decline in his midfifties, when I was still in college. He was so young when he got sick, and the nature of his disease was so prolonged, that I never had the chance to truly get to know him, one adult to another. Stories I have heard from his past remained hazy. Of course I can remember him vividly as a dad, as the jovial traveling salesman who helped raise two sons, but the person—the human being independent of his parenthood status—is an abstraction, an amalgam of secondhand information.

My determination to never let that happen with my mother came because of movies. Of course it did.

One chilly October night in 2018, while I was visiting home, the two of us were in the dining room, eating takeout from the preferred Cantonese-American restaurant of my youth, the amusingly, dubiously named Hong & Kong. Unhealthy fried delights scattered the table. She was nibbling, I was devouring; I used chopsticks, my mother a fork. A merlot was uncorked. There have been few simpler pleasures in life than opening a bottle of wine—a single glass for her, more than that for me—and talking at the dining room table with her as evening gives way to night. These days, alone together in that house, as the shadows outside grow long, it can feel like we're the only ones in the world.

Dinner conversation turned, as it always does, to movies. Leslie is always thrilled to animatedly express disgust at the latest aging actress who has noticeably had "work done," or to sing the praises of some Jennifer Aniston rom-com she's watched for the seventh time—but she's also apt to rummage through her cinematic past with meditative rigor. We started discussing films she grew up with, talking about the differences between

distinct movie eras. Out of curiosity, I asked her which decade
stands out as her favorite.

"The eighties," she responded, barely missing a beat, before
taking a sip of wine.

I fully expected my mother, who was born in 1948, to respond that the 1950s were her personal favorite. After all, that
was the first full decade of her life, and the one in which she
was introduced to the movies—an era of widescreen epics and
glamorous movie stars in full Technicolor. Also I knew many of
her favorites are from that epochal stretch of American moviemaking, from *Singin' in the Rain* (which her mother took her to
see when she was four) to *The Ten Commandments* (a corny epic
today, but a special-effects marvel then) to *Some Like It Hot*. Or
I might have guessed she'd pick the 1960s, because that's when
she was in high school and college; when she opposed the Vietnam War, started hating Nixon, fell in love with my father, and
saw *The Sound of Music*, *The Graduate*, *Funny Girl*, and *Rosemary's Baby*, none of which have ever left her. Or perhaps she'd
go further back, to the 1940s, because, well, *it's the 1940s*, when
Golden Age Hollywood was at its incontestable height; when
Bette Davis and Gregory Peck and James Stewart and Ingrid
Bergman and Claude Rains and Rita Hayworth were doing
most of their greatest work; when "talkies" were not even two
decades old, but cinematography, sound, and performance style
were working in complete tandem to create a perfect world unto
itself, the "Dream Factory" at its dreamiest.

That she immediately seized upon the 1980s came as a surprise. I asked her why this decade, which is not generally re-
garded as a high-water mark for the art of cinema, especially in
the US, and which is perhaps cited more by today's nostalgia-
drenched thirty- and forty-somethings, continues to capture her
imagination. She replied, with almost teary eyes, that this was
the first full decade of being a mother and raising young children. It was also when we first bought a VCR and she was able

to watch movies whenever she wanted—a true revelation, we shouldn't forget. More importantly, she could also share them with her family. "One of my great joys," she told me, "was going to the video store every Friday night and picking up a stack of movies for the weekend."

I remember these trips with longing, especially now that video stores have gone the way of the dodo. Our town's stores came and went over the years, and had ridiculous, grandiose names—Video *Paradise*, Video *Thunder*—but going to each was for me a constant thrill. The already fading brown carpet, the vaguely musty smell of videocassette tape, the blue-and-yellow microwave popcorn tubs offered as last-minute impulse buys, the rows and rows of enticing movie boxes, everything designated so succinctly: the sought-after new releases you were lucky to grab, the older comedies, dramas, horror and sci-fi movies— not to mention that creepy back room I was never allowed to enter. It was all possibility. Somewhere in that store was something that could potentially change my life. And often all I had to do was hold a box up to my mother and ask her what it was. She almost always knew.

I realized this dinner discussion was making her wistful, so I changed the subject. I often do that when something seems like it's getting too intimate. I'm all too willing to give myself over to movies that I know will be emotionally difficult; for me, crying at movies is one of life's great catharses. Yet I would rather avoid such confrontations in life. Who needs an overdose of reality when you can vicariously experience a fictional character's pain?

It was only from this conversation with my mother that I started to really think about the parallel paths of our lives and how those paths converge in revelation. There are many ways our experiences feel connected across decades, most dramatically that her father died when she was twenty-eight—a year after my older brother was born—and my father died when I was thirty-two, forever changing the landscapes of our lives at crucial points in our adulthood. But here I realized something else: her self-realization as a mother and the burgeoning of my self-awareness as a child were inextricably tied to movies, and how she taught me about the world, herself, myself, through their images.

I was born at the tail end of the 1970s, so the 1980s *were* my childhood, and remain a time of intense nostalgia, eliciting in me a mild kind of homesickness. The sense memories linger: seeing *E.T. the Extra-Terrestrial*, *The Muppets Take Manhattan*, and rereleases of Disney's *Cinderella* and *Fantasia* in the thrillingly stygian caves that were the theaters of Chelmsford's now demolished Route 3 Cinema multiplex; endlessly rewatching my very own VHS copies of *Poltergeist* and *Gremlins* and *Ferris Bueller's Day Off*; ordering *The Color Purple* and *Raising Arizona* and *The Lady in White* from our cable network's pay-per-view service and recording (and, yes, endlessly rewatching) them; reading *Premiere*, my first movie magazine subscription, and a thoughtful gift from Uncle Ric, my dad's brother in faraway Ohio. I would indiscriminately tear movie ads from *Premiere*'s pages and staple them to my bedroom wall like some crazed lovelorn teen. Beyond movies, the decade was my first everything: kindergarten and grade school, riding a bicycle and learning how to play piano, making and losing friends, feeling crushes and experiencing disappointments. First feeling uncomfortable in my own skin, and realizing that I didn't conform to the standards of masculinity that everyone—and every film—seemed determined to reaffirm.

When considering the 1980s, many would likely conjure pictures of John Hughes teen comedies or perhaps the muscular actioners that became so central to this most testosterone-fueled era of moviemaking: Schwarzenegger and Stallone, Bruce Willis, Jean-Claude Van Damme, Chuck Norris, Steven Seagal.

Some of those films, like *Sudden Impact*, *Die Hard*, and *The Terminator*, were certainly in rotation in our house, mostly thanks to my brother.

Four years older, Jonathan retains an enthusiasm and glee for movies almost as pronounced as mine, perhaps just a little more savage. While I have distinct recollections of us enjoying many of the same movies, his recurring video picks tended toward the übermale. Lucky for him the swaggering Reagan eighties offered no shortage of cinematic bravado. Hardly immune to the pleasures of a well-choreographed car chase or perfectly orchestrated explosion, I would often join him in these viewings, yet these films implicitly articulated some of the clear differences between us, between the rougher-hewn, macho son and his milder, perhaps more effeminate, and certainly more hyperactive younger brother. I was the kid who preferred to play with girls, who enjoyed being alone in his room. He loved to pummel me in the video game *Street Fighter*; I was more susceptible to the mild charms of *Sonic the Hedgehog*. He liked Metallica; I liked Janet Jackson. He went outside and skateboarded; I barricaded myself in my room and wrote movie reviews.

This is not to say that my brother's taste in movies is bad, or even necessarily strictly in opposition to mine. For example, as much as the next guy, I enjoy the brilliant social satire of *Robocop*, which features a man getting slammed into by a car and exploding after being dunked in toxic waste. Yet I never felt genuinely connected to movies that gave off even the slightest whiff of self-sufficient testosterone. The films that most defined the decade for my mother and me were primarily about and starring women, movies that put their emotional inner lives front and center, movies that seemed to exist so that viewers could glean a greater understanding of another human perspective.

We have long heard the refrain that "there are not enough good roles for women" in American film. This has only become truer as the years have passed. Throughout the 21st century, superhero movies all but overtook our multiplexes, monopolizing a culture geared toward teenage boys and a largely male adult viewership that has been willingly infantilized by risk-averse studios intent on working only from bankable franchises. Looking back, the 1980s feels like a lost paradise. At this time, there had been no shortage of formidable female actors commanding strong leading roles. Women were being given—and in some cases, as producers, giving themselves—multifaceted, headlining parts that weren't merely doting wives or girlfriends, and often acting alongside other women with strong star personas of their own.

The list of these stars is long: the eclectic Meryl Streep, the regal Sigourney Weaver (who created her own brand of muscle-bound action hero in *Aliens*), the homegrown Sissy Spacek, the literate Glenn Close, the nimble Whoopi Goldberg, the brainy Kathleen Turner, the idiosyncratic Debra Winger, the earthy Jessica Lange, the indomitable Sally Field, the no-nonsense Cher, the kinky Geena Davis, the fiery Holly Hunter, the mercurial Michelle Pfeiffer. The names go on to include stars who built upon the inroads they had made in the 1970s to remain top-billed actors throughout the 1980s, like Diane Keaton, Jodie Foster, and Susan Sarandon. Most of them were in their thirties and forties without being forced to succumb to matronly, desexualized roles, choosing parts that were full, rich, complex, and frequently politically engaged.

The films they headlined were midbudget studio films, which existed somewhere between the major blockbusters that were redefining the business—sly, winking entertainments like *Ghostbusters* and *Back to the Future*—and the emerging independent film movement heralded by such mavericks as Jim Jarmusch and Spike Lee. These were movies from which the studio could expect a good enough return on their investment: stories about families and relationships, melodramas and period pictures concerned with the nuances and delicacies of social behavior. Strict cinephiles today might denigrate many of these films as "middlebrow," a category that has now all but disappeared from studio lineups. Indeed, many of these films, whose dramatic tensions pivot on the interaction between adults, now seem like rare beasts. Such films were almost always directed by men, although there were the occasional exceptions: Barbra Streisand's *Yentl*; Randa Haines's *Children of a Lesser God* with Marlee Matlin; Joan Micklin Silver's *Crossing Delancey* with Amy Irving. Nevertheless, even in this male-dominated industry, the force of their stars shone through, and these leading women became their own brands of auteur.

Little did I know at the time that the stars of these movies were benefactors of the battles of second-wave feminists from the previous decade, during which Jane Fonda, Ellen Burstyn, and Jill Clayburgh had been trailblazers, starring in films that tackled chauvinism, discrimination, and inequality head-on. Nevertheless, these were few and far between, and with the rarest of exceptions—such as Diahann Carroll, Cicely Tyson, and Pam Grier—were always white women. The hallowed 1970s American cinema, typified by such films as *The Godfather*, *Five Easy Pieces*, *Chinatown*, and *Taxi Driver*, was undoubtedly a masculine one, with a meager amount of substantial roles for women. That this changed so much in Reagan's eighties suggests that the political discourse of white mainstream culture that controlled Hollywood had moved away from the tragedy of Vietnam and the disillusionment of Watergate and over to more domestic battlegrounds—spaces more commonly considered "feminine"—taking in the economic recession, the spiking divorce rate, and the industrial and agricultural depressions. A new wave of melodramas with an urgent political backdrop emerged, and following the example of 1979's *Norma Rae*, starring an Oscar-winning Sally Field, many of them were fronted by strong female stars, playing undaunted women blazing their own trails. There were also more period pieces set in the not-so-distant American past, such as *Frances*, *Yentl*, *Places in the Heart*, and *The Color Purple*, which focused predominantly on the struggles of women to survive within patriarchal systems that had no dignified place for them. The actresses who played these parts were often socially engaged performers aware of their own power and the significance of their positions.

These were women to whom my mother felt a palpable kinship, and these were also women I looked up to. Surely not incidental to my quite strong feelings of identification with these women (though I wouldn't have known at the time) was my own incipient homosexuality. While mainstream cinema today could hardly be called a gay paradise, back in the eighties gay representation was practically nonexistent, and whatever there was remained inaccessible to a child. There were very few sympathetic gay male characters in the films that penetrated my home, no one to model myself on. As a result, my identification and attraction was displaced onto women, a kind of presexual yearning. When watching *Dirty Dancing*—which, as a kid, I must have seen as many times as I brushed my teeth—I was not lusting after Patrick Swayze, but obsessing over Jennifer Grey's take-no-shit boldness, her drive to get what she wanted. I kept returning to *Adventures in Babysitting* because I was passionately attracted to Elisabeth Shue, for her beauty, but also for her maternal teen bossiness.

I found not only their femininity appealing but also their strength. She may not even have known it, but my mother was teaching me the importance of fortitude. In identifying with these women on-screen, I was implicitly positioning myself against the accepted ideas of what and who a young boy was supposed to be. Coming of age during such a period, I had no reason to assume that women didn't have all the power. Likewise, growing up in a home where my mother was the literate one, the one who all but devoured her endlessly expanding collection of books that barely fit on our already copious shelves, and who actively engaged with the cultural events and objects we took in, women seemed to be in control over the artistic, intellectual, and emotional life of everything we experienced. My father went to work every day; he came home exhausted, read the paper, and drank a beer. There was never any doubt that he cared deeply for me, and that he tried to engage in some of the things that I liked. But it was like he was seeing my life and interests through a glass partition, a distance that unintentionally reaffirmed a disconnection that I had implicitly begun to read as male. With my mother, there was a full-bore immersion into a cultural life outside the home, as though she shone a spotlight on whatever she found interesting at any given moment.

The maternal influence over how I watched and understood movies was clear and pronounced, and not just because she preferred, recommended, and brought home movies starring strong women. By projecting myself onto the strengths and struggles of female characters and stars, I was grasping on to something that I couldn't find in *Rambo* or *Die Hard*: an implicit need to be heard in a noisy universe, and the tools to cut *through* the noise rather than contribute to it. These movies were reflecting shifts in the culture as much as shifts in my own realization of the world. For me, it was the Decade of the Actress, and I don't believe the American movie industry has seen anything like it since.

Even Molly Haskell seemed to agree with me that there was something special about women on-screen in this otherwise politically regressive, reactionary decade. One of the most important film critics of the 20th century, Haskell wrote for *The Village Voice*, *New York* magazine, and *Vogue*, and her landmark 1974 book *From Reverence to Rape: The Treatment of Women in the Movies* is an essential text for anyone who wants to understand the alternating currents of misogyny and empowerment that have followed female stars and characters throughout Hollywood history. If my mother taught me about women's place and prominence indirectly, Molly Haskell taught me about women's centrality and mistreatment directly, through her carefully crafted and researched books and essays.

"In the 1970s, women were speaking the language of liberation, but they were still trying to get out of old roles and didn't know where to go from there," Haskell told me, during a visit in her sunlight-drenched, book-lined Upper East Side apartment she had shared for decades with her late husband, the also legendary film critic Andrew Sarris. "By the eighties, there's a kind of empowerment; they just have a confidence they didn't have, I think. And there were just more roles for them. I think the eighties is a time when they were being listened to, and carving out idiosyncratic spaces."

Leslie Stone was born in 1948, nearly thirty years before me, and she grew up in Boston in the 1950s. Regularly taken to the cinema by her mother, Bertha, she was swept away by Audrey Hepburn in romantic comedies like *Roman Holiday* and *Sabrina*, by Leslie Caron in musicals like *Lili* and *Gigi*, and by Elizabeth Taylor in adult dramas like *Giant* and *Suddenly Last Summer*. Regardless of the much-theorized social and political repression of the era, reflected today in clichéd images of subservient women in strictly domestic, homemaking spaces, representations of female indomitability were nevertheless imprinted upon her. For Leslie, it was actresses such as Hepburn, Caron, and Taylor, as well as Natalie Wood, Debbie Reynolds, Jean Simmons, Joanne Woodward, and Deborah Kerr, that helped define her sense of self. Moreover, movies were an escape from her volatile and itinerant childhood. Despite the trauma of her emotionally erratic home life, she and my grandmother, also a lifelong film fanatic, would bond at the movies. Sometimes Bertha would even let Leslie skip school so she could accompany her to one of the many Boston-area theaters that today light up my mother's memory with intense longing.

When my mother was a teenager, she enrolled in an art appreciation course that was part of her regular curriculum. Though she never went on to a career in the arts, the class proved to be deeply influential. Lessons on Matisse and Picasso, on French impressionism, pointillism, and modern abstract expressionism, on 20th-century modernist architects like Frank Lloyd Wright, were interspersed with presentations of films. She would tell me about this class when I was a kid, but only later did I realize how remarkable this was in the mid-1960s, years before film studies courses were in vogue even in American universities.

This class has long been a source of fascination for me, an apocryphal story of artistic discovery. I have often asked her about the nearly mythic figure of her middle-aged teacher from Newton High, so ahead of the curve, imparting wisdom and knowledge about *The Cabinet of Dr. Caligari* and *Citizen Kane* at a time when few movie-lovers, let alone art instructors, would even have had the basic language to discuss them. "There was no such thing as video yet, so he must have been shown the movies on 16mm projection," I marvel to my mother one night.

"Mr. Schmidt," she recalls his name, though quizzically. A couple minutes later, eureka: "No, it was Mr. *Schultz*!" We went flipping through her high school yearbook—the one I desecrated as a child by scrawling the word *MOM* across my mother's senior class photo—looking for a picture of Mr. Schultz, but to no avail. He only exists in her memory now. Aptly for something recalled with such haziness, the course was taught in the basement; she remembers walking through cement corridors with exposed pipes. Nevertheless, it opened up a new world for her—and, decades later, for me.

Without even knowing she was doing it, Leslie would pass on to me a seriousness of intent, a tacit instruction to look at a film as more than just a couple hours of story-driven entertainment. One forgets how resistant many people are to this idea in our culture, in which a movie is most often talked about in terms of box-office performance, like a gleaming product off the assembly line destined to either "work" or not, like a toaster. Under her influence, I remember trying to look deeper into movies at an early age. I remember chastising other kids in kindergarten when they called Walt Disney's *Fantasia* "boring" because it "had no story." I'm sure I was wildly irritating. I remember when she sat me down to watch *2001: A Space Odyssey* on VHS at age seven it was with the understanding that I would be witnessing *art*. Despite what I would now call an unreasonably small screen on which to watch Stanley Kubrick's mind- and eye-expanding masterpiece, I was swept away and deeply moved. When the film ended, when the Star Child's expectant, impassive face filled up the screen, waiting to return to Earth for some unknown but clearly important reason, my eyes welled up with tears. Tears at the sheer power of art to move something inside you, something you can't touch or explain.

Movies themselves thus had a maternal air cast over them. This could not, of course, produce a full alchemy in which the masculinist film historical narratives we all grew up with—in which men became heroes of mythic proportion and women were supportive at best, subservient and abused at worst—were somehow reversed. But for this gay kid growing up in suburban Massachusetts, it allowed movies to be a wondrous, warm, feminine space in which I could glean an emotional understanding of the world. Throughout my childhood, before I struck out on my own as a rabid cinephile, I wanted to see everything she had seen. I would open the hardcover Oscar book she got me as a Hanukkah present at age eight, go page by page and quiz her on all the classic films listed—not just obvious ones like *Casablanca* and *An American in Paris*, but movies with more exotic, enticing titles: *Leave Her to Heaven, The Valley of Decision, Johnny Belinda, The Snake Pit, Splendor in the Grass, La Dolce Vita, Love with the Proper Stranger, The Prime of Miss Jean Brodie, The Garden of the Finzi-Continis, Days of Heaven.* Perhaps one day I would actually see these movies, but for now it was enough that *she* had. An entire history was slowly coming into focus.

The eighties, then, were for me an era of absorption, taking it all in—to borrow a phrase from the critic Pauline Kael—in a steady, mostly unthinking stream. Later I would become too opinionated about movies to be quite so open-minded. Even in my teen years, even on glorious summer days, when watching movies all alone, up in my room, lonely and hermitized with my weekly stack of videotapes from local libraries, I was often seeing films through my mother's eyes, implicitly understanding them and their situations as projections of her own thoughts, wishes, and fears. Paired with the inherent loneliness and solitude of cinephilia, of the need to retreat into a safe space untouched by the masculine cruelties of daily life, I now see it as the gradual creation of a refracted queer consciousness.

As she approached middle age, and I was graduating college in New York, things changed drastically for her and all of us with my father's diagnosis of early-onset Alzheimer's. The painful, decade-long process, leading to his death in 2011, changed us all immeasurably; acting as his primary caretaker, she struggled with his sickness more than any of us. Throughout all this, my mother and I never stopped watching and talking about movies: old and new, good and bad, inspiring and depressing. Only later did I realize how much we needed movies, and though she never said it to me, what a persistent source of comfort, what an intellectual and emotional escape, they remained for her. At least through movies we could momentarily forget what was going on and redirect our focus to ideas, characters, images, costumes, performances—*other people's* narratives. Movies speak to our anxieties and despair and say the things we don't. They keep our secrets.

As I helped clear the table, putting the leftover egg rolls and spare ribs in Tupperware, I kept obsessing over what felt, strangely, like a revelation: that *my* movie decade was also somehow her movie decade. I wanted to do the research into my mother's past and present, to seek out things I didn't know or learn more about the things I only thought I knew.

I asked myself, What do I really understand of her life before she was a mother? About her various jobs, both before and after I was born? About the curtailed singing career of her youth? How does she define her political selfhood, and her aspirations and dreams, then and now? I really didn't know very much even about her current life as a widow, living alone with that sweet-faced little cat in that quiet suburban house that once burst with family life.

Conversely, what have I allowed her to really understand about me, about my identity as a gay man now and my struggles as a queer kid growing up in the years before homosexuality was much talked about, if at all, in the home or the culture at large?

There are things we've just never spoken about. However, taking a seat and just asking my mother about her life felt like anathema to me. It's not my way. Movies, in effect, started these conversations, and movies would have to finish them. After all, they provided us with a kind of private language.

Sitting down to make a list of the most important female-driven films of the eighties, I realized that my mother had introduced me to practically all of them, brought into the house on VHS tapes, boxed treasures presented to me with anticipation, intrigue, or foreknowledge. Yes, throughout my childhood, my mother was impressing upon me the importance and centrality of Beethoven and Monet, John Steinbeck and Aretha Franklin, but also Sissy Spacek and Jessica Lange, and why not? For families, movies are totems, passed down through generations, and like relationships, how we perceive films deepens with time.

The more I thought about these female actors, and the films they were in, the more I realized that each could unlock a new facet of my mother's life left too long uninvestigated by me. If

I watched some of these movies again with her, we might open up a new dialogue. I'd also have an excuse to visit more often. I wasn't moving back home—heaven forbid—but I would be coming home more regularly than I had in years, which would have the effect of making me feel like I was journeying back in time.

Thus, over the course of sixteen months, we would rewatch and discuss ten female-driven films from the eighties that were either influential on me or which I knew spoke to her on a deep level. There would be one selection from each year, better to give the proper span of a complete decade. They'd vary in genre and tone, from comedy to tragedy, from low-budget to blockbuster; each reveals an aspect of the era's social mores and industrial realities, as well as new things about my mother's life that I never knew. Some are favorites we've shared many times, others she forgot about after first introducing me to them, and still others are films she has willfully avoided since last seeing them in the eighties. As part of the mission—not quite a *game*, but I like to give myself rules and challenges in my writing—I wouldn't tell her ahead of time each new movie I selected, perhaps all the better to let each marinate as its own specific experience with its own particular emotional contours. The project took on a life of its own, naturally weaving its way into the fabrics of rituals and events: holidays and celebrations, health concerns and worldwide crises.

By exploring and discovering truths about my mother's perspective and interior life I may never have known or seen, I was creating a personal history via a pop cultural one. After all, we often wrestle with movies and their meaning more frequently and willingly than we do our own lives. I once watched these films through this forty-something woman's eyes; what does it mean, in this radically shifted world, to watch them through a seventy-something woman's eyes? And what do I acknowledge about myself now, as a married gay man who has entered his early forties, when I revisit these films through this double lens?

And if I do not have children of my own, will these movies as I know them, as *we* know them, get lost to time? For me, the story of film is the story of a mother and a son, and both the fragile and unbreakable bonds that unite us.

With the house appropriately tidied up—leftovers put away, dishes cleaned, blinds drawn—we finally collapsed on the couch to watch a movie. There's no other way to wrap up a day.

The selection tonight, taken from my mother's ample DVD pile, is one that would naturally fall outside the parameters of the project we would soon embark upon, but which we cannot resist: the great 1944 Vincente Minnelli musical *Meet Me in St. Louis*, which we've shared innumerable times since she first brought it home from the Chelmsford library when I was a child. Its seasons-spanning structure and turn-of-the-century American Midwest milieu have always instilled a kind of impossible nostalgia in me, as has its bustling household of caustic but loving siblings, including, of course, Judy Garland as the love-lorn Esther. Sometimes we watch it for Christmas; other years it feels more apt for Halloween. Also, it might as well be a spring movie. My husband and I have made it into a seasonal tradition as well, carrying on the gospel. No matter when I watch it, its depiction of home is always the same for me: aspirational and overwhelmingly poignant, a place that one needs desperately, but knows they must one day leave. And thanks to Margaret O'Brien's morbidly obsessive "Tootie," there's a healthy undertaste of vinegary perversity to cut the potential for syrupy sweetness. The movie contains everything: the comfort of family, the terror of change, the need for both.

It's a movie that's beyond a movie. It's like dreaming about a place I once lived. When Judy croons "The Boy Next Door," longing for her handsome neighbor John Truitt, my heart stands still; when she sings "Have Yourself a Merry Little Christmas," I feel every Christmas of my life rolled into one. The experience of watching *Meet Me in St. Louis* is like a distillation of what movies do: it contains within it all the experiences of watching it before. The family on-screen, the family on the couch.

It's a movie that is as necessary to our emotional makeup, to who we are as people, as any book we've read, any song we've heard, any person we've known. It's not just an essential work of cinema, it's a crucial piece of *our* cinema. It's inside us.

Here it is again, just like we remembered it, but always more vivid and thrilling than what our memories can evoke. The camera cranes expressively and dazzlingly around the studio backlot designed to look like St. Louis's impossibly perfect Kensington Avenue, a place so magnificently unreal that nothing could be realer. Now we can relax. The movie eases my mother and me into the night, into the past.

1980: Work

"Dumb-witted broads."

It was a phrase that, thankfully, I hadn't heard before. And I may have quickly forgotten it, if not for my mother, who wasn't going to allow such words to pass through the ears of an impressionable six-year-old without letting him know that it was quite a terrible thing to say.

The insult is muttered angrily about two-thirds of the way through 1980's slapstick dark comedy *Nine to Five*. It's directed at the film's triumvirate of sympathetically vengeful heroines, played by Jane Fonda, Dolly Parton, and Lily Tomlin, by their misogynist prick of a boss, Franklin Hart (embodied by the expertly mustachioed Dabney Coleman). At this point, he has been nearly poisoned, fired at with a pistol, kidnapped, tied up, and held hostage in his own house. But at the gendered taunt, Leslie drew a line.

She turned to me on the couch and said, "Michael, that's a really *bad* thing to say."

The movie's centrality to my childhood and its unconscious

shaping of my awareness of the world's gender inequities—
as well as its giddy, endless rewatchability—made it the perfect starting point for the cinematic journey upon which I was
embarking with my mother. The voracious, spongelike minds
of children crave repetition, and *Nine to Five* was one of those
films that, in the ascendant VHS era, I watched over and over,
to the point that I had memorized some of the dialogue (and
certainly Dolly's earworm title track). My mother, on the other
hand, hadn't seen it in decades, possibly not in its entirety since
she first showed it to me.

It was a cold January afternoon when we revisited *Nine to
Five* together for the first time in more than thirty years. Dirt-
caked, iced-over remnants of a snowfall from the previous week
crusted the ground outside, and we could still see white glistening on the frozen, spindly branches of the oaks that surrounded
the family room, a space that gets a lot of natural light. If it's a
movie afternoon, we often have to lower the shades to avoid
sun glare on the television; today it was mercifully overcast. We
clutched mugs of tea. Sometimes we'd supplemented our hot
drinks with a cookie or two; this time I needed a free hand to
scribble into a notebook any thoughts that might come to my
head. I was used to taking notes during screenings for movies
I was going to review, not during the joyous comedies of my
childhood. Would such a film as *Nine to Five* hold up to analy-
sis and scrutiny? What was I really looking for?

One thing I did want to discover: I wondered if my mother
would respond to the "dumb-witted broads" line the way she
had decades ago. As it turned out, she let the scene play without interruption. Perhaps as a man nearing forty, I didn't need
parental guidance.

Afterward, I asked her about that line, and she told me she
didn't remember making a big deal out of it. But it was a big deal
for me. It's fair to say that *Nine to Five* was morally instructive to
me as a prepubescent kid. Its antagonist was repeatedly called a

"sexist, egotistical, lying, hypocritical bigot," and though these words formed a rather pleasant *supercali-fragilistic-expiali-docious-*esque timbre when strung together, I had surely never heard at least four of them before. Nevertheless, they were entirely legible. As I learned the words, I also was learning how not to act, how not to treat others, how not to speak to and about people, and specifically to dare not disrespect women.

Nine to Five was my first exposure to the concept of feminism, years before I would learn more about the socio-historical depths of the term, what the struggle for freedom and equality meant and has continued to mean for women. The office drudgery and marginalization that Fonda's Judy Bernley, Parton's Doralee Rhodes, and Tomlin's Violet Newstead had to overcome in *Nine to Five* told a different story, about the joy of catharsis— of screwing over a boss who was always trying to screw over, or just screw, you. As with all the potent female movie stars my mother presented to me at a young age, she seemed to identify with Fonda, Parton, and, particularly, Tomlin, with her take-no-guff demeanor. I knew nothing of the established personas of these three stars; I just knew they seemed to get what they deserved: a little dignity and a little respect, as Violet triumphantly puts it at one turning point.

I grew up in a household with a dominant maternal figure who voraciously read books *and* kept track of finances *and* did the shopping *and* cooked the meals *and* wrote articles for the local paper *and* was an active member of the local chapter of the League of Women Voters *and* performed in local theater when she somehow found the time. It was only years later I would appreciate the fact that she was the only woman in a house with three males and that none of this necessarily came without a considerable amount of emotional balancing.

While never domineering, my father boasted a six-foot-two frame that made my mother's five-foot-one stature seem even more diminutive, so she had to sometimes shout over the noise to be heard. We often thought my mother—her now gray hair once a fiery red—had a "short fuse" or a "temper"; God help the man, inside or outside of the family, who dared tell her to "calm down." The insinuation that she needed to control herself or be somehow pacified only infuriated her more. The reasons for her occasional outbursts don't always remain clear in my memory (usually something to do with my brother for his antagonistic behavior or my father for allowing my brother to get away with it), but some of the results are etched in my brain, such as the entire, freshly delivered pizza she threw against the kitchen window one evening in agitation. Only later that night, when we noticed the string of mozzarella hanging off a shutter, were we able to laugh.

With a personality honed in high school musical theater, Leslie was hardly the kind of person who was going to be made to feel smaller; her bold physical comportment has always been purposefully, provocatively, at odds with her height. She's the type of woman a man might piggishly call a "loudmouth," one not above telling a telemarketer to never call the house again or her husband's boss what she really thinks of him, or, most controversially, her father-in-law—meddlesome and critical about her recent piano purchase—to "go to hell."

In other words, I couldn't quite see my mother being taken advantage of the way Jane, Lily, and Dolly are in the first half of *Nine to Five*; nevertheless, even now, the film made her constantly nod in recognition. I was curious what she was relating to in the film. Our rewatch was surfacing questions that hadn't occurred to me previously. How much did her female identity define who she was, and what did that mean during different parts of her life? And what was her working career exactly, her identity outside of the home, outside of being a wife, outside of being my mom?

From stories told over the years, I was aware of her intermittent professional life, a recurring career made up of different jobs of various shapes and sizes, some part-time, some full-time, all worked around the overwhelming schedule of being a mother. By 1980, the year *Nine to Five* was released, I was one year old, and my brother was six, and she had long stopped working in order to stay home and raise us. I had heard her talk a little about her hospital administration job in the early seventies, but it was only after she began working part-time again in the mideighties, when I was eight, that I first grew aware of her life outside the home. This was her "dream job," as a public relations reporter for our town's school system: it gave her the ability to always be home by the time my brother and I got out of school while also allowing her to do something meaningful that wasn't making beds, folding laundry, or giving me my daily peanut butter sandwich and chocolate milk.

Like any selfish kid, I knew about her job in relation only to my own experience, as much as I only really understood my father's work as a traveling optical salesman because he would bring my brother and me on business trips, granting us a behind-the-scenes view of his day-to-day. There was a thrill of being outside the house, of seeing the less traveled roads of Maine and Connecticut, of staying in motels and getting to watch HBO, of the novelty of eating out at restaurants on my dad's per diem. Most of all, I loved getting to see him at work. My dad's job was tangible and, for a kid, completely understandable: he would carry big cases of eyeglass frames into his optician and optometrist clients' offices, take them out one by one, show off their colors, their temples, their spring hinges, all the while charming them with tales of the road. If the client liked them, my dad simply wrote it down on his order pad, gave them a receipt, and faxed it to the office at the end of the day back at the motel. It was a joy to witness, especially because his accounts always appeared to be so thrilled to see him walk through their doors, as though he were a returning hero, a friendly man of jokes and smiles.

Early on in our re-viewing of *Nine to Five*, my mother casually commented upon the movie's office set, with its rows of identical desks, typewriters, and entirely female staff of stenographers: "I worked in an office just like that."

"You did?"

This was when I really began to realize just how little I knew.

Later, as the closing credits rolled, Parton's title song reprising as toe-tapping exit music, our mugs of tea long gone cold, we continued our trip into the past. Simple questions begat longer and longer answers. Eventually I became just a listener, perhaps for the first time since I was very young. As a child, my mother liked to tell me, I preferred to be in the role of the storyteller. After teaching myself to read at age three, I became restless with the idea of being read to. I would often grab the bedtime stories from my mother's hands and read *Home for a Bunny* or *Goodnight Moon* to her instead.

Now, as my mom elaborated upon anecdotes I had only heard in passing or had never heard at all, and as she went into greater detail about personal epochs I had taken as apocryphal, I had no choice but to take it all in. To be the little child again, the receiver of tales.

My mother's first office stint was a summer job during college in 1967 and '68 at the Boston headquarters for a Midwestern store called Hill's. My grandma Bertha had worked for many years as a personal secretary to one of the owners, and had helped her daughter, Leslie, find some work there. Hill's, located near Boston's South Station, had started as a hosiery company before going big-time as a clothing chain.

Leslie typifies what she did at Hill's as "grunt work," mostly unmemorable tasks like fetching coffee and typing memos and adding up numbers without the assistance of a calculator, while working toward a degree in elementary education at Boston University. "Being a secretary was an honorable profession," she told me, noting how strictly gendered this profession had been. Hill's vast rows of precubicle desks were out in the open, each manned by a woman. The men were the bosses, and they had their own, separate offices. "Women can multitask better than men—period, that's it," she said as she sliced through the air with a definitive wave of her hand.

During her next summer job, she got a more dramatic and disappointing life lesson that reveals a great deal about the entrenched sexism of the American workplace. It was a story I had certainly never heard before, and which, from my supposedly enlightened 21st-century perspective, seemed shocking.

She had been working, she told me, "in the crummy office of a little third-party company that handled the checks that came in for magazine subscriptions, I can't even remember the name." Shaking her head in bemusement and what seemed like mild embarrassment, she said that she was not destined to have the job for the whole summer. There was a slightly older guy who worked there, probably in his early to midtwenties, and the two got along swimmingly. They joked and perhaps flirted a bit— this was enough to attract the attention of the boss, who called my mother into his office. He informed her that this newfound office pal was in fact a married man. Therefore, he regretted to inform her that he had to fire *her* on the spot. Apologetic, as though he had no choice, he placed a wad of cash in her hand, and she left. Leslie says she never related this story to me, or practically anyone else, out of a sense of shame: "I convinced myself it was partly my fault."

After graduating college, she moved out of her parents' home and got an apartment in Allston, an area of greater Boston, with two other girls. She took a bus to work every day to a new job that she had for about a year, keeping records and answering phones at Health Co. Scientific, where they made vials, test tubes, and other products for hospitals and labs. It was hardly glamorous. She worked in a warehouse garage with forbidding cement floors. While there she got engaged to my dad. She had known him since childhood, so it perhaps isn't surprising or strange that their engagement lasted only a few months. She left Health Co., and they got married in March 1972, right in the middle of a blizzard.

After the first couple months of marriage, she says, "I had nothing to do all day and went nuts." This was when she applied for a secretarial post at the personnel office of the Waltham Hospital, a full-time job in a department of all women. It was a place of great camaraderie among the female staff, and her three and a half years there resulted in close friendships, one of which—with her wonderfully take-no-shit friend Evie—has lasted to this day. She stopped working in 1975 when, six months pregnant with my older brother, she could no longer fit behind the wheel of her car.

The gender disparities and segregations endemic to these offices remain indelible to her.

Leslie had come of age during one of the most socially and politically tumultuous times in the nation's history—her high school to college years spanned the deaths of JFK, Martin Luther King Jr., and Bobby Kennedy, the Civil Rights Act of 1964, the 1968 Chicago riots, the escalation of the US's involvement in Vietnam, and the emergence of radical social movements for Black Power, gay rights, and women's liberation. The progression of the latter was of particular interest to her as she entered the 1970s. The struggles and tenets of the second-wave feminist movement were most present to her through the cultural material she read and watched. For a woman who believes she has led a "charmed life" in terms of the strong, relatively uncomplicated bonds with all of the closest men in her life—kind, supportive, and loving father, brother, cousin, and husband—growing aware of the plights of women seemed to her more of a political than a strictly personal prompt. Through the decade she'd find herself deeply affected by the writings of journalist Gloria Steinem and in books that dealt with the repression or abuse of women, nonfiction works like Germaine Greer's *The Female Eunuch* (1970) and G. J. Barker-Benfield's *Horrors of the Half-Known Life* (1976), or novels such as Marilyn French's *The Women's Room* (1977).

Though there were isolated incidents in her youth in which she suffered abuse outside of the home, and there have been times as an adult that she was made to feel unsafe at the hands of predatory men, she considers herself "never one of the victims." It's at this moment that my mind flashed to a strange occurrence from my childhood, one that seems as daylight-harsh and sadly clear today as it was fogged with darkness and confusion then.

My mother and I were at the movies, just the two of us—the specifics, such as the year, the theater, and the movie title itself, now escape me. Suddenly during the middle of the movie she bolted up from her chair and whispered that we were changing seats. Without making a scene, we quietly moved a few rows up. I was bewildered by this uncommon and sudden change, but was finally able to reimmerse myself in the movie. Later, after the movie was over and we were walking back to the car, I asked her why she abruptly made us change seats.

"There was a weird man next to me," she replied.

I didn't know what this meant. It sounded at once innocuous and threatening. Finally, she explained that this weird man had placed a hand on her leg during the movie. I remember noticing that my mother was wearing shorts—this memory must have taken place sometime during the summer—making the violation seem all the more vivid, tactile, and abhorrent. I also remember the general matter-of-factness with which she told the disgusting story, almost as a way of telling me that this was not the first time something like this had happened to her, and that this was the kind of thing that women—"don't call them broads"—had to deal with in this world.

That I was sitting directly *next to* my mother in a dark, public place—the hallowed space of a movie theater, no less—while this was happening made it especially disturbing, a turning point that I only later would acknowledge for me as a kind of trauma. In the moment, after watching *Nine to Five*, after talking about the micro and macro social and sexual abuses women experience at the hands of men, I wanted to bring up this memory, but I didn't. It felt too dark, too private. It might have broken the spell.

Instead, we talked about the 1970s, a crucial, impressionable era for her. As the subject turned to movies from that era, she realized there were a surprisingly paltry number of American movies that featured strong, independent female leading roles, let alone films that adequately reflected the struggles of women in an era of supposed consciousness-raising. Aside from *Alice Doesn't Live Here Anymore* (1974), Martin Scorsese's depiction of an abused wife (Ellen Burstyn) hitting the road with her young son to try and make it as a singer; Martin Ritt's *Norma Rae* (1979), with Sally Field's breakout dramatic role as a real-life North Carolina labor union activist; and, my mother's favorite of these, *An Unmarried Woman* (1978), Paul Mazursky's richly comic evocation of a divorcee's emotional, sexual, and psychoanalytic awakening starring Jill Clayburgh, there wasn't much she had been aware of. It was an era particularly attuned to the inner lives of men, elevating their disillusionments and masculine identity crises to almost mythic status: such movies as *Five Easy Pieces* (1970), *Scarecrow* (1973), *The Godfather* (1972) and *The Godfather Part II* (1974), *American Graffiti* (1973), *The Last Detail* (1973), *Serpico* (1973), *Chinatown* (1974), *The Conversation* (1974), *Lenny* (1974), *Dog Day Afternoon* (1975), *Jaws* (1975), *Night Moves* (1975), *One Flew Over the Cuckoo's Nest* (1975), *Rocky* (1976), *Network* (1976), *Taxi Driver* (1976), and *The Deer Hunter* (1978) all but overwhelmed the cinematic culture, leaving the creative capital and ideological heft with male characters and stars.

Moreover, by the second half of the decade a treacherous, reactionary conservatism was creeping into films that featured women striking out on their own. My mother remembers being horrified by *Looking for Mr. Goodbar* (1977), with Diane Keaton as a sympathetic but promiscuous schoolteacher whose journey through the New York singles bar scene culminates in her getting carved up in a nearly orgiastic bloodletting; and working through conflicted feelings about the Best Picture–winning *Kramer vs. Kramer* (1979), a sensitively drawn but unquestionably male-centric story of divorce that Meryl Streep rescues from the clutches of misogyny by refusing to overly demonize her escapee wife and mother. In both of these films, which became cultural talking points, women are either punished or severely questioned for daring to take journeys of self-discovery.

These anxieties around female independence formed a tentative bridge to the start of the next decade. In July 1980, such activist groups as Women Against Pornography and Women Against Violence in Pornography and the Media were publicly protesting the release of Brian De Palma's *Dressed to Kill*, a thriller in which a middle-aged housewife (Angie Dickinson) is butchered in a New York City elevator after daring to follow her libido. (It must be noted it's a film that my mother and I absolutely adore for its Hitchcockian stylish daring and technical virtuosity, despite its distinct lack of political correctness.) But by December of that year, *Nine to Five* was hitting theaters, telling quite a different fantasy of urban women on a mission, one in which they wielded the weapons, eradicated male privilege, and ended up gloriously on top. *Nine to Five* now seems like a herald, pointing the way to a decade of female stars and characters more fully in control of their narratives, images, and destinies.

In 1973, while the newlywed Leslie Koresky was doing clerical work at the Waltham Hospital, less than twenty miles away, in Boston proper, the women's empowerment workforce movement called 9to5 was born. The grassroots organization, which would directly inspire the movie of the same name, fought for equal pay and collective bargaining and against discrimination and sexual harassment in the workplace. The initially small group eventually expanded by joining independent groups from other cities, and together they formed a national organization called Working Women, which continues to provide guidance and legal counsel in matters related to workplace inequity and abuses of power, while agitating for policy change.

The seeds of the movie were planted when Jane Fonda first became acquainted with this nonprofit group. The Oscar-winning Hollywood star, loved by many—including my mom—yet loathed in conservative quarters for her left-leaning political activism, especially her outspoken opposition to the Vietnam War, had long shed her *Barbarella* sexpot image. Throughout the 1970s, she had been involved in films of social import, including Hal Ashby's Vietnam reckoning *Coming Home* (1978) and James Bridges's antinuclear drama *The China Syndrome* (1979), and, most radically, *Tout va bien* (1972), an anticapitalist post–French New Wave narrative experiment from French filmmakers Jean-Luc Godard and Jean-Pierre Gorin. Fonda, who had been friends with 9to5's cofounder Karen Nussbaum from their days together in the peace movement, became so inspired by the group's activism that in 1975 she decided to begin pitching to studios an accessible, entertaining movie about the female secretarial workforce: a way of communicating something to even casual Friday-night moviegoers about the importance of the women's movement in the US. As Fonda would later say in a 2005 interview recorded for the film's twenty-fifth anniversary DVD release, "The best way to address serious issues is do it through comedy."

Despite the fact that by the midseventies one in three women in the US (over twenty million women) were working, Nussbaum had to create a briefing memo for the studio to convince them there would be an audience for such a female-centric film. At this time, Fonda began interviewing a cross-section of working women from the 9to5 group to try to better understand what motivated them, but also what frustrated them, and whether they felt exploited and abused. Through anecdotal research, it became clear that getting revenge on their chauvinist male bosses was a common thread.

With the scarcest of plots in mind, Fonda was nevertheless beginning to envision the perfect actresses to appear in the film alongside her. Fonda's apocryphal tale of casting the film is a getting-the-band-together movie unto itself. She says that she "fell in love" with Lily Tomlin the night she went to see her 1977 play *Appearing Nitely*, the first one-woman show to ever appear on Broadway, and then, while driving home from the theater, the car radio happened to blast Dolly Parton's "Two Doors Down," from her 1977 album *Here You Come Again*. Tomlin, though best known for such sketch comedy characters as precocious prepubescent Edith Ann and condescending telephone operator Ernestine, had proven herself more than capable as a screen actor in Robert Altman's *Nashville* (1975), for which she received an Oscar nomination, and Robert Benton's *The Late Show* (1977). Parton, on the other hand, had never acted in a movie. Nevertheless, Fonda says in this moment, driving through the city night, coasting on the high from Tomlin's play and the delight of Parton's song, "I had an epiphany," convinced that these were the women to round out the trio: three stars who had forged their own, independent paths in three different sectors of the entertainment industry. (Of course there were backups in mind—for Tomlin they had considered Carol Burnett and for Parton there was Ann-Margret; it's perhaps *too* easy to see them in these roles.)

Another woman crucial to the creation of the film was Patricia Resnick, the film's coscreenwriter. Resnick, who had attended USC film school before being hired by Altman, first as the assistant to the publicist for his *Buffalo Bill and the Indians* (1976), then as a writer for the treatment of his 1977 masterpiece *3 Women*, and then as a coscreenwriter on his wild (and today underrated)

A Wedding (1978) and *Quintet* (1979), had heard about Fonda's project, and about the stars who were potentially attached. Since Tomlin had given Resnick her first writing job, creating two characters and monologues for *Appearing Nitely* (Tomlin thanks her by name in a curtain call speech from the show that's available today on YouTube), and Resnick also had done some television writing for Parton's appearance in a sketch on a TV special with Cher, the twenty-five-year-old woman felt emboldened and experienced enough to lobby for Fonda's project.

Though she followed Fonda's lead that it should be funny, Resnick also initially went a little darker than anyone expected, pitching a film in which the women intentionally try to kill the boss. But, as Resnick told me, "At the time that was considered too dark and scary; they were afraid there wouldn't be enough sympathy for the women." Resnick, speaking with me on a pleasant phone call that kept cutting out as she drove through a canyon in the Los Angeles hills on the way to work, continued: "Sexual harassment was not a big part of it when Jane came in. After I came on, I went to do research because I had not worked in an office. So I went to Twentieth Century Fox's insurance company." Among the women interviewed was the boss's assistant, who burst into tears, telling her that everyone at the office assumed she was sleeping with the boss, and it wasn't true. "This became the Dolly character's story," said Resnick.

In an irony that wouldn't be lost on anyone, Resnick ended up getting sidelined and all but pushed out of the production process once its director, Colin Higgins, was hired. "He came in and rewrote it," said Resnick. "I went to meet with him and he said, 'I write by myself. I don't want you on the set because I believe every ship has one captain.' He let me come to the set once." The project ultimately went into arbitration at the Writers Guild, and Resnick got sole story and coscreenplay credit.

Resnick today says she feels the film, which would be nominally the greatest hit of her career, also represented something "really heartbreaking." She notes that, even after the tremendous success of *Nine to Five*, she wasn't on a career path to directing films, as she had wanted.

Indeed, Hollywood has never been particularly kind to the idea of female directors, and the few who were working on studio films in the seventies and eighties (including Joan Micklin Silver, Amy Heckerling, Susan Seidelman, and Randa Haines) would find themselves struggling to get work, never achieving the heights or successes of their male counterparts. In 1979, the year that *Nine to Five* went into official preproduction, a circle of female filmmakers formed the Women's Steering Committee, a branch of the Directors Guild of America. Called the "Original Six," the group, which included Lynne Littman—who would go on to direct the superb, Oscar-nominated postapocalyptic drama *Testament* (1983) and, unable to get an industry foothold, precisely zero other theatrical features—spoke out against gender discrimination in Hollywood. After a year of gathering research, the group revealed in a 1980 DGA meeting the mind-boggling gender imbalance in the industry: only 0.5 percent of film and television assignments were being given to women. After years of seeing no significant change, the Original Six encouraged the DGA to bring a lawsuit against two studios; by 1985, the case was thrown out on an ironic and rather jaw-dropping technicality: the DGA was discriminatory against women as well, therefore the studios could not be totally to blame.

With this as an industry backdrop, it's unsurprising that even a feminist comedy such as *Nine to Five*, conceived by a powerful female movie star, would be helmed by a male director. There's no doubt that the light-footed comic breeziness of the film has much to do with the slapstick stylings of Higgins, who had previously directed the mediocre 1978 Chevy Chase–Goldie Hawn hit *Foul Play*, but will always remain treasured by cinephiles for his screenplay of the pitch-dark intergenerational comic romance *Harold and Maude*. Nevertheless, the treatment Resnick claims to have felt during the production of *Nine to Five*—that a man took credit for her work—all too uncomfortably reflects one of the film's pivotal plot points: Hart taking credit for "right-hand gal" Violet's highly successful reforms in the department, right in front of both the company's president and Violet herself. In response, she swallows her pride, vowing to play it safe for six months until she finds out about a much-needed promotion.

The job goes instead to an unseen figure named Bob Enright (the name oozes white American male entitlement), over whom Violet protests she has five years seniority. The disingenuous Hart responds that Bob has a college degree and "a family to support," never mind that Violet is a widow with four kids and has worked more than a decade on the job. After claiming he had no choice, Hart blurts out, "Clients would rather deal with men when it comes to figures." In response to her claims of unequal, unfair treatment ("You're so intimidated by any woman who won't sit at the back of the bus"), Hart dismisses her with a swift, "Spare me the women's lib crap." Initially quivering with rage, Violet gradually finds her voice, launching into a short speech that builds to her raising her arms in triumph, demanding respect before making her dramatic exit.

It's in moments as these that one realizes just how much the film relies on the unique power of each of its stars, and how Fonda's instincts for casting these roles were dead-on. As a comedian, Lily Tomlin's singular mix of self-sufficiency and oh-so-slightly hidden vulnerability were key to her eccentric characters; the confidence she displayed was often offset by involuntary tics and mannerisms (Edith Ann playing with the soles of her shoes while swinging back and forth in her oversized rocking chair; Ernestine's expressive snort and mocking tongue) and seemed a mask for some sort of indefinable insecurity. As Violet, Tomlin is given a backstory that indicates the seeds for that insecurity are rooted in a particular social reality. She wants to be allowed to do her job without having to second-guess every word and gesture as a possible sabotage for her career.

For Tomlin, the word *struggle* has had multiple meanings. Her romantic relationship with her professional partner, Jane Wagner, was something of an open secret throughout the seventies and eighties; Tomlin and Wagner, who have now been together for almost fifty years, finally married in 2013 after the legalization of gay marriage in parts of the US. As far back as 1975, with the release of *Nashville*, *Time* magazine offered her the cover story if she'd agree to come out publicly, but she said no, revealing in a 2009 interview in *The Advocate* that she was "not interested in being typed as the gay celebrity." Though out-of-the-closet celebrities were almost unheard of then, Tomlin's queer status was known enough for discussion of it to make its way into my living room. I distinctly remember my mother mentioning, with a lack of perceptible judgment, Tomlin's personal life, quite possibly the first time I ever heard someone say "lesbian."

A female star who constantly had to prove herself while never feeling the need to be part of any boys' club, Tomlin appears to have internalized all her personal pressures in her performance in *Nine to Five*. Even her clear, dynamic professionalism begins to feel like a symptom of the anxiety foisted upon her and, by extension, all women. As my mom affirmed with that definitive hand gesture, women are highly skilled multitaskers; Tomlin embodies this, in one scene juggling multiple phone lines and keeping crucial numbers in her head, all while dealing with phone calls from her kids whining about peanut-butter-and-banana sandwiches, as the camera subtly tracks around her desk in a delirious yet succinct single take.

If Tomlin's adeptness at conveying simmering neuroses helps give Violet's confidence an extra dimension, Dolly Parton brings to the film a similarly contradictory, yet opposite, quality: though presumed insubstantial by others' sexist prejudice, Doralee has a core of steel. Chipper, smiling Doralee is initially objectified, judged on her looks, not only by Hart—who makes constant sexual passes, even literally chasing her around the desk at one point—but also by the women in the office, who all assume she's sleeping with the boss. With her happy-go-lucky office demeanor, brightly colored and patterned dresses, and Parton's famously ample chest (which Fonda's Judy tries not to stare at with intimidated amazement upon their first meeting), Doralee is unfairly dismissed as something of a ditz, having to weather not only Mr. Hart's dehumanizing remarks ("You mean so much more to me than just a dumb secretary") but also the gossip and gawking of the other secretaries. "Everybody treats me like a bastard at a family reunion," she complains to her briefly seen husband one night, giving a glimpse into her confusion and isolation, which Parton plays with effortless sympathy.

Parton's own anxieties around her first movie role also provide essential subtext in these early scenes; as Doralee is desperate for her coworkers to like her, Parton, thirty-three at the time, also seems eager to gain the confidence and trust of the movie's audience, to prove herself an actress and likable on-screen presence—someone who was hired for her natural talent rather than her mere stardom. So inexperienced was Parton in the ways of moviemaking that she showed up on set the first day with the entire script memorized—both her lines and everyone else's—as though it were a play to be performed in one linear run-through. Though her hit title song (the film's one Oscar nomination) plays over the opening credits and, in a sense, gives Parton a certain ownership over the movie from the start, Parton acknowledged she was out of her element. "I don't think I was scared... I think I was *horrified*," she laughed in a 1980 television interview with Bobbie Wygant.

In an exhilarating narrative pinball effect, Parton's first big chance to prove herself comes as a result of Violet's frustration at not getting promoted. In the midst of her unfiltered anger at Hart, Violet loosens her lips, and refers to Doralee as his "mis-

tress" before storming out of his office. This sends Doralee into
her own rage spiral, taking Hart to task for encouraging such
speculations, culminating in Parton's brassiest and finest line
reading, threatening Hart: "If you ever say another word about
me or make another indecent proposal, I'm gonna get that gun of
mine, and I'm gonna change you from a rooster to a hen in one
shot!" Mixing the character's growing sense of self-assuredness
with Parton's own homespun country-girl folksiness, the line is
an instant star-is-born moment, proving Parton a charismatic,
strong screen presence and Doralee a woman not to be messed
with. Parton is, after all, an entertainment powerhouse who has
released over forty top-ten country albums; won nine Grammys;
gone on to star in multiple films, including 1989's era-defining
Steel Magnolias; and even co-owns her own theme park in Pi-
geon Forge, Tennessee, named Dollywood.

Of the three women, Jane Fonda was most playing against type.
After a decade of embodying such fiercely independent women as
unapologetic prostitute Bree Daniels in *Klute* (1971) and her sympathetically adulterous Sally Hyde in *Coming Home*, both Oscar-
winning roles; playwright Lillian Hellman in *Julia* (1977); and her
fearless reporter and would-be whistleblower Kimberly Wells in
The China Syndrome, it was a bit of a twist for Fonda to start the
1980s with *Nine to Five*'s mousy Judy Bernly. Perhaps the least dynamic of the three, Judy is nevertheless, thanks to Fonda's casting,
the biggest surprise, and also the one with the grandest narrative
arc. Prim, proper, and positively out of her element, Judy is new-
est to Consolidated, and perhaps the least equipped to handle the
environment. A recent divorcee who caught her husband having
an affair with his secretary, she's out in the working world for the
first time, and as such is positioned as a perfect audience surrogate. We see the office through her eyes, and, through her astonishment, come to understand its draconian policies (no personal
photos or coffee cups are allowed on the desk) and sexual inequities. "Lady, you're gonna hate it here" is one of the first greetings

she receives, and since it's from Eddie (Ray Vitte), an African-American mailroom clerk, one can readily assume the company treats not just its women with coequal disrespect.

It's the injustice of it all that really rankles Judy—and it's what makes her really not so much different from Fonda. At the nearby bar Charlie's, a sanctuary for the perennially dispossessed and disillusioned, all three women truly bond, kicking off a pot-fueled, giggle-heavy night where they envision their wildest scenarios for revenge against Hart. (It's also here that Fonda, who wasn't shy about admitting her love for cannabis in a 2015 interview in *Du Jour* magazinr, most humorously functions in opposition to her character, who proudly proclaims that she "smoked a *mary-wanna* cigarette once.")

The movie's official transition to its zany broad comic register—pointing toward Resnick's dark vision—is signaled by these fantasies of vengeance, cartoonish slapstick, and gruesome death: Judy imagines hunting him down with a rifle before decorating his taxidermy-festooned office with his own decapitated head; Doralee, dressed as a cowgirl gunslinger, sexually objectifies Hart before spit-roasting him over a fire.

Violet's Disney-esque dreamscape, in which she poisons Hart before tossing him out his high-rise office window, is the most subversive moment in the film. Tomlin is dressed in the iconic garb of Snow White—blue-and-red silken shoulder pads, yellow dress and corset, red hair bow—and flanked by adorable animated forest animals. A central symbol of docile femininity in American cinema, Snow White is here empowered and re-branded as an avenging angel, delivering ghastly just deserts to the man who has kept her under his thumb. Finally we see Violet, Judy, and Doralee, all dressed as fairy-tale princesses, waving from a castle balcony; with the evil male vanquished, they are free to be benevolent leaders of their own matriarchy.

It's a powerful image that will find an echo by film's end, when we are gifted the catharsis of the three women perched behind Hart's desk, popping a bottle of champagne and reveling in their own new, corporate kingdom. Having kidnapped Hart, leaving him to spend his days in literal chains while watching *Days of Our Lives*, they have been able to effect positive, progressive change at the office: instituting humane work policies, establishing an on-site day-care center for working parents, allowing flexible part-time hours, and, as a quick shot of a man in a wheelchair implies, creating a friendly environment for differently abled workers. Sterling Hayden's chairman of the board visits and is delighted, congratulating a flabbergasted Hart on his accomplishments. In a telling aside, however, he whispers to Hart, "That equal pay thing, though—that's gotta go." Some things never change.

We were still talking as my mother was putting the tea mugs in the dishwasher. The sun was about to set, its muted winter rays poking through the tree branches, casting shadows across the frosty white lawn outside. We had to start figuring out what dinner was going to be, but we remained preoccupied with the question of movies that represented women in the workplace. We noted that it seemed such films were more often than not comedies. As the eighties wore on, such depictions would proliferate in Hollywood. Movies like *Baby Boom* (1987), featuring Diane Keaton as a high-powered executive whose life is turned upside down when she inherits an orphaned toddler from a dead cousin, and *Working Girl* (1988), with Melanie Griffith as an ambitious Staten Island secretary who climbs the ladder to corner-office success in a few short months, were in constant rotation on our television, and always seemed particularly appealing to my mother. She can recite certain lines from them by heart.

Yet these allegedly progressive films, which allow Hollywood to pat itself on the back, always come with a sting of conservatism. In *Baby Boom*, Keaton's J. C. Wiatt ultimately realizes that true fulfillment means getting out of the rat race and raising a baby in Vermont. The script still forces her into the traditional gender roles she initially rejected. It's a movie we would return to later, to delve into more deeply.

Meanwhile, in *Working Girl*, the runaway success of Griffith's Tess McGill in mergers and acquisitions is predicated on not only her rivalry with her tyrannical female boss, Catherine (a sly Sigourney Weaver as the film's true villain), reifying clichés of women fighting with other women to get ahead, but also her sexual entanglements with Catherine's lover, Jack (Harrison Ford). Though she loves the movie, there's a passage that makes my mother's skin crawl. Tess, high on tequila and Valium, turns to Jack, whom she's just met at a bar, and purrs, "I have a head for business and a bod for sin." While the come-on produces a priceless reaction shot from Ford, it otherwise does little more than objectify the film's ostensibly liberated protagonist. When I reminded her of the line, Leslie has an almost involuntary spasm, her voice rising to a higher pitch. "I hate that. *What is that?!* No…woman…would…ever…say…*that*. It's absurd. When I hear that line, my whole body just cringes."

Though perfectly crafted escapist entertainments, *Baby Boom* and *Working Girl* are ultimately betrayed by an intrinsic fear of change. Compared to these films, *Nine to Five* dives right into the deep end. In what shouldn't be a radical twist but nevertheless feels downright daring, Violet, Doralee, and Judy are never punished. Perhaps only in the most unreal of comic confections could this even be possible. The film's tone may be broad, but these women are never, ever broads.

When my mother reentered the working world in 1985, after more than a decade staying at home to raise my brother and me, the notion of flexible hours—one of *Nine to Five*'s climactic reforms—was the most important factor for her in taking a new job. Though my father held on to the same traveling salesman job for nearly thirty years, the family could always use extra money to cushion whatever financial blow might be on the horizon. It was only when I was beginning first grade, a milestone marking the moment that her sons would no longer be home during the day, that she started looking for work. Thrilled that her newfound PR reporting job allowed her to make her own hours, she set up a writing space in the house, converting the former bar area in the corner of the basement's rec room—a built-in architectural attribute of many 1950s-era suburban tract houses—into a clandestine office.

Many years later, when I was in junior high school, my mother returned to secretarial work. It was at a company that produced (*clears throat…*) noncontact capacitive displacement sensors, gap sensors, bore gauges, and density sensors with matching capacitance amplifiers. While working here, this forty-something mother of two, who had at this point worked as a reporter and a nursery schoolteacher, who had performed onstage in musicals and managed a household and read hundreds, if not thousands, of books, would find that men would still treat her as though she were a teenager toiling at a summer job. She says she'll never forget when a visiting associate of her boss's gestured to her and asked, "Can your *girl* get us some coffee?"

Throughout these years and the following decades, Leslie—secretary or journalist or nursery schoolteacher or elementary school aid for children with special needs—may have been alighting on different possibilities for income and self-fulfillment, but to me it was more: she was constantly, provocatively, shifting identities. At the same time, I realize now that none of these jobs took over or defined her; none became all-consuming enough that she took the work home, which left the house a hallowed space for thought, for books, for music, for movies.

From my mother's perspective, working outside the home was simply a way of life; she was following her own mother's example. As a child of the fifties, Leslie grew up in a household in which both parents worked, a self-proclaimed "latch-key kid." Left to her own devices, she had to learn to take care of her little brother at an early age, and also to be alone and re-sourceful. Though she looked up to her mother, she always felt caught between admiring her as a strong, independent work-ing woman and fearing her as a parent—a strict, acute narcissist who demanded attention.

One year after *Nine to Five*, there was another movie, featuring a different kind of professional woman emphatically dedicated to her career, who, quite unfortunately, evoked my mother's mother. It would be enough to make her laugh with horror.

1981: Mommie

The wind chimes had just gone up for the season. At the house, that's how you know change is in the air, how you know that the erratic breezes and blusters of spring are about to give way to the tranquil humidity of summer.

An unusually hectic late winter back in New York made it difficult for me to see my mother for several months, and as a result we hadn't been able to make much progress on our movie project. Determined to get the plan back up and rolling, and not to let the caprices of city living get in the way, I bused my way north to Massachusetts. In Chelmsford, I was happy to be met with a lush blanket of verdant lawn and May weather pleasant enough to walk barefoot in. Having lived in the city now for more than twenty years—a *real* New Yorker, as they say—I have come to believe that there are few decadences greater than feeling soft, thick blades of grass against your toes. Along with the swaying of the tall oaks that surround the house and the sound of those gentle chimes tinkling from the porch's ceiling beams, it's enough to momentarily make you want to leave the metropolis once and for all and set up shop somewhere that's green.

Often when I'm back in the house on Walnut Road, experiencing its living, breathing presence and powers of rejuvenation, I am reminded of the meaning this simple, two-floor "Cape Cod" has always had for my mother. Growing up in Jewish enclaves around Boston, Leslie was a city girl, but like little Natalie Wood in *Miracle on 34th Street*—one of her favorite movies and a Christmastime Koresky household staple—she always longed for a little house of her own, nothing fancy, just something imbued with love and warmth. The possibility of four walls and a roof in the suburbs symbolized to her firmer ground, something far away from the succession of seven apartments she lived in as a child.

Leslie's father, Henry, worked six days a week in a shoe store, eventually as a manager. Before getting her full-time position at Hill's, her mother, Bertha, had a part-time job as a salesperson in a department store called Franklin Simon & Co., catering to the upper crust of the Chestnut Hill area west of downtown Boston. As young as age nine, Leslie would often be left alone to take care of her three-year-old brother—who grew up to be known, famously, as Uncle Jeff.

The constant moving around from one small living space to another, and from one school to another, contributed to a life of instability, and left my mother unable to make and keep friends as an adolescent. Because the family was sometimes cagey about following school zoning regulations, her mother discouraged Leslie from getting too close to other children. "They'll find out where you live," Bertha warned. As a result, Leslie envied other kids—those with legitimate phone numbers and addresses who could maintain relationships.

Bertha—who would turn out to be a central topic of our conversation following our next movie—exacerbated my mother's sense of dislocation and unsettled her psychological well-being.

Her behavior toward her kids whipped between occasional tenderness and emotional terrorism. Bertha's manipulation and warfare stemmed from what Leslie would retroactively recognize as profound insecurity. Years after Bertha had died, at age ninety-one, following struggles with dementia, Leslie would armchair-diagnose her mother as having had borderline personality disorder—not in the grand, operatic Livia Soprano way, perhaps, but affecting and consuming enough that it created constant, simmering tension in most interactions between mother and daughter, and, dramatically, between Bertha and Henry, by all accounts a kindly man, who died the year before I was born.

"I was afraid to enter a room and kiss him before I kissed her," says Leslie, who feared her mother's retribution for perceiving that her daughter loved her any less than she loved her father. It was a household marked by yelling and sometimes by hitting; the constant fighting never led to any resolutions.

To escape from all this, my mother would go to the movies—but they were also an escape her mother was happy to take her on. Like me, and my mother before me, my grandmother was a movie fanatic, all the way back to the silent era, to the days of Douglas Fairbanks and Mary Pickford and Lon Chaney (whose makeup and facial contortions in *Phantom of the Opera* terrified her as a child). Bertha was born in 1918. Her father, Isaac, was an itinerant tailor from Lithuania who traveled from village to village with a sewing machine on his back, and had met her mother, Hannah, during one of his trips to Riga, the capital of Latvia. To escape the pogroms that were being systematically carried out against Jews in Eastern Europe and to find better work, they relocated to Manchester, England. From there they rode the steamship *Cedric* all the way to dock in the United States.

Like so many American Jews of first- and second-generation immigrant parents in the early part of the 20th century, they attended motion pictures, and Bertha adored them—she was an avid reader of fan magazines and a follower of movie-star gossip. Films were affordable attractions, and largely the products of Jewish immigrant entrepreneurs who had come over from Europe and struck out for the west. Jews didn't see themselves on-screen, but the studios were being run by them, such men as Carl Laemmle, Louis B. Mayer, and Jack Warner. And who could resist the seductive, commanding actors they primed for stardom? Bertha would tell my mother all about her star obsessions of the twenties, thirties, and forties: Clara Bow, Lew Ayres, Clark Gable, Judy Garland, James Stewart, Jean Arthur, Gregory Peck. They were more than glamorous to her: they were—or appeared to be—wholesome.

Bertha had a particular fondness for Joan Crawford. A working-class Midwesterner from a broken home who had worked her way up from dance-hall girl to bit movie player in silents to bona fide superstar of the "talkie" era, Crawford was a quintessential Hollywood glamour queen, a fiercely independent woman who embodied fire and ice at once. The movie role for which Crawford is best known is her Oscar-winning turn in the noirish melodrama *Mildred Pierce*, director Michael Curtiz's liberal adaptation of James M. Cain's novel about a depression-era waitress struggling to make ends meet while dealing with a viciously ungrateful, status-obsessed daughter. Yet in the larger popular culture, Crawford might best be remembered as the unfortunate subject of her adopted daughter Christina's best-selling 1978 memoir, *Mommie Dearest*, an excoriating catalog of alleged child abuse that would forever taint Crawford's image. Bertha refused to read the book. In fact, she didn't believe Christina at all, tagging her a "liar" and a "troublemaker." There simply was no way that this beloved movie star, this icon of glamour and good taste, was capable of doing the things her daughter claimed.

Perhaps Hollywood's most notorious takedown of a celebrity—and by her own daughter, no less—*Mommie Dearest* was a sensation, inspiring an equally notorious 1981 movie, starring another Oscar-winning movie queen, Faye Dunaway, as Crawford. Of course, Bertha refused to see the movie as well. Like surely so many ardent movie fans, she wanted to keep the Hollywood veneer of perfection intact, to preserve the illusion. But there may have been something more behind this rejection of an abuse narrative, a more deeply personal inability to come to terms with it.

For these reasons, and just for the general nature of the film—which functions as a textbook for how *not* to raise a child—it might come as a surprise that my mother and I came to have a deep connection to this film, one born of both derision and affection. In fact, of all the films we would be sharing for this project, *Mommie Dearest* is the one we have probably watched together the most often. For despite its basis in an ostensible reality, and the vicious explicitness with which it depicts emotional and physical abuse, *Mommie Dearest* allows us to share in a kind of catharsis through laughter and awe.

We're not the only ones who find the film insanely entertaining: since its release, *Mommie Dearest* has gone from detested flop to seminal camp object, beloved by outrageous queer auteur John Waters, producing more quotable lines than any intentional comedy you can name outside of *The Big Lebowski*. There's "No wire hangers," sure, but how about: "Tina!! Bring me the ax!" or our personal favorite, which comes when Pepsi-Cola's board of directors tries to excommunicate Joan after her husband's death: "Don't *fuck* with me, fellas! This ain't my first time at the *rodeo*." These all spew forth from the mouth of Dunaway, whose performance is a thing of breathtaking derangement, not merely an inhabitation but a complete demonic possession. Dunaway both destroys and saves the film at once, and, accordingly, it's a performance that both destroyed and would come to define her career.

As a child, when I first watched—and was terrified by—*Mommie Dearest*, I knew nothing of my mother's complicated relationship to my grandmother. To a kid with no sense of irony, *Mommie Dearest* seems appalling, a pure expression of psychosis and a catalog of horrors. I still knew none of this when, as a teenager, I re-viewed it and found it hysterical, in every sense of the word, even inviting high school friends over to watch it for *fun*: for its shock scenes, its deliciously overripe dialogue, its soap opera corniness, and its general overall willingness to push beyond the limits of taste within what appears to be an eminently tasteful package. Not that the film was made to be funny. As Susan Sontag wrote in her famous essay "Notes on Camp": "The pure examples of Camp are unintentional; they are dead serious."

Nothing can compare to watching *Mommie Dearest* with your dear mommy. That May, one night after my brother, his wife, and I took her out for a two-weeks-late Mother's Day dinner, the two of us sat down to watch it again. I felt both the usual anticipatory delight and, this time, a slight queasiness. Every single time we put ourselves through the experience, during particular scenes, like clockwork, Leslie will quietly shake her head and say, "That's just like my mother." In the past, I had never wanted to dig too deep into what that could possibly mean. Tonight would be different.

Mommie Dearest is so full of pain that its overwhelming artificiality and ecstatic embellishments serve as inoculation. Its hyperbolic padding makes the film not only bearable but also enjoyable, a bumper-car-like cushion from the violence it depicts.

As a biopic of Joan Crawford, *Mommie Dearest* is woefully clichéd; as a portrait of child abuse it's so extreme and cartoonish that its monstrosity is neutralized by camp. The tone of surreal old-Hollywood pantomime is set early, in its evocation of Joan dealing with a career decline and in her relationship with Gregg Savitt, a Hollywood lawyer played by Steve Forrest with all the subtlety and grace of a grizzly bear walking on stilts. As Joan and Gregg stroll on a beach at sunset, in a supremely cornball image of romantic idyll, a slop-bucket of terribly written exposition comes sloshing out. This is where my mother always begins to perk up: Joan reveals she wants to adopt a baby, and that she had lost seven children to miscarriages; Gregg reminds her she hasn't had a hit movie in a long time, that she's been divorced twice, and that she's too "vain" to have a kid anyway. "Hard times is good for people, I tell ya it is," Dunaway purrs like Barbara Stanwyck shaking down Fred MacMurray in *Double Indemnity*. Then Dunaway turns to Forrest, angrily brushes wind-strewn hair from her forehead, and delivers the clincher: "You guys in Hollywood… All you think about is publicity, deals, box office…"—getting seductive—"Why don't you try to understand a *woman*?" She plants a kiss on him.

This exchange never fails to send my mother and me into paroxysms of laughter, as does a later bedroom fight scene for which the term *overripe* is an understatement. Joan sneers at Gregg like she's Shere Khan: "You're nothing but a rotten, crooked lawyer supplyin' the *grease* that makes this shitty business work." Then, after an intense physical and emotional altercation has subsided, she reclines on her bed and, wildly confident in her come-hither abilities, gestures to him with a nod of her head: "I'm waitin' for ya." In their glamorous bedroom suite, he doesn't succumb to her charms; on our living room couch, we howl with appreciation at her brazen badness.

The arch corniness of both actors, which felt wholly out of place in the landscape of the more naturalistic approach of eighties American cinema, contributes to a sense of near-parody. This feeling is enhanced by the deliberate, studied manner in which all of *Mommie Dearest*'s actors speak and move; the sometimes outrageous costumes, including a Little Bo Peep bonnet at a children's birthday party that makes Joan look like a deranged echo of Bette Davis's Baby Jane; and the guessing—perhaps it should be a drinking—game of the thickness of Dunaway's painted-on eyebrows from scene to scene. The movie functions as horror, as melodrama, but, for us, almost exclusively as comedy. Yet it's not satire; if it had been made with more self-awareness, it wouldn't have worked as hellishly well as it does. Parodies can get awfully tiring when you feel that the filmmakers are trying too hard to make you laugh: think of Mel Brooks's *Robin Hood: Men in Tights* or Garry Marshall's *Airplane*-like soap riff *Young Doctors in Love*. This, on the other hand, is a pure dose of seemingly unintentional burlesque. You can't fake that kind of dedication.

Most of that dedication comes directly from its gorgon-like lead performance. Dunaway was so single-mindedly invested in becoming Joan that she swallows up all reason; it's a remarkable performance—every gesture, every eyebrow arch, every word, *ev-er-y syll-a-ble*, primed to hit her costars, and viewers, in the solar plexus. Many took it as simply "bad"; it would even end up garnering Dunaway a Golden Raspberry Award for Worst Actress of the Year (the movie also won Worst Picture). Yet simply dismissing what Dunaway—a former Oscar winner for *Network* and nominee for her nuanced performances in *Bonnie and Clyde* and *Chinatown*—has achieved in *Mommie Dearest* as "bad" implies that she was confused or lost or didn't know what she was doing. Dunaway is firmly in control here; the performance might ultimately have been a miscalculation, but it's not one that can be given by accident. And knowing that Dunaway's major, highly respected career was all but ruined because of it lends the role a poignant, Icarus-like tragic dimension.

There's an outsized, almost incongruous joy that comes with her fiery interpretation of Joan as a malignant, raging narcissist. And for a while the movie—and our experience of it— coasts on that delightful perversity. But for Leslie, about a half hour in, it momentarily slows down, gets too real, and begins to evoke her own past.

At this point, Joan has made the fateful decision to adopt a bouncing baby girl. We've flashed forward to Christina—or as she's often screamingly addressed, "Tina!"—around the age of eight, and are gradually getting a sense of Joan's unhealthy approach to mothering her. A seemingly relaxing Sunday morning by the pool takes a nasty turn when Joan challenges Christina to a swimming race. Even after allowing her a head start, Joan handily beats the blonde tyke, who rightly claims it's unfair for her mother to keep winning since she's bigger and stronger. Angrily tossing her towel at the injustice, Christina is met with rage. "Don't you *ever* use that tone with me. Who do you think you're talking to?"

It's here that my mother's hair raises on her neck. "That's *just like* my mother." It's the tone, it's the face twisting into domineering rage, the apoplexy at being questioned by one's own child, and being anything less than subservient. Joan gives her a couple of smacks and locks her in a closet. From this point forward—with Joan's insecurity, egocentrism, and victimization of her daughter laid bare—the movie becomes a slightly different experience for us.

In a later scene, Joan comes upon Christina sitting at her mother's vanity table, playacting as though she's won an Oscar. Joan, sweat-drenched from one of her intense, body-punishing jogs, is not flattered, taking it as an insult, accusing her of going through her things, of "making fun of me." Again, my mother shakes her head with recognition; the response of an acute narcissist is depressingly familiar. It's good that what comes next always gives us a cushioning chuckle: Joan punishes Christina for her transgressions—and for gooping up her hair with mommy's setting lotion—by scissoring off her locks. But a series of continuity editing errors don't cooperate, as the girl's hair goes from long to short to long to short again from one shot to the next. That's bad cutting in more than one sense.

The combination of horror and hilarity my mother and I feel throughout *Mommie Dearest* reaches its hyperbolic zenith later on. Christina, now a young adult played by a righteously scowling Diana Scarwid, seethes with rage after her mother has forced her out of boarding school and lied to a *Redbook* reporter that she was expelled. This leads to Scarwid's infamous, stoic line reading of "Why did you adopt me?" which in turn incites Dunaway's guttural, anguished scream: "Why can't you give me the *respect* that I am entitled to?! Why can't you treat me like I would be treated by any *stranger* on the *street*?!" According to Leslie, this is almost line for line something her mother would say to her, a recurring reminder that Bertha craved a dignity that, in her mind, her children and husband refused to give, that she was forced to martyr herself for a family that didn't respect or understand her authority, her sacrifices, her unconditional love.

As my mother explains to me after the movie has ended, Bertha's own psychological makeup is difficult to define. Her Boston childhood was certainly one marked by its own trauma. The second-to-youngest of a whopping ten siblings—all four sisters shared one room—she had to deal from an early age with an alcoholic older brother. And when she was very young she was witness to the harrowing sight of her younger sister burning to death after playing with matches. Bertha was partly defined by a desperation for attention that extended into adulthood, a demand for love that Leslie says made it feel like growing up she was "living with a needy five-year-old."

If feeling unloved, Bertha would gladly speak ill of her own family to strangers, her eyes blurred with tears, angling for sympathy. My mother vividly remembers being accosted as a teenager by a middle-aged woman at a family gathering, who said to her, accusatorially, "You should be ashamed, the way you treat your poor mother." Bertha was, my mother tells me, a woman who, after seeing the movie musical *Gypsy*, vociferously sided with Rosalind Russell's character—the most famous stage-mother monster in all of American theater—and criticized victimized daughter Natalie Wood for her selfishness.

Insecure and unhappy, Bertha looked for acceptance and compliments anywhere she could get them. At the same time she rarely offered kind words for others, correcting her husband's grammar—"He'd say things like 'He weren't gonna come,'" my mother remembers—and finding something negative to remark upon about his coworkers, especially if they were women. Bertha took jobs to contribute to the family income, as they went through years of serious financial difficulties. She always wanted better apartments, nicer neighborhoods, even as they remained out of reach—before she found work, they were buying groceries on credit.

Bertha loved her children, but had trouble trusting them—or anyone else. When she was employed as a private secretary, she would do her best not to interact with other women, habituating a snobbish attitude to convey a sense of superiority. "She acted like someone who came from a high-class, moneyed family," Leslie told me, "looking down her nose at people who seemed 'less than.'" No matter that they were strictly working class. If Leslie ever felt bold enough to bring friends home, her mother would interrogate them. She remembers the day she invited a sweet classmate from elementary school over to play. As my mother recalls, Bertha looked her up and down, disapproving of her clothes. The friendship didn't last long: "When the girl left the apartment, my mother looked at me and just said, 'No.'"

This level of attempted control over Leslie's life extended into adulthood, when Bertha took over the planning of her daughter's wedding, resulting in a guest list that was almost entirely her own, refusing to make space for Leslie's own friends and vetoing her choice for maid of honor. Then, as the wedding approached, her mother became angry that she wanted her father, as per tradition, to walk her down the aisle. She refused to understand why she didn't want both of them to walk her, flanking her on either side. As my mother explained: "She always thought, 'Why not me, too?'" Bertha would outwardly accuse Leslie of loving her father more than her, and her covetousness of Leslie's love for Henry lingered into adulthood. My mother still regrets not having spoken at her father's funeral when she was twenty-eight; at the time she was too afraid of her mother's jealousy to do so.

It was a household marked by unresolvable conflict, the tone set by a mother who would fly off the handle at even the slightest perception of criticism. Nights out eventually devolved into screaming matches between her parents. Years later Leslie would learn that the abuse was known beyond their walls, and that a beloved aunt and uncle would address her and her brother, Jeff, as "those poor children."

This night, long after the credits on *Mommie Dearest* had rolled and the dishes were still piled in the sink, my mother was revealing more than I'd ever heard.

Bertha's treatment of my mother's father seems to hurt her the most all these years later. She would often tell Leslie that she had "settled" for Henry. Furthermore, she would say inappropriate things about Henry to Leslie to try and turn her against him: "awful, even sexual things," my mother said, astonishing herself—and me—as she remembered this. During such moments, my mother said, "I'm standing there thinking, Is there a hole I can fall into?"

On this night, she first told me about a particularly painful memory from childhood, one of her most traumatic moments: "I was five years old, and they were having a row, screaming as they so often did. Suddenly, she came into my room and said to me, 'Your father's leaving us. *You* tell him not to go.'

"I ran into their room, desperate. I saw his suitcase on the bed. It was packed. I sobbed and begged, 'Daddy, don't go.'"

That night, her pleading worked. To this day she wonders if he truly would have left had she not cried out.

I had never heard that story before. This viewing of *Mommie Dearest* was as riotous and enjoyable as ever, but our postscreening conversation had unleashed demons. By sheer force, the spectacle of Faye Dunaway channeling Joan Crawford reached across decades, into our living room, and revived this long-buried chapter.

The now widely related mistreatment of Christina Crawford

by her mother is, of course, based on the belief that her book is a work of documentation rather than fiction. Bertha was hardly the only person who preferred not to believe Christina. Reflective of a culture that has long tended to discredit outspoken victims of abuse—a culture that has significantly begun to change over the past five years in response to the #MeToo movement—Christina's book has always been cast in a shadow of doubt. In a 2010 book, Joan Crawford biographer Donald Spoto took Christina to extended task for factual inconsistencies and for essentially writing the scathing memoir as an act of retaliation after she and her adopted brother, Christopher, were cut out of their mother's will upon her death in 1977. It's understandable why Joan Crawford partisans and superfans would remain angry at Christina: so powerful is *Mommie Dearest*'s hold on the culture—partly due to the can't-look-away extremity of the film adaptation—that for generations Crawford has been remembered more for being an alleged child abuser than a movie star.

Joan Crawford's drive, ambition, and ability to forge her own path during Hollywood's early years reveal her to be a figure irreducible to mere "Monster Mom." Born in San Antonio, Texas, and raised in Lawton, Oklahoma, Crawford came into this world as Lucille LeSueur. Abandoned as a baby by her birth father and sexually abused as a prepubescent by her stepfather—who would eventually be taken to court for embezzlement—Lucille kept pushing ahead, undeterred in her dream of becoming a dancer. By the midtwenties she was hoofing it in chorus lines on Broadway, and would soon be spotted by talent scouts. In *Conversations with Joan Crawford*, an invaluable 1980 collection of interviews conducted during the sixties and seventies by Roy Newquist, Crawford explains her persona in those early years of Hollywood: "I was only a contract player, one of maybe thirty kids who hung around the studio waiting for the simplest assignment or some sort of break... Finally I was so bored and scared I raised so much hell they started putting me in pictures, as a chorus girl, naturally, a symbol of flaming youth, the flapper who danced 'til dawn, the I-don't-give-a-damn girl."

Lucille had a last name that sounded too much like "le sewer" for Hollywood's taste, so it was changed via a "Name the Star" magazine contest sponsored by MGM. In 1925, just two years before the first "talkie," *The Jazz Singer*, would forever alter the course of film history, she had already appeared in five movies; by 1928, with the release of director Harry Beaumont's silent drama *Our Dancing Daughters*, Joan Crawford officially broke through, making her mark as a foxtrotter, the height of rule-breaking roaring twenties cool. There's an unfettered, fresh-faced joy to her performance that might take contemporary audiences by surprise; there's no trace of the hardened, seen-it-all diva many now associate with her persona.

One of a handful of established silent-movie stars who successfully made the transition to sound, Crawford began to take on more serious roles in the early thirties, and thanks to such hits as *Laughing Sinners*, *Possessed*, and Best Picture Oscar-winner *Grand Hotel*, she became one of the top stars of the decade. Much of her popularity lay in her relatability to a populace still suffering through the Great Depression, as the star herself would explain in Newquist's book: "I think a million or so girls with nothing in their pocketbooks and a head full of dreams paid to see a Joan Crawford picture because, let's face it, between MGM publicity and the parts I played, I was the rags-to-riches girl and if they were lucky they could make it, too."

However, moviegoers are fickle, as are studio execs, and Crawford's star began to fade midway through the decade. After a handful of flops, she was officially dubbed "box office poison" in a May 1938 article in the influential industry trade publication *Independent Film Journal*, a traumatizing label directly evoked in *Mommie Dearest*. Unhappy marriages to Douglas Fairbanks Jr., and Franchot Tone, the latter marked by seven miscarriages, contributed to Crawford's sense of unease in an industry that loves you on Monday and tosses you out with the garbage on Tuesday. Two years after being released from her MGM contract in 1943, she fought for *Mildred Pierce*, her comeback at Warner Bros. To this day, that film remains the greatest showcase for Crawford's mix of salt-of-the-earthiness and imperious glamour, and by making the character's foe her own nasty, selfish, class-obsessed daughter (played with curt snobbery by Ann Blyth), *Mildred Pierce* would for decades paint Crawford as a kind of martyred mother figure—an image that *Mommie Dearest* would handily dismantle.

In 1977, during one of the last interviews before her death, and a year before *Mommie Dearest* was published, Newquist asked Crawford about the stars of the moment, and whether any of them had the pizzazz or potential of the Golden Age luminaries of the old studio system. Her response: "Of all the actresses— to me, only Faye Dunaway has the talent and the class and the courage it takes to make a real star."

Joan Crawford was a role that Faye Dunaway, coming off her *Network* Oscar and at the height of her powers in Hollywood, was convinced she was perfect for. The film's producer and writer Frank Yablans had initially approached Anne Bancroft to play the role, and one can easily see Mrs. Robinson herself doing a fair embodiment of Crawford, both the take-no-prisoners strength and the cracks of neurotic vulnerability. According to Yablans, who died in 2014, Dunaway wanted it the most: he claimed in a video interview on the film's 2006 DVD release that when he showed up to first talk about the possibility of her playing the role, Dunaway answered the door in full Crawford garb, including thick painted eyebrows and a flower in her hair. "She wanted so much to be Joan that she took on her persona and airs," remembered Yablans. She was undeniable, and her commitment would only grow more intense during filming.

In her autobiography *Looking for Gatsby*, Dunaway remembers it differently: "When I was being pushed to do *Mommie Dearest*, I would have given the world to be surrounded by people who would have argued against my doing it."

The discrepancy in memory between these accounts—his claiming she lobbied for the part; her insistence that she was all but coerced into taking it—makes for a considerable gray area. It also speaks to Dunaway's much remarked-upon disavowal of the role, which she has declined to talk about in interviews for decades. In her book, Dunaway writes on the film how one might write about physical and emotional trauma. She recalls finally being convinced to do it when Yablans and director Frank Perry assured her that their adaptation would be a balanced, sympathetic portrait of Joan, as much about the terrors and challenges of being a major female star in Hollywood as about Joan's abuse of Christina. Adding to the emotional intensity of the experience was that in the summer of 1980, as she was preparing to take on the challenge of playing Joan, Dunaway had become a parent for the first time, creating another parallel between the actress and the person she was about to embody.

Despite whatever hesitancy she says she had about taking the role, Dunaway, a reported perfectionist and a method-trained actor who believes in fully inhabiting her characters, reaches into the guts of the part with a fury and heedlessness often reserved for superhero villains. Except for formidable little Mara Hobel, who holds her own as younger Christina, just about everyone orbiting Dunaway in *Mommie Dearest* comes across as stranded and hapless—from Scarwid, with her often robotic, stalwart delivery; to Forrest's blustery, swaggering parody of masculinity; to Rutanya Alda's sheepishly supportive housekeeper Carol Ann. There's no way for them to avoid the gravitational pull of Dunaway's Crawford; it becomes an inescapable, insanely entertaining force.

According to Alda, this is reflective of the atmosphere fostered on set as well. In her own memoir about the experience, Alda claimed that Dunaway so mistreated crew, especially hair and makeup workers, that even legendary costume designer Irene Sharaff left the film. Alda also wrote that Dunaway hated being looked at while acting, so she forced costars to turn their backs during shots where they wouldn't be in the frame. While I was writing this chapter, Dunaway became embroiled in a theater controversy that would seem to generally corroborate some of Alda's accusations: in summer 2019, Dunaway was fired from the Boston production of *Tea at Five*, a Broadway-bound one-woman show about Katharine Hepburn. As reported in the *New York Post*, Dunaway "slapped and threw things at crew members," who became "fearful for their safety."

Whether or not Dunaway would deny that she bred such distress on the set of *Mommie Dearest*, she fully admits the film took a toll on her: "In this movie, I lost myself for a while… I don't think there's any wonder that I fled this country after that movie. That I yearned for, went looking for, and found during the eighties, a softer, gentler, more human world."

Of course, one can't discuss *Mommie Dearest* without the notorious, and quite spectacularly insane "wire hangers" scene, for which Dunaway reserves special treatment in her memoir. Even after decades of hype, this jaw-dropping set piece lives up to its reputation. It's a minor symphony of pain and overwhelming noncatharsis; nested within the whole, it's confounding and completely self-sufficient as its own short film, never referred to again by any of the characters. Just a scene earlier, Crawford has won her Oscar for *Mildred Pierce*. Her joy doesn't last long.

As if driven by booze and some kind of unstoppable inner torment, she launches into an explosion of obsessive-compulsive rage, waking up Christina in the middle of the night, screaming at her for allowing wire hangers in her closet (how a little girl would choose what kinds of hangers would be in her closet is a question too logical for such an impassioned bout of looniness), beating her with one of the dastardly objects, and then forcing her to scrub an already noticeably clean bathroom with an inordinate amount of Old Dutch powdered soap, with which she also beats the poor child and then herself in a kind of ecstatic self-flagellation that leaves the room looking like the aftermath of a napalm raid. Amid all this, Dunaway's face is caked in cold cream, her red lips poking through a white face, giving her the aspect of a snarling kabuki mask. The scene is so willfully grotesque and out of the bounds of reason or believability that the emotion it engenders, rather than sympathy, is awe.

In his book, Spoto claims that the wire-hangers scene isn't based in any sort of reality, a complete invention. Yes, Crawford hated wire hangers, but according to the biographer, the dry cleaners were strictly instructed to return all her clothes on her nicer, regulation-style hangers. Anyone who has seen *Mommie Dearest*—*many* times, for those of us so inclined—knows this is beside the point anyway, and to take this scene, and indeed the entire film, as some sort of documentary portrait of a real woman's life is to both give it too much credence and to not appreciate it on the level it best works: a bizarre, mottled facsimile of Hollywood glamour, the gross, tasteless underbelly of family life and of a certain kind of decadent LA domesticity.

"'No more wire hangers!' Those words remain, even now, an ugly wound on my psyche," wrote Dunaway, who also provides an account of the scene, in which she very clearly blames the director for not harnessing her. "No one else had stopped it, or shaped it, or done anything to modulate the scene," wrote Dunaway in her memoir. "It was camp that had gone way over the edge… Everything about this production was out of kilter, off-center, and somehow I could never find my way back to some sort of middle ground."

Many have credited *Mommie Dearest* with all but ruining Dunaway's career. In another parallel to the character she was playing, Dunaway would thereafter be deemed something akin to "box office poison." This would be her last major starring role in a Hollywood studio picture of the eighties, and she would never again ascend to the heights of reputable stardom. Perhaps rather than haggling over how to define what Dunaway accomplishes here—is this one of the worst performances of all time, or is it somehow one of the best?—we should ask whether this was fair treatment for an actress who had so beguiled as *Chinatown*'s long-suffering, reluctant femme fatale or *Network*'s brawny, no-bullshit TV exec. Some delighted in her downfall, due to rumors of her difficulties on set as well as the perception that she had simply gone *too far* with this performance; the palpable schadenfreude of the situation can often feel like a double standard in a business in which male stars are often given second, third, and fourth chances after box-office belly flops. Imagine if Dustin Hoffman was never given any more lead parts after *Ishtar*, or George Clooney was never allowed to come back after the early mistake of *Batman and Robin*. There are numerous bitter pills to swallow while freely and gleefully enjoying *Mommie Dearest* as a train wreck, not the least of which is witnessing the slow-motion demise of a woman's career.

Another strange sensation, of course, is laughing so wholeheartedly with your mother at the astonishing spectacle of bad parenting. Is it some form of catharsis? Is it a relief to be reminded of what you escaped? I asked Leslie if, as a young parent, she made a concerted, conscious effort to not parent like her mother had, to not intimidate, manipulate, or give in to neediness and insecurity, emotions that we're all capable of, after all.

She told me about a time from my childhood when my older brother was "pushing all my buttons." Perhaps the more rebellious and willful of the two of us from the start, Jonathan was the kind of kid you'd call "a real handful." On this occasion, she says, "I grabbed him and started to whack him. Suddenly I stopped myself. I called a friend and asked her to take him for the day. I told her, 'He's making me so angry that I'm afraid to be near him.'" Fearful of the anger that may have been inside

her, she made the concerted effort—the decision—to not respond with the behavior she had seen modeled for so many years.

I'm sure I had my own infuriating moments as well, yet never
do I remember any punishment being out of bounds or at all
frightening. I was a somewhat hyperactive child with tireless
energy that verged on the destructive—according to my mom, I
scribbled on the walls with crayons and tore pages out of books.
For my mother's album collection, I broke records for most records scattered and stomped upon. Yet, tellingly, I was able to
most calm down when watching a movie, especially in the dark-
ened hush of a movie theater. My mother remembers taking me
to my first movie, a rerelease of Disney's *Cinderella*, at the very
young age of two. Admittedly nervous due to my propensity
for running, spinning, and talking a little too loud and a little
too often, she was pleasantly surprised, astonished even, to see
me sit stock-still, eyes wide open, at the moving images dancing before me from the light of the projector. Serenity washed
over me that day in 1981, the first inkling of a kindred movie
spirit between us.

The movies also provided an anchor for my mother and
grandmother. Sometimes they influenced the tumult, ascending their day-to-day altercations into the realm of melodrama.
My mother recalls a shouting match during which Bertha, in
high-toned Crawford/Dunaway fashion, screamed imperiously
at her: "I gave you everything!" To which my mother replied,
"Everything but *love!*" before being summarily slugged. Today,
my mother believes this was in imitation of *Imitation of Life*,
borrowing the phrase from Sandra Dee in Douglas Sirk's 1959
tearjerker.

At other times, movies were the calm in the center of the
storm. In delineating all of the difficulties, manipulations, and
abuses that marked her household as a child, my mother was
also quick to remark upon Bertha's positive aspects and caring
nature. "My mother was a good mother in some very basic im-

portant ways," she insists, helping me better recall the mellow, loving grandmother of my childhood whose passive aggressions and borderline personality disorders were invisible to me. "She always told me when I looked nice, and wasn't critical of my looks or voice. She was supportive. That's big. I've come to realize she just had her demons, and they came out in ways that weren't healthy."

Most of all, she fondly remembers the movies she took her to see throughout the fifties. Since Henry came home so late from the shoe store, they would often end up at the movies, and no matter which Boston-area neighborhood they were living in there was a local theater to frequent. "I played hooky a couple times with her. In the morning, she'd whisper to me in bed, 'Want to go to town?' We never called it Boston. We called it 'town.' She'd take me to lunch, a movie. *Sleeping Beauty* in downtown Boston. It was like Christmas."

Back then movie theaters were grandiose temples to the cinema—reverential and church-like experiences before the takeover of the American multiplex transformed the industry. Many of these single-screen palaces now exist only in my mother's memory, and she speaks of them—the Franklin Park and Morton theaters in Dorchester, the Paramount in downtown Boston, and the Oriental in downtown Mattapan—with the passion one might use to talk about a Sunday service. The latter, she tells me with ecstasy, was decorated as though a Chinese village, its ceiling adorned with clouds and sun that turned into a starry night sky when the lights went down.

The act of sharing movies with one's child betrays the belief of movie-watching as an essentially lonely activity. While I would harbor a guess that a majority of the films I've seen have been alone—many of them viewed as a solitary teen in my bedroom while the sounds of the unimaginably happy neighborhood kids bouncing basketballs and riding bikes wafted through the window screen—there's a peculiar, marvelous feeling to being introduced to something and not just seeing it but also feeling it alongside someone else. For all its inherent trauma, its bruising personal reference points, its vengeful origins, *Mommie Dearest* is a film that my mother simply likes returning to, and our mutual, even spasmodic enjoyment of it brings with it a charge of sly conspiracy. There's a participatory aspect to watching it, and it's felt every time my mother lets an "Oh, no..." escape her lips whenever a new, ridiculous supporting character appears or when she points at the screen at Dunaway angrily scrubbing the floor and says, "That's how my mother washed the floor... in high heels."

There's something more, which has been clarified for me over the years, as so many things are when one is more willing to wipe the fog from one's mirror. Unbeknownst to my mother and me throughout my childhood, *Mommie Dearest* has long been recouped as an outrageous queer classic. A May 1998 *New York Times* article chronicles a special "Mother's Day" event at New York's Town Hall auditorium that featured not only a screening of the movie but also appearances from Tina herself, the infamously catty gay critic Rex Reed, and the drag artist Lypsinka—aka John Epperson—in full Joan Crawford regalia. According to the *Times*, Crawford "has become the 20th century's greatest camp heroine. She is beloved by female impersonators, who are in thrall to Faye Dunaway's staggering performance in the 1981 film." The event benefited Gay Men's Health Crisis, then the most prominent organization raising money for AIDS treatment and research, and featured the unusual spectacle of Christina bestowing a "hand-decorated wire coat hanger" to Lypsinka as though a fairy-tale wand.

It's not a leap to suppose that our bonding over the movie's excesses, our unbridled, shared joy at Dunaway's haughty shoulder pads, superchunky eyebrows, and fierce, fuck-it-all delivery—all of which pushes the film into near-drag territory—was somehow related to our tacit understanding of its queerness. The films of

John Waters would have been too extreme for us to share; Pedro Almodóvar's too labyrinthine and postmodern. In the absence of explicitly queer cinema, *Mommie Dearest* now seems like the outré gay film we never had, and years before I ever came out of the closet, we were able to share in its abhorrent delights as though they were part of some as yet untranslated language.

The night was drawing to a close. The complicated exhilaration of experiencing the movie had long given way to reflection and rumination, and those dishes still had to be done. The astonished laughter of *Mommie Dearest* had been supplanted by personal memories—both painful and pleasurable—as evening gave way to night. They had seemed to pour out of my mother. One moment she would be marveling at how, despite everything, Bertha "was also a very good mother," and would often show true support and maternal affection. The next, Leslie would suddenly recall some odd, long-buried anecdote, like the time that, during a dinner party, Bertha didn't make a space at the table for her husband, excommunicating him instead to a humiliating snack table in front of the couch. And the time that, in the midst of slapping her, Bertha's ring caught her, breaking the skin, prompting her to implore her daughter, "Don't tell Daddy." She never did, because she didn't want them to have another fight.

And then: "One day I decided to leave home. I was ten.

"I had an altercation with my mother, and I was angry and fed up. So I walked out, went down the street, out of our apartment building, which was on the corner of a huge main artery going right through Dorchester and Mattapan. I walked and walked for I don't know how long.

"Finally I thought, 'Where am I going, what am I doing here?' I turned back and went home. As it turned out, she didn't even notice that I had left."

I would guess that most kids want to run away from home

at some point in their childhoods. To drop everything and go somewhere. For me, growing up in the eighties, that impulse was mitigated by technology. If I ever felt misunderstood, the escape that I needed was readily available, and easy to access with a videocassette and a remote control play button.

Loneliness is inevitable for a child, even with a supportive mother. As I entered my pubescent years, feelings were beginning to stir in me that made me feel different, though they were vaporous, illegible, attractions that would take years to fully process. Movies didn't offer solace in this regard; I didn't even know that movies could show me anything reflecting reality. I had already spent so much of my time looking at screens that I hadn't yet bothered looking for myself.

1982: Found

I've often wondered if other kids were seeing themselves on movie screens. For me, movies were an escape, not a mirror. I felt an estrangement from what I was seeing, comfortable in the fact that these were other people's stories. Husbands and wives, people who worked hard in very adult-looking offices to have their two-car garages or palatial city apartments; men and women who had bouts of marathon sex, who went on expensive vacations, who remodeled kitchens and paid for elaborate weddings, who raised adorable children who never resented them. For reasons as yet unexamined, none of that seemed in the cards for me, so I saw movies as time marching forward, vessels for a linear progression perhaps not meant to include me.

Coming to terms with one's own desires can be terrifying, especially for the young. The teenage years are allegedly fueled by raging hormones; in my case, I felt dulled, somehow inured to sex. I don't remember feeling any overwhelming urges. I never had a wet dream. Movies about teenagers, especially those in the eighties, were so preoccupied with matters of the body and the ins and outs of sex and dating that they felt as culturally alien to me as Sylvester Stallone rampaging through a jungle or Bill Murray busting slimy, green ghosts. In retrospect it's clear I was suppressing something. Little moments have come back to me in memory shards over the years: the photo of a shirtless Marlon Brando from *A Streetcar Named Desire* that was in a little book of movie quotes I kept tucked away like a secret love letter; the quiet fascination I had for the sensitive bravado of Michael Biehn's bug-squashing military grunt in *Aliens*; the strange drive I had to befriend cool Corey Haim. The obsessions of childhood are easy to write off as quirks, so these fetishes at the time seemed as natural as my recurring dream about being buddies with Jabba the Hut. (In my version, he lived in my bedroom and was a really nice guy.)

Unaware of—and disinterested in—the underlying sexual nature of such idolatries, my preteen self instead indulged in fantasies of identification. Looking back at it from today's vantage, my nascent fascination with Ellen Greene's stiletto heels and skid-row-glam outfits in *Little Shop of Horrors*, the laser-beam-like attraction I felt for Melanie Griffith's jangly bracelets and Louise Brooks's bob in *Something Wild*, and my inability to resist the visual lure of Madonna (yes, reader, I once kissed her on the lips, or at least a photo of her on *The Cable Guide*) might all seem to give off code-pink warning signals, but at the time I was simply a little boy craving images of women, for whatever reason.

Throughout my tender years in the eighties and nineties, sex wasn't really brought up, either at home or at school, aside from the usual schoolyard taunts and one paltry, exclusively hetero sex education class in seventh grade. The less technical, more complicated matter of *sexuality* was even less discussed. There was straightness, and everything else was an aberration. Even in a household with a mother who was politically liberal, there was little for a budding gay kid like myself to grab on to, nothing that might help him fully understand or embrace such fuzzy feelings. While my parents never pressured me as a small boy into gender normativity—allowing me to play with traditionally "feminine" toys like baby dolls and an elaborate and a very exciting plastic kitchen set alongside my *Ghostbusters* and *Transformers* action figures—such openness did not segue naturally into discussions of sex and identity.

In this era, movies were of little help. Gay characters were even less visible in mainstream American cinema than they are now at the start of the third decade of the 21st century—which is to say practically nonexistent. When the odd gay person somehow made their way into my visual peripheries, it seemed like an intrusion, or a mistake. If there was ever a sexual component to such a character, like a mutual touch or, heaven forbid, a kiss, I didn't know how to react. Was I intrigued or repulsed? And if I felt intrigued was it because I was susceptible to such feelings? And if I felt repulsed was it just because that was how society told me I had to feel? Either way, I was afraid—afraid of being intrigued, repulsed, or a combination of the two; better to not have to see two men kiss on-screen so I wouldn't have to wonder what I was feeling at all, a self-fulfilling avoidance.

As I entered the nineties, and my body and mind matured, I became increasingly curious and open to occasional representations of homosexual characters, though not necessarily in a way that I saw as applying directly to my life. Gay men often turned up as lovable foils for strong, open-minded women: I adored Nathan Lane's sympathetic gay best friend to Michelle Pfeiffer in *Frankie and Johnny* and Robert Downey Jr.'s hyperactive gay brother to Holly Hunter in *Home for the Holidays*. Especially crucial were two movie theater outings with my mom: *The Crying Game*, for which Miramax quite successfully and, perhaps, cravenly sold the Jaye Davidson character's hidden trans identity as a shocking twist, and *Six Degrees of Separation*, in which a young Will Smith—a kid-friendly superstar for my generation due to the hit song "Parents Just Don't Understand" and the sitcom *The*

Fresh Prince of Bel-Air—is found in bed with a nude male hustler. These were movies that refused to judge their LGBT characters. In my mind I would keep turning these films over and over like prisms, letting the light shine on them from different angles to reveal nuances. These characters didn't feel weird to me. Wasn't I supposed to be one of the normal ones who stood in opposition to them in my mainstream privilege?

Then there was a special delivery. I had been given a subscription for *Entertainment Weekly* when I was about eleven, and had grown fond of the magazine's passionate, in-depth movie reviews. In September 1995, they released an issue with the words "The Gay '90s: A Special Report" emblazoned on the cover, surrounded by an image grid of gay and lesbian cultural touchstones of the moment. Keeping in mind that this was even before Ellen DeGeneres came out of the closet, one must realize the unusualness of an entire issue devoted to what the editors believed was an ongoing revolutionary mainstreaming of gay culture. The evidence of this alleged shift could be found in the rise of music icons like k.d. lang and Melissa Etheridge; the inclusion of gay characters in such TV shows as *Friends* and *My So-Called Life* as well as movies like *Clueless*; the ubiquitous homoerotic ad campaigns of Calvin Klein; and the textual queer readings of pop culture figures as disparate as Batman and Robin and, yes, *The Lion King*'s Timon and Pumbaa—the Bert and Ernie of a new generation. Whether or not I was persuaded by every detail of this state-of-the-arts exclusive mattered less than that I was suddenly engaging with questions around gayness. It didn't seem like it applied to me, but I was *very* interested. Decades later I would discover that this special issue was partly the brainchild of a critic and author I admired, Mark Harris, then working as an editor at the magazine. Fortuitously, I had held on to the issue all those years and would be able to quote it back to him, a little sheepishly—like it was still a secret.

The Gay '90s may have been happening, but they were happening somewhere out there, and certainly not in my house. Pop culture was less politically minded than it is now, and questions around gay marriage, equality, and gender fluidity were unthinkable as nightly dinner-table conversation. If I had been more fully conscious of my identity then, I may have felt even more isolated; as it was, I was awash enough with the general alienation that comes with growing up—discomfort with my lumpy body, confusion over the future, and the awareness that I didn't quite belong in any of the groups in which other boys my age seemed to gladly take part. Hating team sports and fearing public-facing group activities like theater or debate clubs, I buried myself in activities I could do all by myself: writing, reading, playing piano, and watching movies, all kinds and as many as I could get my hands on. If there was a gay-straight alliance of any sort at my high school I wasn't aware of it, and I only heard rumors of one kid coming out of the closet before graduation.

With its lack of outward sexual difference, life in Chelmsford, Massachusetts, didn't seem particularly abnormal; this was just the way it was, here and presumably across the country. The culture had begun to change incrementally in the nineties, but small-town American life, reliant on maintaining the monoculture and the long-held capitalist standards of living that implies, was resistant. There was no indication that things would ever change.

It was only when I visited my mother in early June for the next installment of our movie pilgrimage that I really began to consider how much things had changed in Massachusetts. The town was in full bloom, with summer right around the corner. Upon arriving on a Saturday, my mother asked me a dreaded question: "Would you like to come to church with me tomorrow morning?"

She had asked me this a few times over the past year, and each time I recoiled. I couldn't get used to the idea. My parents were raised Jewish, as was I. Even though we had not gone to the synagogue for decades, I continued to feel a cultural connection to my Jewishness, and I had it in my head that going to church was somehow an affront to our heritage. Furthermore, I have long rejected and even quietly disparaged organized religion, and self-righteously wanted nothing to do with what I perceived as the rampant hypocrisy that can infect all faiths like a virus.

Churches weren't entirely alien to me; I had been inside them a handful of times over the years, for weddings and funerals, of course, but also during a couple of Christmas services with my husband's family in Milwaukee. Even my older brother, whose wife, Melanie, comes from a Catholic family, was married in a church. Nevertheless, I puzzled over why my mother had suddenly found a new faith, aside from the appeal of singing in the choir. It felt like a major change late in life.

"It's Unitarian," she insisted. "They don't even have a cross on the wall."

Out of curiosity and my newfound commitment to understanding more about my mother, I agreed to accompany her, knowing full well that part of the outing would necessarily involve her introducing me to a cadre of new church acquaintances—my role would have to be the supportive, loving son returned home for the weekend from New York to visit his mother.

That Sunday morning the sky was overcast, the temperature hovering around an unseasonably chilly fifty degrees. My first happy discovery of the day was that the First Parish Unitarian Universalist Church was in an edifice I knew very well, but which, despite having lived in this town for the first seventeen years of my life and visiting consistently for the subsequent twenty-three, I had never set foot into. Driving into Chelmsford center, the church is unmissable; its tall steeple, a weathercock perched at the top, all but presides over the town as its welcoming beacon. Founded in 1655—just three years after Chelmsford was settled—it was for many years the only church in town and for nearly two centuries its vestry served as the town meeting space. It remains the primary visual marker of Chelmsford's historic district and an emblem of small-town New England pride. As pagan as I may be, I can't deny the symbolic power it holds.

Though I had never been inside, I had often tromped around the Forefather's Burial Ground, the centuries-old graveyard that abuts the church and which had been a source of fascination for me and my friends—a good place for a scary round of late-night hide-and-seek for kids, an even better place to escape to for teenagers looking for somewhere to go. Splayed out in front of the First Parish is the town green, a well-maintained square patch of grass, trees, and benches that provides the space for community concerts, Fourth of July pageantry, and an annual Christmas tree lighting. As a child, I thought this expanse of lawn was enormous, enough to contain an entire town's worth of spirit and solidarity; today I see its modesty, taking not even a couple of minutes to walk its perimeter.

As I stood on this lawn, struck by the brisk wind and light mist of rain while I waited to go inside, I glanced across to the other side of the green at the Old Town Hall, which had in the past decade been transformed into the town's Center for the Arts. Fluttering on this once municipal building was a rainbow pride flag. No, wait, there were *two*. The meaning was unmistakable.

Inside the First Parish, I was more than a little relieved to learn that my mother hadn't lied to coerce me on her new Sunday morning ritual: the Unitarian Universalism was indeed properly nondenominational. Bright and spare, unburdened by sacred vessels and accoutrements or obscuring stained glass, the nave of the church is a pleasantly puritan, wide-open space that would have been even cheerier that morning if not for the preponderance of clouds. Its tall, wide windows once must have given a clear, pastoral view of untouched, verdant New England land. Today, I could see that pride flag across the town commons, a slash of color against an otherwise drab day.

As I walked in I noted my mother already taking her place in the choir, preparing for a hymn—an unusual image for me to be sure, but something about it already felt calm and right. As I sat down, the pew creaking under my weight, an elderly woman next to me turned and, despite a curious look that acknowledged she had never seen me here before, gave me a warm smile. Looking down at the pamphlet I had grabbed on the way in, I noticed the following words, underneath all its contact information, right there in bold and italics: *First Parish is a Welcoming Congregation committed to welcoming and celebrating the presence of bisexual, gay, lesbian, and transgender people.* Sure enough, its reverend, Ellen, spoke of LGBTQ+ rights in her sermon, as though to underline the point. Did she know I was coming? Or maybe, just maybe, I wasn't the only gay person in town anymore. Or maybe, just maybe, I never was.

She also mentioned the importance of community leaders of all faiths and ethnicities, of Islam and Judaism and Hinduism and Christianity; she name-checked MLK and Gandhi in the same sentence as JC. Suddenly, the choir's singing "Spirit of life, come unto me/Sing in my heart the stirrings of compassion" took on a whole new meaning. I opened the hymnal and began to sing along.

Momentarily blinded by what seemed like my hometown's sudden symbolic acceptance of the queer community, I had somehow forgotten that this was the beginning of June; I was not aware of anything called "Pride Month" growing up, and felt a sudden pang of jealousy that younger generations of Chelmsford kids would. I had also not realized that the movie I had put on the roster to watch with my mother that weekend was, serendipitously, a film that had taken me aback as a child for the sympathetic queer character prominently at its center.

When my mother brought home Robert Altman's 1982 ensemble drama *Come Back to the Five and Dime, Jimmy Dean, Jimmy*

Dean from the video store one day thirty-something years ago, she hadn't known what to expect. And, unlike *Mommie Dearest*, it was a film that we had *not* watched together again in the ensuing years. I wasn't even sure she'd remember it. As predicted, when we sat down for our re-view, she admitted she only had the foggiest recollection of it.

For me, it had proven haunting. The film is about a group of James Dean superfans who reunite at their preferred hangout twenty years after the star's tragically young death: an old five-and-dime shop in a tiny Texas town near Marfa. There they find themselves caught in an escalating whirlwind of intense emotional revelations. I remember that as the film began I had been unsettled by its eerie, claustrophobic atmosphere: Was it ever going to leave the confines of this dusty variety store? Making things even more disorienting was the film's tendency to time-hop without warning, even within single shots, jumping between the fifties and the seventies, and relying on the audience's imagination to make those leaps understood—the actresses never change their clothes despite playing twenty years apart. But the one detail that rattled me the most, and which I would remember most vividly for years to come, once the details on its maniacal twists, turns, and reveals vanished from my memory, was that within its main, almost entirely female cast, one of the characters was once biologically male. Years before I would know the word *trans*, here was such a character on-screen, and I was undeniably drawn to her.

As a boy I knew nothing of Robert Altman, though by the time I was an eighteen-year-old heading to school to study film, he had become a favorite of mine. With *Come Back*, Altman was in his experimental eighties phase, wading somewhere between the critical and commercial breakouts of his seventies films like *M*A*S*H*, *McCabe and Mrs. Miller*, and *Nashville*, and his nineties resurgence with *The Player* and *Short Cuts*. As the seventies came to a close, Altman's idiosyncratic style—large ensemble casts, complexly recorded and often overlapping dialogue, and curiously roving camerawork—was growing out of fashion, and this coincided with the shift in the American movie industry from ambitious, director-driven films to more commercial, less risky studio efforts intended to appeal to the widest possible audiences, typified by *Jaws* and *Star Wars*. Altman also was the rare director of the era to give prominent, complex roles equally to men and women. His dreamlike 1977 film *Three Women*, for instance, featuring unforgettable performances by Sissy Spacek and Shelley Duvall as southwest outcasts who undergo an almost supernatural personality swap, is now widely considered a masterpiece, though at the time, despite earning Duvall an acting award at the Cannes Film Festival, was a commercial failure and indication that oddball auteur visions were on their way out. In the early eighties, one project after another fell apart for Altman, and he found himself increasingly disinterested in trying to create products that the major studios would be willing to finance.

Altman's years in the wilderness drove him to the theater for a spell. He accepted an invitation to direct a pair of one-act plays at the Los Angeles Actors' Theatre, the first time he had worked on the stage since the fifties, back when he was in Kansas City. His reignited passion for theater led him to *Come Back to the Five and Dime, Jimmy Dean, Jimmy Dean*, written by Ed Graczyk in 1976. Altman was enticed enough to bring this odd chamber piece to Broadway, even if, as he said in an interview in the 2006 book *Altman on Altman*, "I didn't think it was a great play."

Come Back appealed to Altman for its visual and dramatic possibilities, but even more as a showcase for its female ensemble, who would have a chance to sink their incisors into a heaping helping of psychological warfare. "It had a Tennessee Williams/ William Inge aspect to it, with each character having their say," the director continued. "And I thought that would be interesting for the actresses." On-screen Altman doubles down on the

theatricality of the work. If the film feels unmistakably like theater, with heightened artificial sets and clear dramatic entrances
and exits, that's because Altman literally shot the film one week
after the play ended its short Broadway run—just fifty-two performances—with the same cast, on two adjacent sets that were
mirror images of each other, less than a million dollars on super
16mm film. Hardly a mere gimmick, the constant negotiation
between the past and present creates a distinct, porous visual
style, but it also speaks to one of the play's underlying themes,
which is the ongoing dialogue between the fifties, marked by
hope and political naïveté, and the seventies, an era of political
and social disillusionment, of Watergate and the Vietnam War.

This bold gambit pays off: the roles feel deeply lived-in, and
the actresses were already accustomed to the muscular chore-
ography that Altman conceived for stage and screen, utilizing
an elaborate network of mirrors and lighting effects that allows
the narrative to take place in both time periods at once. On
the page, the revelations and confrontations could become exhausting, but the mesmerizing women make the play's excesses
often exhilarating. Sandy Dennis—already an Oscar winner for
playing the mousy Honey, victimized by George and Martha
in 1966's *Who's Afraid of Virginia Woolf?*—stars as Mona, who
seems to live in a kind of fugue state, claiming to have given
birth to the son of James Dean after a one-night stand that took
place while he was filming *Giant* in Marfa. Alongside her are
two eventual Oscar winners giving hints of the film careers to
come: Cher, in her first dramatic role following more than a
decade as a pop and television star, as open-hearted sexpot Sissy,
who's hidden a life- and body-altering illness from everyone;
and Kathy Bates as tougher-than-nails bully Stella Mae, who's
married into big money and hasn't lost her nasty edge. Others
who have returned for the Disciples of James Dean reunion include milquetoast Edna Louise (Marta Heflin), pregnant with
her seventh child, and the older Juanita (Sudie Bond), an in-

tolerant Bible-thumper who has never come to terms with her late husband's alcoholism—she's a character who feels situated on the cusp of the American evangelical movement that would flower throughout Reagan's presidential term.

Towering over all of them—both in my child's eye and in my contemporary estimation—is Karen Black's mysterious arrival, Joanne. Dressed in a sophisticated white pantsuit with matching leather gloves and stylish sunglasses, Joanne is an ethereal presence, unrecognizable to the other women yet oddly familiar and somehow armed with a wealth of knowledge about them: much to Juanita's chagrin, she knows where her ex-husband stashed his secret bottles of liquor behind the counter. Arriving in a yellow sports car and giving off an air of urban sophistication, Joanne is clearly a fish out of water. It becomes evident that Joanne is the reunion's missing piece.

As she gradually reveals, Joanne was once Joe, the mild-mannered teenage store clerk (played in flashback by Mark Patton) who was the only male member of the Disciples. Mercilessly teased and bullied by the community for his effeminacy, he had been fired by the bigoted Juanita and her husband for being "shameful" and "not right." In the mirrored flashbacks, Joe is wilting, tearful, and tremulous; Joanne, however, is confident, fierce, and unafraid of a stare-down. It's initially unclear why she's returned to the site of such trauma, but Joanne suddenly has the fearsome strut of a cigarette-smoking avenging angel. And this out-of-towner's got a killer line for these Texas bumpkins: "Unlike all of you, I have undergone a change."

As a child, I found this woman—who refuses to be mislabeled and is quick to correct anyone who might not call her a "she"—fascinating, to say the least. Watched today, Altman's film might not contain the most enlightened embodiment of a trans character: *Come Back* is too studied and symbolic, too pressurized and reliant on reflections and doublings and high concepts, to function as a realistic portrayal of any woman's life. For instance, Sissy's big narrative twist, enacted superbly by Cher—who was initially courted by Altman to play Joanne, but lobbied for Sissy instead—is that she's been hiding the fact that she had a double mastectomy following a traumatic battle with breast cancer. There's more than a touch of cruelty, not to mention an overly symmetrical conceit, about this revelation, creating yet another mirroring effect, this time between the two women's transformed bodies. And Joanne's relationship to her own body postsurgery, as envisioned by the play's cisgender male writer, is dubiously reliant on faux psychologizing. When Stella Mae asks her if she ever regrets the decision, Joanne's response to this nosy intrusion is both vague and complex: "Only when I think about it."

Nevertheless, the singularity of this character and her centrality in this small but significant work in the career of a major Hollywood director remains remarkable. Simply put, Joanne is a landmark role, one of the extraordinarily few multidimensional trans female characters in American movies, which also includes Roberta Muldoon, the postop former football player played by John Lithgow in *The World According to Garp*, released just a few months before Altman's film. At the time of these films' releases, the Diagnostic and Statistical Manual of Mental Disorders, last updated in 1980 (DSM-III), classified transgender people as mentally ill, using the term *gender identity disorder*. Representation in mainstream cinema was more typified by something like Brian De Palma's blood-drenched *Dressed to Kill*, which featured Michael Caine as a murderous Norman Bates–like psychiatrist whose desire to become a woman is depicted as a function of split-personality disorder—when he gets sexually aroused, he assumes the identity of "Bobbi," a killer blonde wielding a razor blade.

Exquisitely crafted, terrifying, and utterly disinterested in making concessions to sensitivity, *Dressed to Kill* would end up making a very big impression on me when my mother—in a lapse of judgment she laughingly regrets to this day—rented it from the video store one fateful night for us to watch. Following the überviolent, erotic fever dream finale, she turned and asked cheerfully, heedlessly, how I liked the movie. As she recalls the incident, I slowly rotated my head toward her, revealing an ashen face that looked as though it had just seen a ghost. To this day, it's the only incident from our past she says she would classify as "child abuse."

The existence of a little movie such as *Come Back to the Five and Dime, Jimmy Dean, Jimmy Dean* can do a lot to mitigate the impact of a flashy hit like *Dressed to Kill,* a film that's often cited today by trans critics as having been damaging to the trans queer community. (In a 2018 online discussion about the film between trans critics Caden Mark Gardner and Willow Maclay, the latter wrote, "There are more instances of trans women appearing as murderers in movies than there are good films featuring actual trans women in meaty, acceptable, dense roles that approach their humanity with something resembling respect for the difficulty it takes to be trans.") Joanne, as played fearlessly by Black, is not merely sympathetic—she's a disruptor and a truth-teller. Before the term *pride* became a centerpiece of the gay rights movement, Black seems to embody it in much of her performance; it's in the way she moves through the store, holding herself with an air of grandeur, as though she has narrowly avoided tragedy and wants the other women to know it, to feel it. She's no victim. Partly due to her experiences as a bullied youth, she's likely also the kindest of all the women, as evidenced when she takes a beat to say to the mousy, oft-denigrated Edna Mae, "You glow brighter than anybody in the place"—a moment of recognition from one misunderstood, bullied human being to another.

Karen Black, who died after a battle with cancer in 2013, was best known for her Oscar-nominated breakout in *Five Easy Pieces* alongside Jack Nicholson; for other viewers, she's best remembered for her camp freak-out in the 1975 anthology horror TV movie *Trilogy of Terror*, in which she's terrorized by a diminutive "Zuni fetish doll," a goofy, colonialist revenge story in miniature that surely no one who has seen has ever forgotten. For me, her Joanne is the career-defining role; though one would hope to see an actual trans performer, rather than a cisgender woman, in the part today, Black radiates compassion and psychological curiosity, and her performance all but sets the tone for a film that might have otherwise devolved into delirious melodrama.

I found—and still find—the strength of all of these women intoxicating, though, and a lot of that has to do with their performativity, a fearless, outrageous style that has its origins in American theater. As the eighties wore on, I would see more of this, in a plethora of movies based on plays, many of them featuring casts almost entirely of women who—in the hothouse Tennessee Williams tradition—also seemed to revel in chewing on thick wads of Southern accents: *Crimes of the Heart*; *The Trip to Bountiful*; *'night, Mother*; *Steel Magnolias*; and an HBO recording of a play called *Vanities*, which my mother had taped on VHS. Whether centering on mothers and daughters, sisters, or tight-knit groups of friends, they communicated an appealing sense of intense female togetherness, which would often intensify into the kind of bickering that can flower from intimacy. The unapologetic feminine emotionality of these highly verbal films hit me on a deep level, speaking to some untapped well of identity that went way beyond entertainment value. I knew that, because of my gender, I might always be somehow left on the sidelines, cut out of this sisterhood.

Loving movies about women felt somehow wrong, like a social maladjustment. After all, if girls were meant to play with pink and yellow plastic dolls and boys with blue and steel-gray toy trucks, then surely girls watched girl movies and boys watched boy movies, whatever those were. The guarding of gender binaries is especially a scourge when enforced on children, as their every desire is inherently judged before it's even formed. Just as kids are taught to play with the "proper" toys, they are instructed what is sexually "right" and "wrong," and it's a subtle, nasty form of social brainwashing. I learned from an early age—from slapstick movies and comedy sketch shows, and from my family's response to those movies and shows—that the act of a man kissing another man was "gross," the kind of unwanted visual intrusion that, if it ever showed up on-screen, warranted either maniacal laughs or a desperate lunge for the remote control in order to expedite fast-forwarding.

This form of conditioning is so strong that, years later, long after I had been comfortably out of the closet, it still feels odd—and even incongruous—to vocalize the feelings of attraction I might have for men on-screen around family or largely hetero-sexual groups of people. In 1999, still several years before coming out as gay, I remember seeing *The Talented Mr. Ripley* in the theater with my mother, which would prove some kind of turning point in my self-awareness. Based on lesbian author Patricia Highsmith's 1955 novel about a sociopathic killer and identity thief, Oscar-winner Anthony Minghella's film was marketed as your average Christmastime prestige pic; we—and I would hazard to guess most of the audience—were taken by surprise to find that the film was a homoerotic buffet, with the lion's share of its hypersensuality directed at up-and-comer Jude Law. Playing Dickie Greenleaf, the spoiled-brat scion of a wealthy industrialist who becomes the target of Matt Damon's repressed gay title character, Law was the definition of "golden boy," exquisitely lit and framed by the adoring camera, his skin bronzed by the film's Mediterranean sun, his lithe, hirsute torso often in various states of undress.

Jude Law's gorgeousness was so unavoidable, and so much a central aspect of the film's point, that when the film was over, I remember my mother and I remarking at length on his looks. Her ideals of female movie-star beauty—Elizabeth Taylor, Natalie Wood, Michelle Pfeiffer—had long been topics of conversation. The perfection of Tina Turner's legs were often remarked upon in my house, by both mother and father; never did anyone talk about the exciting contours of Marlon Brando's arms or Denzel Washington's abs. This was the first time I could recall ever having that kind of discussion about a man. It felt scary and exciting to even be talking about it, somehow brave, like I was slowly pushing on a door that would take a few more taps, then a few more shoves, to get fully open.

A few years after college—and five years after *The Talented Mr. Ripley*—I came out to my mother over the telephone. I had reached what felt like a crisis point, partly triggered by that singular feeling of postcollege loneliness, as so many of my closest friends were leaving New York. It's hard for me to remember the words I used, or what exactly I was saying or trying to say. But I recall standing in the crummy kitchen of my floor-through apartment in the Lefferts Gardens neighborhood of Brooklyn—for which I paid what now seems like an obscenely low amount of five hundred bucks a month—and barely getting out the words. I remember the phone having an actual cord that I was nervously coiling and uncoiling, but my memory may have invented that.

"Mom, there's something I need to talk about," I must have said, before stammering and delaying for a few more agonizing minutes. She interrupted. "Michael, are you gay?" She made it easier on me.

"We knew before you did," she told me fifteen years later, after the credits had rolled on our rewatch of *Come Back to the Five and Dime*. "I remember saying to Dad, when you weren't around, 'I think that Michael is gay. If he is, would that bother you?' And he said, 'Nah.'"

I don't remember exactly how I responded in the moment of that fateful phone call, so dazed was I. Eventually I would feel relief, of course, but in the moment I was only mortified. The scrutiny is too much, too sudden. Closeted people spend years and years doing their best to keep the spotlight off them. When the instant illumination shines on you, you long for the protection of shadows. On certain days, I still wish I was that boy, safe and alone in his bedroom with stacks of movies to watch on a thirteen-inch television, blocking out the world as he immersed himself in the lives, hopes, dreams, and desires of unreal people.

Coming out is a contradiction. It's an act of becoming your best, true self, but at the same time it takes you outside of yourself, maybe for the first time. You're no longer hiding, isolated, and solitary; you're suddenly part of history, a lineage and a community that's long been marginalized. You're an unavoidably political being. If you're lucky, it may bring you closer to your parents, but even in the best-case scenario of complete parental love and acceptance, it also creates an unbridgeable divide: you're suddenly a defiantly sexual being with an identity that stands definitively apart, in most cases, from the family that raised you. Sex and identity are far too personal to ever completely share, especially with a parent; the truth both excites and unmoors you from the past, from the parent.

My recent sexual experiences with both men and women had put me into a state of confusion; it was time. Life isn't like a movie, with easy narratives, beginnings, middles, and ends. Sexual attraction is fluid, but by that point I had to admit that while I physically admired both Jude Law and Elisabeth Shue, it was Jude Law who got the blood rushing. It was that picture of Marlon Brando from *A Streetcar Named Desire*. It was John Gavin, not Janet Leigh, in *Psycho*. It was Tony Leung, not Maggie Cheung, in *In the Mood for Love*.

The story of the movies is basically one, long, heterosexual romantic epic, an unceasing love story between a man and a woman continuing on, decade after decade. It has never given gay viewers very much of an olive branch, even though the Hollywood dream machine has long been fueled by a kind of unspoken, closeted queer desire. When there has been the unusual outwardly gay-themed drama, more often than not it has ended in tragedy and violence: *Mulholland Drive, Brokeback Mountain, Milk.* Films from around the world—from Spain, from Taiwan, from Thailand—were speaking to my queerness on a profound level, but American cinema was still way behind. It was only in the very late year of 2018 that a major Hollywood studio put out its first coming-out teen movie, the charming if necessarily bland *Love, Simon.* The movie was white, bourgeois, and as edgy as a Starbucks latte in a paper cup, but following decades of countless cookie-cutter boy-meets-girl high school comedies, it still managed to feel like a poignant breakthrough. I cannot help but wonder if the trajectory of my life would have been different had *Love, Simon* been released in the nineties, when I was in high school, or even in the eighties when I was just beginning to understand the world.

Movies have an intense power; we follow them by example, even if we don't know it. Just as they can impart bigotry, movies can teach compassion. It's a byproduct that even the most cynical aesthete (me, sometimes) can appreciate. *Come Back to the Five and Dime, Jimmy Dean, Jimmy Dean* encouraged my mother to express delight at how far things have come in terms of acceptance and representation of the transgender community. The fact that she was saying this at all reflects how much things had changed; it's a specific language of empathy my mother would not have had in 1982. In fact, one of the few things I can remember her saying about Altman's movie way back when she first brought home that VHS from the video store was that the movie was "weird." Sure, she could have been referring to the stage-bound atmospherics, the overheated melodrama, the bizarre narrative twists; but it was the presence of Joanne that was the purposefully destabilizing element. Even if she felt relatively comfortable with the idea of homosexuality, my mother would unlikely have had any experience with trans people, to this day the most marginalized and endangered of the LGBT community, even with considerable strides made.

My mother wasn't entirely ignorant of the queer world, though until I came along—and came out—homosexuals were always viewed by her as distant others. In movies she would have seen in the sixties, gay people were either repressed sad sacks—Don Murray's clandestine closeted politician in Otto Preminger's 1962 *Advise and Consent* or Shirley MacLaine's suicidal lesbian in William Wyler's 1961 *The Children's Hour*—or the flouncy, limp-wristed butts of jokes, as with Christopher Hewitt's admittedly hilarious Roger DeBris in Mel Brooks's 1968 *The Producers*. To even the most apparently compassionate straight person, these stereotypes can stick.

Outside of movie screens, my mother remembers various gay men in her life, I discovered during our postmovie conversation. She talks about them like vaporous ghosts of the past. "When I was in college I had a really good friend who was gay. A dead ringer for Tony Franciosa. He was a nice guy. His name might have been… Eric?" I asked if he was out. Of course not. "But he was gay. I knew. He wasn't saying anything; he spent summers on Fire Island." She also got wistful when she recalled her experiences doing summer stock: "I worked with a gay guy at Falmouth Playhouse. He lived in New York, I think, and he very well may have been one of the AIDS casualties. He was a good singer…what was his name?"

Then there was the younger brother of one of my father's childhood friends; the two families lived on the same street in Newton, Massachusetts—the legendary Theodore Road that I was told so much about as a kid. When I was growing up, I had heard his name spoken in somewhat hushed tones, usually accompanied by a sad little headshake. "He had a big job in New York at CBS; he had a partner, I think. They put it in the paper as 'died after a long illness.' We knew it was AIDS. I don't know how we knew, but it was understood."

My generation of gay men, coming of sexual age in the late nineties and the first years of the 21st century, is lucky. With just a few years difference, we largely avoided experiencing the horrors of those who came before us, of having to witness our friends and lovers get sick and painfully die, all the while being politically ignored social pariahs under an uncaring president. The trauma—for those who managed to live through it at all— is unimaginable to me.

I distinctly remember my mom bringing home the movie *Longtime Companion*, the acclaimed 1989 drama about a group of gay men coming to terms with the rising AIDS crisis. The film had received an Oscar nomination for Bruce Davison (incidentally, an actor my mother had met during summer stock) and was deemed an important milestone, the first accessible, semimainstream movie to take the ongoing epidemic as its main subject matter. The increasing prevalence of AIDS on the nightly news during the eighties had made the subject of male homosexuality inextricable from sickness and disease for much of straight America, and I was part of the generation raised among this awareness. Even for non-Bible-thumpers, gayness itself was discussed as though a death sentence. *Longtime Companion*, a sensitively handled, beautifully evoked portrait of the decade directed by Norman René, who would die from AIDS-complicated illness just a few years later at age forty-five, was an unlikely film for us to watch together in the Koresky household: all the principal characters in its ensemble were gay men. I remember watching it with unease and fascination; I also remember being momentarily sent out of the room during the one montage in which things get mildly frisky between some of the men—meaning a kiss or two and a few embraces. I don't recall such parental protections happening during most of the infinitely more explicit "straight" sex scenes that peppered the films of my childhood.

For even the most apparently accepting parents of gay children, it may come as a surprise—or for some perhaps a confirmation of their private fears—that we retain a certain level of resentment into adulthood. I'm well aware that my particular coming-out story is, to most eyes, ideal: my mother's kindness in speaking the words I couldn't manage, and the lack of fireworks or drama thereafter. At the same time, questions inevitably nag: if she claims to have known even before I did, maybe even since I was a child, why did it take her or my father so long to say something? Isn't it our parents' responsibility, their only charge, to protect their children, to make the world a more comfortable place for them? I ask these questions not as personal accusations, but as larger social queries. The tyranny of our culture has long been the demonization of anything outside of the mainstream, and for gay people specifically the message that sexuality is somehow something to be ashamed of, to hide, not discuss. If we live in a strictly demarcated society in which heterosexual values have been centralized—in movies, TV, art, politics, sports, religion, and every other aspect of culture one can imagine—to the point of largely eradicating images of all alternatives, then it's up to parents to remind their children, from an early age, that they matter regardless of identity or sexual preference. Yes, each child, each person, must come to their own conception of their self on their own, but I've come to believe that children must be taught values of love and self-acceptance, and that discrimination can begin in the most minute, undetectable ways in the home.

I asked my mother if she had been aware of even the concept of homophobia as a younger person. "It never touched my life," she responded. What about the treatment of gay characters in movies? "There weren't any to notice. I didn't think about it; it wasn't on my mind. If there was a gay character, it was a joke, in a comedy. I have to admit to you that I laughed just as hard as anybody else."

As did I, which is partly social conditioning and partly a sense of solidarity with outrageous "others." Witnessing flamboyant gay stereotypes, whether it's *The Producers* or Sean Hayes on *Will and Grace*, or Damon Wayans and David Alan Grier's snap-happy "Men on Film" duo on the sketch comedy series *In Living Color*—a Koresky household staple in the early nineties—can trigger an appreciative camp response in even the most diligently proud viewer. Almost two decades after an entire episode of *Will and Grace* satirized the impossibility of showing two men kissing on television, it's become almost commonplace to see two men or two women disrobing, kissing, and fondling on prime time, on such dramatic network series as *How to Get Away with Murder* and *Pose*, or streaming breakthroughs like *Orange Is the New Black*, which are enjoyed by viewers of all ages and identities. When I was visiting that June, my mother was especially excited about the imminent second season of a CBS police procedural called *Instinct*, starring Alan Cumming as the rare main character to be incidentally gay—and a detective to boot. She loved the show largely because the protagonist's gayness made it so that "he and his female partner had no dumb sexual tension." Even more, she said, "He has a *fabulous* husband."

It's no surprise that parents breathe huge sighs of relief when their children "settle down" with someone and "make a life for themselves." I use quotation marks because these are terms I've heard my mother—and other parents—use over the years. Parents of a certain generation who have gay offspring seem to feel this desire acutely, as if having a steady relationship goes a long way to "normalizing" queer people. Luckily, I do indeed have a *fabulous* husband, and my mother is right in adoring Chris. I met him not long after coming out, and he is inextricably tied to my sexual identity. We are pleased to enjoy the social freedoms and acceptance that earlier generations would have thought impossible: Chris and I got hitched at Brooklyn Borough Hall less than a year after gay marriage was legal in New York State.

One of the many things that movies have taught me is that American culture can feel homogenous, constricting, and terribly limited, focused on procreative forward motion at the mercy of anyone who falls outside the boundaries of heteronormativity. As in the movies, gay people have long felt like the supporting characters in the larger, straighter narrative. Now, we'd love to have our own stories. And I don't mean that in the manner of streaming giants like Netflix or Hulu, in which identity-driven programming has become another virtuous box to check. Rather, I'm talking about being part of the complete social fabric, not just an errant thread that's constantly sticking out.

Throughout the eighties and most of the nineties, I wouldn't have assumed there was any other way. The lives of gay men were not part of the story of cinema, and, after all, these women's pictures were enough for me. I wasn't sure how or why, but I aspired to them. I aspired to their emotional transparency, to the unabashedly feminine bond they shared. They didn't resolve arguments with guns; they hugged. Sometimes they even kissed. Mostly they talked. And not in the alienating, words-as-machine-guns way that guys seemed to talk, in movies like *Diner* or *Glengarry Glen Ross*; this wasn't about sexual conquests or arcane trivia or pulling a con. These women seemed to be getting in touch with some deeper parts of themselves and using them to connect to others. The actresses seemed to be doing the same. Jessica Lange was going deep, as was Sissy Spacek. As were Cher and Sandy Dennis and Kathy Bates. And Karen Black, who may not have been trans, but was digging down into something real within herself. She clearly felt it; I felt it.

The world has moved on from *Come Back to the Five and Dime, Jimmy Dean, Jimmy Dean*, and in some ways that's a good thing. But Joanne has never left my world. I can still see her out there somewhere, downing whiskey shots and making people feel wonderfully, purposefully, uncomfortable while also somehow managing to glow brighter than anyone in this place.

1983: Lost

I had been anticipating our next movie with a bit of anxiety. It was sure to open up a can of worms. I just didn't realize I'd be opening it up so soon after arriving for the weekend.

As we chatted on the highway during the drive home from the bus station, I was talking to my mother, as always, about what new movies I'd recommend to her. My husband and I had just been to the theater to see Lulu Wang's *The Farewell*, an independent American drama about a second-generation Chinese immigrant (Awkwafina, whom I knew my mother had enjoyed as the zippy comic sidekick in *Crazy Rich Asians*) living in Brooklyn. She returns to her family's hometown of Changchun after her grandmother is diagnosed with terminal cancer. The twist is that the family, due to long-held cultural custom, does not plan on telling the elderly woman that she is dying; instead, they have all convened under the false pretense of a cousin's wedding, which they carry out in full, an extreme length to go to cover the truth.

"I think I've heard of that one," my mother said, while keeping her eye on the road and two hands tightly gripped on the wheel as usual. "What's it about again?"

I reminded her of the premise. There was a silent pause as the car rattled down Route 3.

"You know I never told your dad he was sick."

I hadn't known this. I had wondered, but never inquired. It was clear that he knew something was wrong with him. That there was a reason he was going to the doctor so much, that they were asking him so many questions, that they were adjusting and readjusting endless cocktails of medications, year after year. But the nature of a deteriorative cognitive disease such as Alzheimer's makes the patient's knowledge and self-awareness ambiguous.

"Were the doctors okay with that?" was all I could think to ask, a kind of distancing strategy for my own self-protection.

"I never even asked them. What good would it do?"

Would it have done any good? All those years my dad was sick, his mind gradually disappearing at such a cruelly young age, would it have mattered if he had known his fate? Would he have given up sooner, and therefore might we have lost him earlier? From the first sign of something wrong—a sudden and severe depression—to his final months in a nursing home, was eleven years. I know my mother would not have wanted to lose a single one of those years, however impossible they became.

Any time my father's disease or his death comes up in conversation, I always feel the urge to change the topic, like finding a quick escape hatch—easier to talk about TV, the weather, *movies*. This weekend, though, I had decided I was intentionally heading into battle. I had begun going to therapy about a year and a half earlier, partly to help with my own emotional evasiveness. My therapist, Jason, had helped me excavate some of my traumas—some of the things I had never spoken about with another human being. This hadn't left the confines of Jason's office, though, with its readily accessible Kleenex box and the caring, nonjudgmental stare that greeted my every blubber.

This weekend promised to be about tackling such things head-on, without the help of a professional. I hadn't yet told my mother which movie we were revisiting this time—not because it was going to be a delightful surprise for her, but rather because I didn't want her to run in the other direction. That July, I already had a lot on my mind. My fortieth birthday had arrived, an event almost as dreaded as the next movie on our list.

One couldn't exactly call the expression on her face elation when she found out what it was. There was none of the glee that had accompanied the prospect of watching *Nine to Five*, none of the anticipatory excitement of descending into the camp hell of *Mommie Dearest*, or even the curious fascination of revisiting that half-forgotten dream *Come Back to the Five and Dime, Jimmy Dean, Jimmy Dean.* Instead, when I gingerly revealed that the 1983 title would be *Terms of Endearment,* my mother let out an "Oh…" that was like the sound you make when you get a box of raisins in your trick-or-treat bag. "That's a tough one."

Though a movie beloved by many, James L. Brooks's domestic tragicomedy starring Shirley MacLaine and Debra Winger was kind of an untouchable object in my house, spoken of in hushed tones and headshakes. I actually cannot remember when my mother first showed it to me; it's one of those movies that's just always been there. Its title is so iconic at this point that it even seems to have lost its specific and elegant double meaning. *Terms of Endearment.* It's just…a title. Out of the almost one hundred Best Picture Oscar winners, it's one of the very, very few that one could ever call a "women's picture," and the only one in the history of the awards that centers almost exclusively on the relationship between a mother and a daughter—stories of dads, sons, and godfathers are more the speed of traditionally masculinist Hollywood cinema. It's not an aesthetically difficult film by any measure, yet my mother remembered *Terms of En-*

dearment as a challenge, even radical in what she perceived as a betrayal of the audience's trust. "We were sitting in the theater laughing *so* hard, and then…" She trails off. "I thought, what *is* this? We were shocked. We felt like we got punched in the stomach."

As we're about to willingly lean into that punch once more, so many years after she told me she could *never watch that movie again*, my mother insists that this was the first film that ever combined comedy and tragedy, paving the way for other tearjerkers of the era, more shameless emotion-exploiting genre-hoppers like *Beaches* and *Steel Magnolias*. The snobby film historian in me wants to correct her, to find all of those instances of tragi-comedies that anticipated Brooks's film. Even as I write this I'm still trying to think of one. She may be right. In this very particular, American way, in how it swings for the fences as both broad comedy and intense tearjerker, nothing else before it comes close. "I think I had some resentment," she admitted. "Like it had pulled the rug out from under me. I never thought a movie could so definitely be one thing and then definitely another."

Selfish, foolish son that I am, I was about to put her through this experience again. Though after so many years, I wondered how different that experience would be. When the film came out in 1983, she was roughly the same age as Winger's young mother, Emma; now she's older than Emma's mother, Aurora Greenway, played by MacLaine. She's also now, like Aurora, a widow whose children have long since moved out of the house. Would time cushion the film's blows, or would it hit harder than ever? Making things more potentially claustrophobic was the weather: the oppressive heat of July made it less likely that we would be spending too much time out on the peaceful back porch. Instead, we'd end up huddled inside in the air-conditioning, which never seems to do enough to cool off the often sun-drenched family room.

As we remembered, the movie is funny, often very funny;

what we both forgot is just how much of it is funny. For about
ninety minutes—which is, after all, the length of a full movie—
Terms of Endearment is unmistakably a comedy; yes, it's couched
in the truths and anxieties of everyday lived experience, and yes,
it affords its characters the strength and dignity and respect one
would associate with what people usually categorize as drama.
Yet, as befitting the directorial feature debut of James L. Brooks,
who cut his teeth on such centerpiece television sitcoms of the
seventies as *The Mary Tyler Moore Show* and *Taxi*, it's also a work
of screwball idiosyncrasy, packed with colorful characters who
spout one-liners in short, expertly edited scenes that get to the
point without much fuss. This is a marked contrast from Larry
McMurtry's dialogue-heavy source novel, which, taking its cues
from Aurora's punctilious, long-winded self-satisfaction, feels su-
persized with endless conversations and argumentative rapport.

In form, Brooks's *Terms of Endearment* is an eighties movie
for sure, much slicker than anything a moviegoer might have
seen in the seventies; even my mother's first comment after the
movie starts, shaking her head as she takes a swig of Earl Grey, is
"This sounds *so* eighties!" She's referring to Michael Gore's driving, insistent minor-key score, immediately recognizable from
those first four descending notes, and from the countless trailers and Oscar montages it's accompanied. When one thinks of
"eighties movie music," there are probably other more instantly
evocative madeleines, like the synth score in *The Terminator* or
Ray Parker Jr.'s "Who ya gonna call?" refrain from *Ghostbusters*.
For my mother, it's the emotional swells of *Terms of Endearment*
or the sweet pop lullaby of Bill Conti's *Baby Boom* score or the
triumphant surge of Carly Simon's *Working Girl* theme song
that gets the heart pumping, the era unthinkable without such
bordering-on-kitsch aural transcendence.

Once I wished away the anticipation of its horrible revelations, the most striking aspect of *Terms of Endearment* remained
the power of its two still-revelatory star performances. A perfect

match for the general causticity of the screenplay by Brooks and McMurtry, MacLaine and Winger are far from typical Hollywood stars. At this point in their careers a veteran and a newbie, respectively, MacLaine and Winger are hugely responsible for the lack of overt sentimentality in a film that nevertheless had audiences weeping in the aisles.

MacLaine brings her own, very curious brand of sangfroid to Aurora, a Boston-born aging Southern belle who naturally attracts and then swats away male suitors like mosquitos. At a dinner party scene early in the film, upon finding out that Emma is pregnant with her first child, MacLaine first chuckles sarcastically and then, with a rising torrent of uncontrollable, wittily terrifying anger, a knife clutched precariously in one hand, screams, "Why would I want to be a *grandmother*?!" and you've never believed anyone more in your life. Winger's Emma is an odd duck all her own, first seen the night before her wedding getting high and singing along to a recording of Ethel Merman doing Cole Porter's "Anything Goes" from behind a haphazard bridal veil. These are two idiosyncratic actors, and they consistently confound and surprise in the way they deliver or twist a line. Together they create a cinematic mother-daughter pairing singular in its mix of intimacy and emotional erraticism.

MacLaine makes Aurora's dissatisfactions readable, but not completely sympathetic, and the arm's length at which she keeps the audience is all to the film's benefit. Since making her film debut in 1955 in Alfred Hitchcock's autumnal death comedy *The Trouble with Harry*, MacLaine never settled for cutie-pie roles, even early in her career taking on parts with pathos and substance, most remarkably in her Oscar-nominated performances in Vincente Minnelli's *Some Came Running*, in which she plays a good-souled but damaged girl who can't catch a break, and Billy Wilder's *The Apartment*, as an elevator operator unlucky in love; for both characters a bubbly personality masks desperation, emotional struggle, and suicidal tendencies. In those parts, and in her sensational work in Bob Fosse's 1969 directorial debut *Sweet Charity*—in which she very bravely took a part tailor-made for Gwen Verdon onstage—MacLaine's stock-in-trade was vulnerability. Her Aurora, on the other hand, is the picture of steely recalcitrance, and it feels born of life experience; she's untrusting of outsiders, determined to keep her life exactly where she wants it. When, in the film's final passage, the dam breaks—and does it ever—it's all the more disturbing, as though their lives, and the well-balanced, structural integrity of the film itself, might never be repaired.

Only three years earlier, Winger had her first serious starring role, opposite John Travolta in 1980's *Urban Cowboy*, which showcased her unusual brand of appealing self-sufficiency and eccentric charm, and which, like *Terms of Endearment*, was set in Texas—her twangy, denim-and-plaid dive-barfly Sissy was an unlikely breakthrough for an Ohio girl raised in an Orthodox Jewish family. Even in a dingy establishment best known for its whiplash-inducing mechanical bull, Winger's sharp intelligence charges through the screen. The Steinbeck adaptation *Cannery Row* and the megahit romance *An Officer and a Gentleman* followed quickly in succession, the latter scoring Winger her first Best Actress Oscar nomination, a testament to her ability to inject complexity, depth, and motivational ambiguity to what on the page might have seemed like a thankless girlfriend role.

Winger makes her *Officer* character, Paula Pokrifki, a factory worker who lives near a US naval base and becomes romantically involved with Richard Gere's troubled aviation officer candidate, more layered than the male protagonist—even if he's meant, per the title, to ultimately embody two kinds of men. Nevertheless, Winger's rising star had at this point been tagged to roles that were essentially written as love interests. With *Terms of Endearment*, she broke away from that convention: her main costar was, unusually for Hollywood, another actress, and her romantic partner in the film, Jeff Daniels, is relegated to a supporting role. As her wishy-washy husband, given by McMurtry the perfect dud of a name "Flap," Daniels is a quintessential dissatisfied suburban husband, a corduroy-jacketed English professor who's less unkind than he is unremarkable, even in his philandering.

Once Emma has fled the nest, following Flap to a teaching job in Des Moines, where their family grows to five—two sons and a daughter—the long-widowed Aurora starts going through her own romantic dramas. Unlike Flap, Aurora's next-door neighbor would seem to be a remarkable icon of manhood; even his name, Garrett Breedlove, reeks of virile hetero masculinity. Yet Best Supporting Actor Oscar–winner Jack Nicholson plays Garrett as a dissolute, mischievous drunk resting on his laurels as a retired astronaut, all too happy to recount his long-vanished outer-space heroics. It's a tactic that works better for the too-young women who frequent his house than for the eternally unimpressed Aurora; it's her lack of idolatry that seems to most possess Garrett. After many years of living mere feet from this overweight, if charismatic—it's Nicholson, after all—blowhard, Aurora finally agrees to have lunch with him. This leads to the film's only true outright slapstick sequence, a legendarily awful first date that climaxes with the two of them driving across the shoreline of a vacant beach, Nicholson steering the wheel with his feet while propped up through the sunroof, before Aurora stops the car short and sends him flying into the water. This doesn't stop him from making an unwanted pass, shoving a hand down a none-too-pleased Aurora's blousy, windblown dress. "Would you like to see me again?" she asks nonchalantly after they miraculously make it home in one piece. "I'd rather stick *needles* in my eyes," he hisses. At this point, my mother is laughing uproariously, seemingly heedless of the shift to come.

As pairs, Winger and Daniels, and MacLaine and Nicholson, appear on-screen together more often than Winger and MacLaine, who are mostly, practically and poignantly, separated by vicissitudes of life and the cruelties of narrative plotting; nevertheless it's the latter pair that anyone who remembers *Terms of Endearment* would first recall. When mother and daughter are on the phone, it's hard to imagine that the actresses were not actually shooting their scenes alongside one another on set, so distinct is their chemistry. Yet Winger and MacLaine's relationship was decidedly less than harmonious, as has been reported in various stories over the years. In a 1986 *New York Times* profile that characterizes Debra Winger as "fiery" and "difficult"—coded, sexist words frequently used against women who stand up for themselves in male-dominated industries—the younger actress admitted about her relationship with MacLaine, "I can't deny that we fought. We're not having lunch together today. We challenged ourselves, and when we got tired of challenging ourselves, we challenged each other. But I think there was always a respect between the two of us." In her autobiography *My Lucky Stars*, MacLaine was more direct, relating a story in which, after the two fought about hitting their marks, Winger "lifted her skirt slightly, looked over her shoulder, bent over, and farted in my face."

By Oscar night, things between the women seemed civil enough. When MacLaine won the Best Actress Oscar, on her way to the podium, she grabbed fellow nominee Winger by the cheeks with a firm grip and kissed her; in her speech MacLaine tellingly thanked the younger actress for her "turbulent brilliance" (a cut back to the audience shows a chuckling Winger, apparently both moved and amused), but she also, perhaps pointedly, then exclaimed, "I deserve this!"

The friction between the two clearly contributed to the essential and productive unease in the performances, as the characters' fighting feels unforced, as natural a part of their rapport as a hug or an involuntary smile. Because of the constant undercurrent of prickliness between the two, there's even more of a release and joy when Aurora and Emma's mutual love shines through. There's a beautiful midpoint moment in which Emma comes home to visit Aurora after many years in Des Moines, and as the daughter swiftly exits the car's passenger side door and jumps into her mother's arms, Brooks's cinematographer Andrzej Bartkowiak switches to a handheld camera. In a movie of mostly static frames with very little movement, this changeup in shooting style suddenly communicates a sense of intimacy, capturing an almost desperate love between these two women. At this juncture, Emma has had three kids, has seen her marriage begin to disintegrate, and has embarked upon a short-lived affair with a timid married man, played by a never-demurer John Lithgow; meanwhile, Aurora has abandoned her host of suitors to begin a romance in earnest with her next-door astronaut.

Life has been rich, unpredictable, sometimes frustrating, but always manageable. Then Emma goes with her toddler daughter for a flu shot. In touching Emma's arm, the doctor feels an ominous lump. Life sneaks up on you.

In fall of 2000, I was entering my senior year at NYU. Though my focus was cinema studies with a minor in dramatic writing, I had for the previous couple of years been working as much as I could on the film sets of my friends in the filmmaking department, taking on different roles: producer, assistant camera, assistant sound, music composer, even actor. It seemed apt that I should gain this kind of experience while I had the opportunity. Looking back I'm eternally grateful for having been able to glean so much about the filmmaking process, especially in a predigital era, when the school was still predominantly having students shoot on 16mm film and editing in-house on big, beautiful, clunky old Steenbeck flatbeds.

During this semester, I had been invited to produce my friend John's short, *Hell's Kitchen*, a clever dark comedy with a great student-film premise: a sprightly teen and his chowderhead buddy stumble upon a portal to the underworld at a local restaurant where they're working summer jobs. Since John and I both came from Chelmsford, we shot the movie back in our hometown, recruiting local actors and filming in the old standby restaurant Town Meeting, a wall-to-wall carpet and wooden chair affair that was by the turn of the 20th century one of the few nonchain restaurants left in town. It has since been replaced by a Walgreens pharmacy. For the all-important climactic scene—in which the intrepid young protagonist bursts into the dining room to frantically announce that the establishment is owned and operated by Lucifer himself, only to be coerced by the patrons into giving in to his needs and sitting down for a meal—we needed a restaurant full of willing, diabolically friendly extras.

John had the idea that my dad should be one of them, and that he should be given a prominent speaking role to boot, as, of course, the kid's father. I had been in perfect agreement. My dad was a dad's dad, as they say. Jovial, almost always smiling, he put people at ease with an unintimidating masculinity and a warmly sarcastic sense of humor that never pushed over into cruelty. His job—a traveling salesman—was dad-like; his interests—cars and airplanes—were dad-like. He seemed to enjoy mowing the lawn, waving at neighbors as he pushed the machine around the yard. He loved *Seinfeld* and *The Shawshank Redemption*. He loved Roy Orbison and Simon and Garfunkel. He adored his friends; he adored the cats. When he died, one of his closest friends since high school gave a eulogy that was literally just a list of things that he loved. It was endless. I keep a printout of that speech in my desk.

Even, or perhaps especially, for a student film, moviemaking isn't quite a breeze. The collaboration of a crew working toward a shared goal is inspiring in the rearview mirror, but on set it can be merely tiring. And before digital video, with which you can shoot and shoot until the actors are blue in the face, filmmaking was slightly more anxiety-provoking, as film itself was expensive and precious, and any out-of-place element—sound, lighting, camera movement, performance—could throw off an entire scene.

My dad only had a couple of lines in his final exchange, the dramatic crux of the film, but he wasn't getting them quite right. And the more he was flubbing them, the more sweaty and frustrated he was getting. It was late in the day; evening had fallen and all of the extras, my dad included, had been sitting in their place for hours, waiting for everything to be just right for shooting. Spirits had gone from high to dubious—a common feeling from every NYU film I had worked on. John was filming my dad in medium close-up, hoping to just be able to insert his lines into the scene later, but even this was proving difficult. The agony of not being able to get the scene right was beginning to show on his face, and it manifest as a distressed expression I had never seen him wear before; his face looked hangdog, his mouth trembling, almost like he wasn't able to smile. It gave me a hollow feeling, like some shift had taken place but I couldn't put my finger on why. He looked different, but in the moment I chalked it up to the novelty of seeing my father act; my mom was traditionally the performer, but never my dad. He preferred being out of the spotlight; sometimes he seemed happiest being in the back row of a theater watching my mom sing, content to be part of the audience.

Yet here he was, all lights on him, the pressure bearing down. The evening was wearing on, and at one point John gave everyone a short break to get some fresh, cool air away from the light stands. In the parking lot, my mother came up to me.

"You need to hurry this up," she said.

"I know it's taking a long time, but John needs to get his shots." We didn't have the restaurant location for more than that day.

"Your father is having a hard time," she said. At first, it sounded like a response to the difficulty of the moment, a literal reaction to the prolonged shoot and his annoyance at continually tripping over or forgetting his lines. But she meant something more general, something hidden, something I wasn't witnessing because I was away at college. *Your father is having a hard time.*

The haunted urgency with which my mother told me this has stayed with me. *Hell's Kitchen* ended up just fine, and, through judicious editing, my dad knocked it out of the park. Other people who watched it—especially those who knew him—enjoyed the naturalism and charm of his cameo; my response to it was always complicated: I could see the uncharacteristic anxiety on his face, captured forever on film. That struck me as unfair for someone who never seemed like he had a care in the world.

What was the nature of his hard time? I'll never be able to speak to this part of his experience with anything like confidence, so caught up was I in my new independent life in New York, immersed in cinema and in a new group of friends. But my mother was there; she had to live with his sudden overwhelming depression, his inability, after thirty years on the job, to rise in the morning and get out of the house. This went past disgruntled or dissatisfied; this was chemical. His brain patterns were betraying his happiness, overtaken by apathy and a loss of interest in activities and hobbies, and most especially his work. Within the next couple of years, I had graduated college, moved to an affordable part of Brooklyn, and was able to parlay, with the support of editor Gavin Smith, an internship at *Film Comment* into an assistant editor job; at the same time, my father—then in his late fifties—would take an extended leave from work. My mother began making a series of phone calls to doctors to help him deal with his depression, leading to a Prozac prescription. At least from my remote vantage point, things seemed better for him throughout the early 2000s; though by 2004 he decided to head into early retirement. He was always on the road, and the life of a traveling optical salesman had become simply too difficult to maintain.

I was in my early twenties, only about a year and a half out of the closet, when my mother told me what was really behind all of my dad's health problems. By 2005, I was the copy chief at the storied *Interview* magazine, working under its fearsome edi-

tor, Ingrid Sischy. I was merely twenty-five and I was tickled to
have my own office with a closing door—never mind that the
door was frequently opened so certain colleagues could come
into the room to confide in me, and often literally weep, about
how abused they felt on a daily basis by the powers that be. It
was behind this closed door that I remember my mother calling me in the middle of the day, on my office phone, to reveal
the truth: "Your father has dementia."

I don't think I could have responded with much more than a
quizzical, "Okay." What could I have known about such a word?
It sounded vague, abstract, something that old people get. I remember my friend Mike's grandmother had dementia, and when
I stayed in his house, I would hear her wandering around in the
middle of the night, making confused, tragic noises. But she was
in her eighties or nineties, certainly. My father was a virile man
who had only recently turned sixty. Aside from a hernia opera-
tion in his forties, he never seemed to be sick at all. Clearly, this
dementia thing was something that could be overcome, a short
blip on the radar to the happy, healthy retirement that my parents had for so many years been planning and saving for.

Soon enough I learned to gradually accept that the way I had
long interacted with my father would now exist only in the past.
My own relationship with Bobby had been defined greatly by
the business trips he allowed me to accompany him on. Starting in my childhood and continuing all the way through to
the end of high school, during July and August, I would perch
in his passenger seat, joining him on his voyages to Maine or
Connecticut, destinations that were never more than two hours
away but which might as well have been the Alaskan tundra for
how exotic and far they felt: the thrills of motels, the delights
of restaurants with salad bars, the time and luxury the car rides
gave me to devour my stacks of books. During these trips, my
father proved to be wildly indulgent of my movie obsession,
kindly stopping at every video store we passed on the road so

that I could pop in and peruse their shelves for previously viewed VHS tapes. It was also during these trips that, after checking into the Red Roof Inn and grabbing dinner, my father and I would occasionally go to the movies, just us. And though my father's taste didn't necessarily tend toward the overtly macho—my mother was always thrilled to boast to her friends that her husband would happily accompany her to any female-driven romance or melodrama—more often than not the films we saw together on our trips were titles that my mother didn't care to see: *Arachnophobia*, *The Rocketeer*, *Lethal Weapon 3*, *Blown Away*, *Braveheart*. These evening hours spent in unfamiliar movie theaters scattered about New England remain vivid in my memory, precious for their anomalousness, private shared gifts.

Now, my father and I could still maintain some of our routines, such as taking him Christmas shopping to buy my mother's presents, which he had always needed assistance with anyway. But concurrently things were changing irrevocably. The rest of the first decade of the 21st century was a series of milestones, both awful and poignant: the decision in 2007 to take away his car, a major and sorrowful turning point for all of us, since my dad was so auto-obsessed; October 2008, when he first had to be checked into a psychiatric hospital to get his medications adjusted; July 2009, when my parents both came to New York, a surprise that Chris had secretly arranged for my thirtieth birthday, a visit to the city that we all expected would be his last. It was that weekend that Chris captured my second favorite photograph of the two of us, from the roof of the Metropolitan Museum of Art, smiling before a blue sky, which sits framed in our apartment in Brooklyn. (My number one favorite is the photo in which I'm perched in front of him, a tiny, smiling blond five-year-old, on his beloved Honda motorcycle; he must have been the same age then that I am now as I write this.)

Scattered about these moments are smaller memories related to movies that are no less vivid. There are good flashbacks, like the family outing to see the relatively little-known Meryl Streep movie *Prime*, which he loved so much ("a nice Jewish story!") that it seemed to zap alive something dormant in his brain, if only momentarily. Then there are the more foreboding ones: one evening, we tried to watch *Howards End*, starring Emma Thompson, a household favorite; this time my father repeatedly, angrily, proclaimed his confusion at following the plot, remarking over and over, "I have no idea what the *hell's* going on in this movie!"

And there was the fateful couch viewing I had with my mom of *Waitress*, a lightweight romantic comedy starring Keri Russell. After the end of the film, which put a smile on my mom's face, I decided, selfishly heedless of her fragile emotional state, to inform her of the movie's sad behind-the-scenes truth: that director Adrienne Shelly had been brutally murdered in her apartment not long after the film's success. I watched as she broke down into heaving sobs—in retrospect a surprising rarity during these years. It was only in this moment, after having enjoyed with her an otherwise innocuous movie, that I realized the extent of what she was living through.

My mother was the one in the trenches: a five-foot-one woman helping a six-foot-two man into the bathroom in the middle of the night; assisting him as he bathed and dressed; dealing with his night terrors and his occasionally threatening behavior bred by frustration. I had the guilt-inducing luxury of living back in New York, surrounded by the distractions of love and friends and films and work and holiday gatherings and the other social commitments that all but weave the loom that is your twenties. If I wanted to be angry about something, I could direct my frustration at George W. Bush and Dick Cheney, whose war in Iraq was the political cause of our generation. With my dad, I could somehow pretend that, despite everything, it would still all be okay. Or at least that he could plateau and we could all live together for a good while, in relative happiness.

That wasn't to be. After many years of slow disintegration, he suffered a rapid decline. By early 2010, things finally felt irreversible. Too many bad scares, too many potentially destructive moments. He had to have a gallstone removed, for which his doctors had given him anesthesia, a risky decision for someone with dementia, and he never quite recovered. I remember coming home in April that year and my mother surreptitiously telling me that he had mistakenly peed in the backyard bushes. She took him to the doctor again, but this time was different.

"I was sort of in denial," she told me. "Hoping they'd find a drug combination as they had last time and that I'd be able to take him home. I remember sitting in that room, and the doctor came in and said he can't go home. After that she left, and I was in the room all by myself; I just lost it."

When she told me this, we were having dinner in the dining room: corn on the cob, string beans, tomatoes—as many fresh summer vegetables as we could find at the local farmer's market. Our re-viewing of *Terms of Endearment* was still humming in our brains from the night before. The movie had proven effective as ever. Watching it all these years later, we didn't feel that Emma's cruel fate—to die of cancer while still a young mother of three—were the machinations of sadistic screenwriters angling for tears, but the natural expression of life's unpredictability. "If there had been foreshadowing," my mom says, "like if it had been a childhood illness coming back, it would have been a different film." This made me think of *Steel Magnolias*, in which the tragic death of Julia Roberts's diabetic Shelby is telegraphed from the beginning. Of course this doesn't make it any easier on the audience when her mother, played by Sally Field, is screaming "Why??" at the burial. The pain and catharsis of such movie scenes function like the adrenaline of action movies or the anxious anticipation of horror movies: psychologists have connected such emotional responses to the release of oxytocin hormones, which make social interactions and even sexual reproduction possible. It's a workout for your empathetic nerve centers.

The scene in *Terms of Endearment* that had most emotionally devastated her the first time remained the killer: Emma saying goodbye to her sons in the hospital, and imploring her more difficult older son to not feel bad when one day he realizes he never told his mother he loved her. "I know that you love me," Winger tells him, sitting up in bed with wide, blue, tearless eyes. "So don't ever do that to yourself." It's the kind of movie moment that can cause gasping, ugly sobs. "This scene was so hard to watch," said my mother. "I had two little boys about that age."

For me, there's a deadlier scene, and it's even shorter: Aurora beseeching the hospital's nurses, with increasingly frenetic movement, to administer her daughter's morphine. We never see Emma in this moment of pain; we don't need to, as it's written clearly all over Aurora's face. Finally MacLaine balls her fists together and screams with indignant fury, "Give my daughter the shot!!" It shoots chills up the spine: at once an expression of a mother's uncompromising love and the ultimate representation of Aurora's "difficult" nature being used for its always intended purpose—to protect and nurture her only daughter.

I can very easily see my mother doing this if my brother or I were in Emma's situation, and refusing to take "no" for an answer. Of course, life is never as clean as a Hollywood movie, even one that wants to make you cry. Often there is no simple morphine shot that will take away the pain, even temporarily. And there isn't that perfectly arranged moment when a parent can perform her rehearsed goodbyes to her children. Instead, it can be ugly and sad and chaotic.

Life snuck up on my dad. It snuck up on all of us. By summer 2010, he had been moved into a nursing home about twenty minutes from the house in nearby Lowell. When he went in, he was mentally unwell but apparently still physically fit. Whether it was being out of his routine and element, or the combination of sedatives and other medications he was getting, he became a different person almost overnight, largely vegetative. He would live in the nursing home for only a year and a half.

Today I have a hard time summoning an articulation of the dread and anger I felt during those drives to visit him there. The only way I could get through the visits would be to convince myself this wasn't him anymore; almost like those outer-space pod people from *Invasion of the Body Snatchers*. This was just his shell of a body, I had to believe, used by some invisible being for ends I couldn't comprehend. For the first couple of visits, he seemed to recognize me, or at least understand I was someone he once knew. As the months went on, even those glimmers of recognition faded, and nothing appeared to be registering. He mostly slept in bed with the shades drawn or went to the bathroom or just sat in a chair, his eyes either closed or open and clouded. He didn't seem to comprehend the world anymore. Neither did I.

I turned forty without much fanfare. In Chelmsford, while we were still visiting for the Fourth of July, my mom baked a chocolate cake, we ordered from Hong & Kong, and watched *When Harry Met Sally* for what must have been the seventy-ninth time. Back in New York, Chris took me out for one embarrassingly spectacular meal and amassed a group of local friends willing to hear me indulge in karaoke—always a good substitute for emotional histrionics.

Leading up to the big day, my thoughts turned to mortality: my dad's, my mom's, my own. Suddenly each decision I made seemed like it had new weight, like it signaled some kind of irrevocable doom. Everything seemed fragile, even happiness, and the slightest raw thought seemed to send me into anxious, tearful paroxysms. My poor therapist was more than earning his co-pay that summer.

In my twenties, thoughts of death hadn't gripped me all that much. That was soon to change. One early morning in September 2011, as I was packing for a flight to Toronto that was leaving in just a few hours, I got a phone call from my mother. My father had taken a turn for the worse, had contracted pneumonia. It was best that I come home. Perplexed and in denial, I sat with Chris at a diner in Brooklyn, poking at some pancakes. There was no way this was really the end. I'd rush home, miss the all-important Toronto International Film Festival, and everything surely would be fine. Right? Chris gently shook his head. "You need to go."

The rest of the day is a blur. I quickly got a bus ticket. That evening, by the time I made it to the hospital in Lowell, where my brother, Jonathan, and his wife, Melanie, were already sitting vigil, my father was unconscious, eyes closed, hooked up to a morphine drip. At this point, his care would be strictly palliative. My mother had been there all afternoon, so she stayed home to rest. The three of us sat by his side. I have no idea how long we were there. Nothing about it seemed real. There was no movie moment where he opened his eyes and smiled ever so tenderly. There was no cinematic revelation where he died right there in front of us—as happens to Emma in front of Aurora and Flap. There was no unexpected catharsis. We didn't have a proper goodbye. Due to the nature of the disease, we felt like we hadn't really spoken to him in years.

I was awoken the next morning to a shocked cry. It sounded like my mother had been stung by a bee, but as I bounded downstairs I discovered she was just holding a telephone. My father had passed away. We took a moment to cry and hug, but there was so much suddenly to do. We had to call Jonathan. We had to call my father's high school buddies Marshall and Michael. I had to call Chris, so he could get the next bus to Massachusetts. We had to call Karen; my father's—and my—dear cousin, who lives in New York, was born three days before him. I can't describe how I felt, partly because I don't know if those feelings can be articulated, and partly because I can't remember.

My mother had lost her father when she was twenty-eight. I was now thirty-two. Before that day, such a loss always had been an abstract notion to me.

Nothing would make his death more tangible than seeing his body at the funeral home. My mother couldn't bring herself to do it, so I took on the responsibility. He was downstairs, at the end of a room that surely isn't as long and tunnellike as I remember it. The lighting was dim; I don't recall seeing anything other than his tuckered cheeks, so thin, and his enshrouded form, which looked light as a feather.

In movies I'm always distracted by the image of a dead body. I simply wait for its eyelids to flutter accidentally or its chest to quietly heave, something to break the illusion.

Earlier that summer, just two months before my father died, my mother visited New York, and I took her to see *The Tree of Life*. I had already been three times to see Terrence Malick's astonishing film of personal and aesthetic ambition, in which a portrait of an American family in the Southwest in the fifties is intertwined with nothing less than a dramatization of the creation of the Earth. Though it's about the human response to loss, Malick's movie is cleansing, a search for answers that is unfathomably expansive yet also infinitesimal, parable-like. It's at once secular and spiritual, mixing Christian imagery and Darwinist determinism, and its portrayal of small lives juxtaposed with cosmic inquiry hit me at just the moment that I was questioning so many things about the universe, a feeling that would only intensify. Seeing the tears in her eyes after the movie validated my intense response to the film. We both knew what we were feeling and what we were thinking about. We didn't really have to say it.

That fall, in the months immediately following my dad's

death, movies continued to be an escape for me, but due to my emotional state I also came to resent many of them. I loathed art-house hits of the season *Drive* and *Melancholia* and *Shame* for what I saw as little more than stylish nihilism. I just wanted to watch *The Tree of Life* over and over. The world had closed in on me, and I wanted movies to be there to reinstill color and life where I saw grayness, to bring back motion where I felt stasis. Movies had a job to do, and I'd accept nothing less than their full beauty.

That July weekend, Leslie told me something I already knew: retirement isn't quite how she expected it would be. "We didn't have any huge plans, but we wanted to see the country. He loved to drive. He just wanted to drive all over the place and see the country. Everywhere. That would have been fun." Nevertheless, life is far from dull, considering her friends, her singing, her books, her occasional travels—she finally saw Paris during her first trip to Europe—and her tireless helping out of neighbors and friends with their own life challenges.

When I was home that July, my mother told me about her own latest condition. While giving her a blood test on account of her atrial fibrillation—or A-fib as it's called—a rapid-heart-rate condition that causes poor blood flow, the doctor discovered she had a high platelet count. Which meant, of course, there was another term I had to memorize: *myleoproliferative neoplasm*.

"Is it serious?" I asked.

"Hopefully it won't *get* serious." She shrugged.

There's a framed photograph that hangs on the wall in the house on Walnut Road that no one can believe. It was taken around 1949 or 1950. In it, my mother is an infant, standing in her crib. Standing next to the crib are a little boy and girl, both about six years old. The girl is my cousin Karen, now in New York. The boy is my father.

People have always been amazed and delighted by the photo,

as it proves that my parents, who grew up as neighbors, have known each other their whole lives. But it also indicates something else, an automatic feeling one doesn't need to verbally articulate: that my mother and father were *meant to be*. It sounds awfully romantic, even though they never had their official first date until 1968, when my mom was twenty, my dad twenty-five.

Her lifelong connection to my dad makes it crystal clear why my mother has put her foot down about ever dating again. This is just one of many ways she's nothing like fellow widow Aurora Greenway. It goes beyond not believing she'll fall in love again; she says she also doesn't want to end up taking care of another elderly person. She's been through that, even if my dad never got to be technically elderly. She's seeing it everywhere now: her close friend's husband has a bad form of Parkinson's and is now in a nursing home; and one of my dad's best friends from high school has also been diagnosed with Alzheimer's, and his wife has to care for him.

"I enjoy looking after myself and not having to answer to anybody," she told me while munching on a corncob, certifying her independence.

"So you like being a widow?"

"Well...no," she snorts. "It's a lousy word."

She's been living on Walnut Road now for almost forty-five years. My dad may not be here anymore, but his picture is everywhere, and his presence is felt throughout a home he helped construct.

"I do miss someone being here to take care of me when I'm sick, and it's nice to have company. I liked sitting on the sofa with him and just cuddling. You know that it's wonderful to have a partner who gets you. I feel blessed that I had that. Some people never have that, ever."

She continues, wistfully: "At one point when he was home, he wasn't connecting well...but he loved me so much, and I remember realizing in that moment: I will never be loved by any-one this much ever again."

I think of Chris, my husband. I feel the same way. It's hard to imagine anyone loving me as much, and it's impossible to con-ceive of myself loving another as much. My mother and I must be hopeless romantics.

1984: Home

During my visits home in recent years, I've noticed that my mother has begun talking to the television. She's always been a vocal watcher, with little emotional responses to what she sees; even when she's reading she tends to let out snickers and head-shakes. Increasingly, though, she seems like she's actually trying to directly engage with the screen. Rarely does an hour of TV news go by without an "Oy vey…" or an "Oh, brother!"

In early 21st-century America I can't imagine that this is an unusual way of being. While Leslie has remained resolutely, even virulently, against using social media (a momentary dabble in Facebook didn't end well, but it surely ended), she's as suscepti-ble to the brain-worm phenomenon of cable news as any of us. She's well versed in the nightly progression of liberal pundits on MSNBC, with particular regard for the labyrinthine precision of Rachel Maddow and the dewy-eyed charms of Ari Melber. Some years ago, I began regulating my intake of the endless cycle of preaching-to-the-choir cable news media, realizing it was sending me to be bed with a case of nightly *tsuris*. At one point, my mother felt the same way, telling me during a phone call, definitively, "That's *it*! I'm not going to watch this stuff anymore." The next time I was home, Maddow and company were back in heavy rotation.

The impatience and righteous consternation with which my mother has surveyed the political landscape in the Trump era has precedent. Growing up in Ronald Reagan's eighties, I would often overhear her fed-up comments about the men in power. Her despising of Nixon in the late sixties and early seventies had produced a dyed-in-the-wool Democrat. And since Reagan's two terms and George H. W. Bush's one term covered the expanse of the first twelve years of my life, I grew up not really thinking there was an alternative to these Republicans who, according to my mother, were wreaking financial and moral havoc in our country. Of course, I didn't comprehend any details about any of this: I distinctly recall thinking, when I was five and Reagan was elected to his second term, that a presidential race was a literal *race*, and convinced myself that I had seen footage of Reagan in a tank top, arms raised in triumph as he broke through marathon finish-line tape—an invented image lodged in my brain to this day. Nevertheless, based on my mother's constant indignation at the state of things, I at least had a fairly strong emotional sense that our Washington leaders weren't necessarily looking out for our interests.

The Trump era brought out an entirely new side of disbelief in her, as it did for so many Americans. Refusing to allow his blatant racism, his inhumane treatment of immigrants, his childish tantrums, his almost involuntary propensity for constant lying, his attempts to scale back LGBTQ rights, his business conflicts of interests, his craven nepotism, his war against the media that dared to criticize him, his admiration of international fascist dictators, and his general flagrant disregard for ideals and standards of democracy, my mother felt that keeping up with the news was an act of vigilance. I had seen her face twist in disgust over Reagan's deregulations; I had seen her shed tears over George W. Bush's needless wars in Iraq and Afghanistan. But I had never seen such wide-eyed astonishment as she had over Trump's laying waste to everything. A well-versed reader of history, with a special interest in thick tomes detailing the rises to power of Hitler and Stalin, she was fearful of the patterns of scapegoating and despotism that she saw being repeated in our own country.

Despite her engagement with history and politics in newspapers, TV shows, and books, I wouldn't say that political cinema is among her preferred genres. In part this must be because overtly political American moviemaking tends to be leaden, self-conscious, and inelegant—soapboxing social justice message movies that pummel the viewer into submission, leaving little room for nuance. So it was somewhat unexpected that our next movie, while telling a deeply personal, character-driven story, would shine a light on so many political realities that persist to this day. *Country*, starring and produced by Jessica Lange, then at the height of her stardom, is the best kind of political film: it wants to make the viewer aware of the daily socioeconomic injustices being experienced by Americans, but filters its messaging through a prism of one hardscrabble family.

When my mother showed it to me as a kid it made me sad and confused; it was too sophisticated for a youngster, too adept at conveying the minutiae of everyday struggle. When I watched it as a newly weary forty-year-old, it summoned ideas about home, nationhood, sustenance, gender, domesticity, work—and how these things are all interconnected and inseparable.

When I had been home in July, my mother somewhat proudly informed me that earlier that week she had cheese and crackers as her evening meal. Now in August, I was informed, "I had an ice cream cone for dinner!" Not wanting to know any more about what I began to privately call a "widow's diet," I told her

I was going to take her out for her seventy-first birthday. All the food groups would have to make an appearance.

My mom seemed to be taking her early seventies in stride, or at least more so than I was taking my early forties, which made me feel like a bit of a whiner. Why should I be feeling more threatened, more irritatingly existential, than her? After she had informed me of her newly diagnosed condition the previous month, I had made the mistake of looking up *myleoproliferative neoplasm* on the Internet, where it's commonly categorized as a serious blood condition that has to be routinely monitored. Did it scare her? I was too afraid to bring it up during what I had hoped would be a relaxed dinner. I would rather she focus on enjoying her food.

We went to a very 21st-century, open-kitchen, farm-to-table restaurant a few towns away with the very 21st-century name Forage and Vine. I was delighted to witness her tuck into a significant meal of hefty portions: a prosciutto and pear salad, grilled oysters, filet mignon, and strawberry shortcake. It was maybe the least birdlike I've ever seen her eat, her tacit admission of a general hunger.

As we've gotten older we both seem to enjoy food more; growing up, meals always felt to me like mere sustenance. Our family wouldn't close out a day without a meat and a starch. In that commonly American way, my mother did all the cooking; my dad grilled during the summer and occasionally made waffles for weekend breakfasts. Leslie ensured there would be a meal on the table every evening, and that all four of us were present and accounted for. I took such consistency for granted, assuming that all houses operated in the same way, which of course I've come to realize is wildly untrue. If I ever had to fend for myself at dinnertime, I don't remember it.

My memories of the movie *Country* have long been related to food, because that's what my mother remembered about it first and foremost. In fact, until I watched it again as an adult, very few images had been impressed on my brain aside from Jessica Lange's main character, Jewell Ivy, presiding over the stove in her farmhouse's modest kitchen, preparing breakfasts and lunches for her family. The film's first postcredits shot smoothly tracks out over the griddle where Lange, a spatula in one hand and an infant tucked under her other arm, flips hamburgers and, all in one take, places them on slices of white bread slathered with mustard and Miracle Whip; she then wraps the sandwiches in wax paper and separates them out for her husband, Gil (Sam Shepard), teenage son, Carlisle (Levi L. Knebel), and preteen daughter, Marlene (Therese Graham). It's a streamlined process she's clearly done every day for years, and the scene seems intended to convey neither earth-mother veneration nor domestic drudgery; rather this is just the way it is—this is work.

As the film goes on to show, Jewell is the one who keeps the lifeblood of the household pumping—she's the heart, but also the rational, practical, and empathetic soul, of the home. At the sight of that first kitchen scene, which my mother has invoked for years but which she hadn't seen in decades, she couldn't help but say out loud to the TV while shaking her head in amazement: "I love this." In a later scene, while she makes pancakes, her lack of makeup and the curlers in her hair only enhancing Lange's earthy, natural beauty, my mother added, "I could watch her forever."

As we took in *Country* again after so many decades, my mother's strong identification with the film seemed to have remained unbroken, even if her experience as a wife and mother in suburban New England seemingly couldn't be further from the hardships experienced by a Midwestern farmer trying to keep her family together despite mounting economic anxiety and dread. Filmed in Readlyn and Waterloo, Iowa, *Country* is vivid and authentic in its drive to articulate to viewers the specific plight of its rural family, with real-life Midwesterners Jessica Lange and playwright-actor Sam Shepard—newly a couple after meeting on the set of Lange's previous film, *Frances* (1982)—bringing conviction and subdued, lived-in passion to their roles. The Minnesota-born Lange was dedicated to the project, functioning as both producer and star. Having grown up in rural farm communities in Minnesota, she was particularly drawn to the plight of the Ivys.

The viewer is made to feel the threats to the family's livelihood from the very beginning, when a harrowing tornado descends upon them while they're out in the fields harvesting grain, lifting and tossing their truck and wheat thresher, and almost killing Carlisle, who is found buried in a pile of corn once the funnel clouds clear. Yet the true gathering storm is coming via something unnatural. After Gil stops by the local feed and supply store on his weekly rounds, he discovers that the US government agency Farmers Home Administration—often called by its increasingly terrifying moniker FHA—has put his family on a list due to some "discrepancies" in his loan, which ominously are under review. Suddenly his operating budget is being called into question, and the FHA states they now have to approve his purchases moving forward, as he has been unable to pay back his loans. Confused and sidelined, Gil argues he won't be able to pay his bills without buying feed and equipment, putting him in a catch-22. He vows to get his paperwork in order to get this resolved, but visible to the viewer, if not Gil, are the words *Work toward voluntary liquidation* written in red on their loan review form. According to the government at least, the Ivys' fate seems to be sealed.

Jewell finds out about Gil's confrontation with his loan officers that night during a town barn dance, after which the couple ends up sorting through multiple desk drawers of paperwork and receipts. It's a powerful scene of domestic desperation, a search for evidence to confirm their own responsible behavior that will ultimately prove fruitless: the government has already decided that the Ivys are expendable and the FHA wants to cut their losses before they get in too deep. The agency claims that the family's estimated net worth in 1980 was $450,000 and that four years later it's half that; Jewell insists that they never had that net worth in the first place, and that they live on just $9,000 annually, depending on medical bills. For the first time, the FHA won't release money to help them pay their debt.

"It's a way of life," explains Gil about the borrowing and lending practices that have long kept his farm and livelihood afloat. "No, it's a business," replies the loan manager, crystallizing the essential dilemma for the Ivys and the progression of American life as we know it. "This is why people voted for Trump," my mom interjected at this point. "This is the root of what we're dealing with now."

As the film progresses it becomes clear that Jewell is the household's real fighter. The farm has been in her family, not Gil's, for more than a hundred years, and she's the one with enough measured anger and levelheaded resolve to be the David to the banks' Goliath. Gil turns to alcohol and succumbs to internalized self-loathing; he comes home late for dinner one night, the ultimate insult, drunk on scotch and his own wounded masculine pride. After a letter in the mail informing Gil and Jewel that they have thirty days to pay off all loans, he's ready to give up, allow the banks to liquidate their assets and auction off their equipment; Jewell, on the other hand, keeps pushing against the brick wall. She goes directly to the local bank, but they tell her they can't approve loans anymore now that they're part of a chain. You see, that would have to be approved way up in Des Moines.

Watching *Country* now is not just to get caught up in the story of one fictional family but also to witness, with inexorable mounting dread, the slow disintegration of a way of life; to watch the process of a country transforming forever, even as people rail against the dying of the light. This was the country then, and this is the country now—here were the insinuating beginnings of "big agro" and the corporate farming industry that has left people like the Ivys in the dust. The film elicits well-springs of empathy in my mother, who spent most of it shaking her head and muttering—both to me and herself—about how things don't change.

Lange, in an interview on a local affiliate television broadcast from Lincoln, Nebraska, that aired at the time of the film's release, makes the film's political intentions fairly clear: "People are not aware of what's happening to the independent family farmer. I just hope that somehow this film can bring it to their attention." The situation she's talking about is now commonly referred to as the farm debt crisis of the eighties. Thousands of families in America's rural heartland lost their jobs and homes, some took their lives, as a result of soaring costs, high interest rates, low crop prices, and diminishing land values. Banks foreclosed on farms, pushing families out of businesses that had been operating for generations.

By the end of the eighties, a quarter of a million farms failed and hundreds of rural, independent banks closed. There had been optimism for the future of American agriculture in the seventies, which, along with low interest rates, helped plant the seeds for what was to come, encouraging the spending that the government would refuse to bail out in the next decade. And this wasn't initially so clearly drawn along party lines: President Jimmy Carter's grain embargo on the Soviet Union as retaliation for their invasion of Afghanistan in early 1980 gave even left-leaning groups of farmers reason to vote for Reagan later that year. When in office, however, Reagan did little to help the radically crumbling farm economy, allowing the rash of foreclosures to continue on unabated.

There's a scene somewhere in the middle of the movie that prompted my mother to put her hand on her head and gasp. In the local bar, where Gil often goes to drown his sorrows—a very rural eighties kind of place, boasting a Ms. Pac Man arcade game—he confronts his local FHA manager, defensive and sheepish about what his job has become. To his captive audience, Shepard, beer bottle in hand, bemoans the political situation: "Here comes the government putting embargos on foreign sales... If we were getting decent prices for our crops, there wouldn't be a damn FHA, and you know that." As it ever was: just earlier in the week that August, my mother had been decrying Trump's escalating battle with China and the US's sky-rocketing tariffs on the growing superpower's goods. China's subsequent freezing of US-grown imports, plus consistent bad weather and lowering prices, was creating a crisis in the contemporary farm economy, especially growers of corn and soybean. An August article in *Forbes* reported a rise in loan delinquencies and bankruptcies, as well as a concurrent rise in suicides among farmers. Earlier that summer, a farm in Wisconsin had plowed a message into its famous corn maze that could be seen from above: Your Life Matters, plus the number for a suicide prevention hotline.

Late in *Country* something happens that terrified me as a child, and which I recall vividly prompted me to get up and leave the room. The Ivys' neighbors, we learn, are going through the same crisis, and it has taken a particular toll on one named Arlon (Jim Haynie). At one point, Jewell visits Arlon in his barn, where he sits solemnly with a cat in his lap and a rifle in his hand; she tries to coax him out, insisting they can figure this out. He assures her that he'll be fine. But as she walks away, we hear the shotgun blast. It's a terrible scene, utterly despairing; instances of death—especially gun violence—rattled me horribly when I was young, especially when they emerged unexpectedly out of otherwise realist dramatic narratives, as in *The World According to Garp* or Robert Altman's *Nashville*, which might as well have been horror movies to me. In *Country*, this moment felt hopeless; I'm not entirely sure that I watched the rest of the movie during that first viewing, leaving my mother to finish it on her own.

Having already seen the film, my mother, on the other hand, knew that narrative redemption was on the horizon for the Ivy clan. Jewell's rabble-rousing gumption culminates in a Capra-esque scene of little-guy triumph, in which, set to atypical soaring music, she turns her family farm auction into a protest, with the farmer community organizing against the FHA under her guidance. Arlon may have killed himself, leaving behind a wife and mentally disabled son in the process, and Gil may have opted out in his own way by drinking himself into a stupor, but Jewell refuses to give up. As Lange said, "When we were doing our research and we were talking to these families, in the majority of cases it was the woman who struck out first… We found that within these families the man really turned in on himself in most of the cases, whereas the woman recognized it as an external force threatening her, like a primitive, almost animal reaction of something coming into her territory."

In the way that Lange's character proves herself more capable and committed than the men, my mom told me she considers *Country* "absolutely a feminist film." At one point, Jewell even wields a wooden plank to defend herself and her child from a suddenly abusive, swaggering Gil—a scene that must have had personal echoes for Lange, whose alcoholic father was given to severe mood swings when she was a child. "When men feel like they can't provide anymore they lose their masculine center. Because that's what they were always told they had to do," my mother said during the movie. "But she never loses her cool, always keeping things as sane as she can."

Once our viewing ended, my mother was beaming. For her, Lange embodies a kind of pragmatic American perfection in this film: "Mother Earth…that's what she is to me. With a soft voice." It was her most deglamorized role to date, yet she is somehow more beautiful than ever. It's difficult to conceive now, as she is firmly in the pantheon of great American actors, but Lange had struggled in her early career to be taken seriously. It was only eight years earlier that she had made her memorable, if artistically inauspicious, debut at age twenty-six in the silly Dino De Laurentiis remake of *King Kong* as the captive beauty mercilessly pawed at by the big beast—a role that resulted in viewers and casting agents assuming she was little more than the latest blonde pinup.

In retrospect *King Kong* registers as an unlikely first role for the practical, independent-minded Minnesotan, and says a lot more about the parts offered to women in Hollywood than it does about her expectations about her own career. She hadn't expected to arrive at film acting: after dropping out of the University of Minnesota, where she had gone on an art scholarship, she began to travel the world, trying her hand at painting in New York, and then mime performance art in Paris, studying under Étienne Decroux. It was because of a reluctant modeling gig that De Laurentiis spotted and cast her, a reminder that male producers in Hollywood often cast female stars based on looks.

Her next screen appearance was in Bob Fosse's miraculous 1979 *All That Jazz*, in a small but crucial part as the Angel of Death, a role the choreographer-director created for her after the two had a fling. She's sensual and symbolic, an effectively inhabited role that nevertheless extended the conception of Lange in patronizing terms of visual impact. In *King Kong*, tied up in tattered clothes, she was branded a sexpot; in Fosse's film, she was the angel, into whose open arms our tortured male hero gets to ultimately spend eternity.

It was with the one-two punch of *Tootsie* and *Frances* in 1982 that Lange entered a new phase: in the former, she portrayed Julie, the soap opera star whose determination and beauty both pose quite a challenge for Dustin Hoffman's secretly cross-dressing actor; in the latter, she gave fierce physicality to the harrowing true story of early Hollywood star Frances Farmer, whose outspokenness and nonconformity were tragically silenced forever by a monstrously sexist and unforgiving industry. The roles showcased the two sides of Lange's talent and personality, the butter-soft and the chalkboard-hard. She received Oscar nominations for both, winning in the Supporting Actress category for *Tootsie*; she may very well have won in the leading category as well, if not for Meryl Streep's juggernaut work as a traumatized Holocaust survivor in *Sophie's Choice*, one of the defining roles of the decade. Nevertheless, Lange had made such an impression that year that her brief pinup persona was all but erased in the blink of an eye.

Country, which made its world premiere in the prestigious opening night slot of the 1984 New York Film Festival, was her next starring role, and thus highly anticipated. The film was also noteworthy for being the second release from Touchstone Pictures, the newly formed "adult" production and distribution arm of Walt Disney, a reminder that *Country* might seem small-scale—the kind that would be a quintessential "indie" film in the coming decades—but it had major studio support behind it. It also registers today as ironic that a film with such staunchly anticorporatist ideals would be the product of a company that would become the biggest conglomerate in the industry, swallowing up the movie business almost whole following its 2019 merger with Twentieth Century Fox and, before that, its acquisitions of Marvel Studios and Lucasfilm Ltd.

Lange's producing role was also noteworthy, an indication of a strong female actor taking a prominent position in the industry. Reviewing the film upon its NYFF unveiling, the *New York Times*' Vincent Canby wrote, "With *Frances* and now *Country*, Miss Lange joins Barbra Streisand, Jane Fonda, and Goldie Hawn—that small group of American actresses who have successfully shown that they are the most important 'authors' of their own careers." It's both an encouraging and sad statement; one can't imagine a prominent male critic of the era writing such a thing about movie stars of the other gender; in that moment, Robert Redford, Warren Beatty, Dustin Hoffman, Eddie Murphy, and many others were widely considered not only actors but auteurs, men firmly in charge of their own careers. That a woman doing the same was considered a novelty is telling—and has unlikely changed in the thirty-plus years since. Lange would remain a major screen figure for the next decade or so, her presence becoming an instant bellwether for a certain seriousness of intent. In such films as the Patsy Cline biopic *Sweet Dreams* (1985); *Music Box* (1989), in which she plays a lawyer reckoning with the truth about her father, accused of war crimes; Martin Scorsese's effectively gonzo thriller *Cape Fear* (1991); and the high-anxiety *Blue Sky* (1994), for which she finally won a leading Best Actress Oscar, Lange deepens and complicates what might have been standard or overbaked, melodramatic roles. She is never one-note; she plays full octaves, with all the notes in between constantly trilling.

Lange has a very particular tone of voice when her characters are on the verge of tears. You can hear it in *Frances, Tootsie, Cape Fear, Blue Sky*, and certainly in *Country*: almost like her throat and nasal passages are tightening up and she has to fight to keep her airways open. There's a moment late in the film when Jewell should rightly be overcome with emotion. She has already had to kick out her drunk husband—"Get out. We don't need you anymore"—but not before he has slapped her in the face. With the bruise still fresh on her lip, she sits with her children and father at the kitchen table and tries to explain the situation, the camera tracking in closer. They are surrounded by paper Thanksgiving decorations, the overflowing cornucopias teasing their plight with promises of bounty. She holds back those tears, showing enormous strength as she explains, "We're caught in the middle of something that we didn't even see coming; it just hit us head-on." Yet she insists, "What we have to think about now is how we're going to keep this family going." It's an impossible conversation about an impossible situation, especially incomprehensible for children who only see unhappiness, squabbling, and pain. At this point in the narrative, we may feel more than a twinge of pessimism about this family's prospects, financially and emotionally; but, as embodied by Lange, Jewell's strength is never in doubt. She's going to fight for the only home she's ever known.

If presented with anything like this situation, I cannot imagine my mother doing any less for the house on Walnut Road, where she's lived for more than forty-five years and which is the only childhood home I've ever known. Being able to return to Chelmsford with relative frequency, to leave the hectic, overwhelming excitement of New York, to close my eyes and feel cradled in the loving slower pace of green, tract-house suburbia, has been a privilege I take for granted less and less as I get older.

The home was especially a refuge for me as a child. Not athletically inclined and tending more toward solitary activities like reading, playing piano, and, of course, watching movies, I always preferred to be inside, away from the neighborhood boys whose competitive, loud machismo was about as inviting to me as a trip to the dentist. I became obsessive about writing down every movie I saw, a process of listing and categorizing and ranking that gave structure to my days, and resulted in endless piles of papers shoved into my desk. Acquiring my brother's afternoon paper route when I was thirteen became an important step in helping me overcome the mild case of agoraphobia that was developing as I entered my teenage years. I always felt exposed and vulnerable when out in the neighborhood; after delivering the newspapers I'd run back to the house, safe and sound once again, at least for another day.

I look around at the house's rooms now, and see all the places that are brimming with memories of their former uses: the staircase where I'd sit and talk on the phone for hours with friends, pulling the cord taut from the kitchen; the basement that was once a playroom overflowing with toys; the versatile little room at the end of the hall that became a TV room, then my brother's bedroom, then an office, then a guest room; the kitchen where, every year, my mom and brother squabbled over when to take the Thanksgiving turkey out of the oven. They still do. But there's a time limit on everything, and the house will one day fall out of our hands; it will not be ours, it will not be mine.

After *Country*, my mother and I sat on the porch eating a lunch of tuna fish sandwiches and iced tea, while the wind chimes gently jingled in the warm August breeze. The movie had inspired us to talk about the house, and she looked crestfallen.

When my father's disease had deteriorated him so much that he was moved into a nursing home, my family's financial realities changed forever: to help pay for his stay at the facility—which cost an incredible ten thousand dollars a month—the state took a great deal of the money my parents had been saving for retirement over the prior decades to supplement what Mass Health was willing to pay. It required a lot of finagling for my mother to remain solvent at all. "Alzheimer's is killing the economy," my mother said, and she has said this on more than one occasion. "They take everything that's in the patient's name. So you have to get what you can out of his name and put it in a different account, and to do this you have to pay an enormous amount of taxes."

As a result, Leslie, who at the time was working as a public school teaching assistant for children with learning disabilities, took out a reverse mortgage on the house. Now that she's retired, she lives off the equity of the house, giving her a cushion while allowing her to pay her bills. For the remainder of her years there, she'll be drawing down on the house's worth, which had been appraised by the bank while my dad was in the nursing home. Finally, it will go back to the bank. It gives the house the fragile quality of an hourglass.

I remember distinctly the pride my parents felt when, in their fifties, they had finally paid off the house's mortgage after so many decades. It seems like an eternity ago. "I feel guilty every time I get money from the house," she admitted to me. "I'm sorry you won't get it. I was desperate at the time. They were talking about throwing him out of the nursing home if I didn't." She doesn't have to explain. I've long disavowed myself of any notion of inheritance. There's so much more we inherit in this life than money or property.

The plight of the farmer and the economic and emotional reality of foreclosures in America's heartland were so prevalent a topic by the mideighties that a movie subgenre all unto itself sprung up. In 1984, *Country* was part of a triumvirate of female-driven films about women fighting against all odds to save their farms, the others being the Depression-set *Places in the Heart* with Sally Field and *The River* with Sissy Spacek. The Oscars that year would offer up a bounty of hearty pioneer women: Lange, Field, and Spacek were all nominated against each other for Best Actress, with Field ultimately taking the prize and giving the infamous "You like me" speech. Movies about the American rural experience—and, more broadly, movies about our citizens working far from urban centers and bourgeois enclaves—thus became as essential a part of the landscape of 1980s cinema as much as the burgeoning teen comedy genre or the drama of metropolitan upward mobility. Actors like Lange and Spacek fit into these roles so well because they gave off a sense of regional specificity, which would become increasingly rare in an ever more homogenized American film culture treating cinema as just another export. *Country* is an emblem of Lange's cultural singularity, a reflection of her essence, as well as her political conviction.

In an unprecedented move, Lange, Spacek, and Jane Fonda came together in May 1985 to testify before a congressional Democratic task force about the agricultural crisis and the toll it was taking on the livelihood and emotional well-being of the American farm family. With homegrown warmth, Texas-raised

Spacek earnestly intoned, "I would be naive to assume this is a simple problem with simple answers, but one thing I'm sure of is we can't turn our backs on these people who have fed us so abundantly and so cheaply throughout our history." Fonda would compare the current situation to the Depression-era bankruptcy and humiliation of American landowners as embodied by her father Henry's performances in John Ford's 1940 *The Grapes of Wrath*, and specifically accused President Reagan of ignoring the farmers' needs in favor of giving more subsidies to defense contractors. Lange, meanwhile, sporting medium-length brunette hair and a simple navy blue blouse, seemed to be at times forcing back tears. Footage shows Fonda next to her wiping her own wet cheek as Lange summons calm. "These people are living in a kind of modern-day slavery," Lange insists during her testimony. "They are being made to feel and made to believe that they have failed. That they've failed their families, their heritage, their country, and they have failed their land."

Republicans—who, pointedly, had not been invited to the caucus—called out the Capitol Hill event as little more than a publicity stunt. Republican Representative of Kansas Pat Roberts was quoted in the Associated Press as responding, "Apparently we're going to play *Hollywood Squares* in the Agriculture Committee." There seems to have been a double standard in considering it gauche, showboating, or counterproductive to have three Hollywood actresses speaking out about a political issue, especially during a period of time when the White House was literally occupied by a former Hollywood actor. Later that year, Reagan would triumph in his reelection bid, trouncing Walter Mondale, a Democratic senator from Lange's home state of Minnesota who had made agriculture a major issue in his failed campaign—and who had selected Geraldine Ferraro as his VP, the first female major-party national nominee.

Though the title *Country* is perfect in its double meaning—it's about "country" folk but also about the state of our country—it easily could have been called *Home*. "We're staying right here," Lange proclaims to the federal authorities in *Country*'s rousing finale. Her baby is tucked under one arm, as ever. She has successfully thwarted the auction, and she's going to appeal. But as an FHA stooge reminds her, "There's no way to stop it." Also, as the dreary gray skies and light snowflakes promise, winter's coming. In the final image, the camera captures Jewell and Gil in a long shot, perched on a bed upstairs, their backs to the camera. They hold hands and embrace; no words necessary. The scene fades out. Like those of so many families undone by larger external sociopolitical forces, Jewell and Gil's future remains uncertain. Some last-minute on-screen text informs us that on February 16, 1984, a federal judge in North Dakota ordered the US government to stop all foreclosures "until the farmers of this country receive their rights of due process under the law." Such an injunction was a drop in the well, as the political realities of the coming months and years attested. A blast of triumphant trumpet music closes the film, indicating that the fight goes on.

In 1975, my parents bought the house on Walnut Road for $35,000, talked down from $40K; it had originally sold for $13,000 when it was part of a new suburban tract land in 1957. Back then, a fireplace cost an extra $500, an expenditure they couldn't justify. They were initially paying around $300 a month for everything—not a huge jump from the $225 for their small apartment in the Boston suburb of Waltham.

"When we bought the house we had a thousand bucks left to our name. So if something worked, it stayed." This included, for many years, the kitchen's storied deep-red linoleum floor and the living room's shag carpeting. Over the decades, they put on a couple of additions, including a porch that became a family room, and my father's deck, which later became a screened-in porch. But other than moving from shingles to siding, the house has otherwise basically stayed as is.

The deep connection and love my mother and I have for the house has nothing to do with its size. A two-floor in the symmetrical Cape Cod style, topped with gabled roof, the house is of the type they don't build anymore, a largely extinct species of modest domicile. With anxieties over maintaining skyrocketing land values and general keeping-up-with-the-Joneses 21st-century materialism, the proliferation of houses all over the Northeast have almost exclusively followed the bigger-is-better mentality. Comfortable, unostentatious houses are no longer built outside of affordable housing communities, and even those are often vetoed by neighborhoods and community boards fearful of their land being devalued and their utilities strained.

Because of this, houses like the one my mother lives in are hot properties for middle-class families who don't want to break the bank. "Houses in this neighborhood sell in days," my mother said while looking around the well-maintained lawns and still-standing oak trees of her neighbors. "Two, three days and they're gone, because there's nothing else like it out there."

The thought of anyone else living in this house strikes my heart with horror—a horror I'll likely have to come to terms with at some point in my life. A couple of years ago, my husband's parents sold their also modest house in Milwaukee and moved, along with his older sister, to an apartment. Similar to my experience, it was the only house he'd ever lived in, so I had assumed that Chris would at least become poignantly reflective if not devastated. It was a shock to my nostalgia-overloaded system when both he and his parents moved on with don't-look-back pragmatism. His mom, dad, and sister are enjoying their apartment complex, with its more spacious layout, its pool, its new neighbors. Home is where you make it, or so I try to convince myself.

My mother always looks closely at the houses in movies, the details inside and out. (For my dad, it was cars.) Often we'll be watching a movie together and she'll remark upon the construction or interior decoration of a house or apartment. That movies are so often shot on sets and soundstages only enhances one's appreciation of the illusion of cinema. Especially if it's a movie you've seen over and over, there's a comfort to be had in continually returning to the same house.

I feel like if I walked into the house in Minnelli's *Meet Me in St. Louis* or Spielberg's *E.T.* or Jodie Foster's *Home for the Holidays*, I'd know exactly where to go to watch TV or grab a bite from the fridge or which closet contains the broom. In fact, the only confusion I remember my mother ever having about the show *The Sopranos*, which she otherwise adored, was that no matter how many times she watched she couldn't figure out the interior layout of that house, and which room connected to where. The comment has stuck with me, and I still think of Carmela and Tony's house as a puzzle—though I'm sure many of its obsessive fans have already solved it. I sometimes think my mother could have been an art director, creating homes for the screen that approximate not just the look but also the feel of those places in the heart.

My idea of home changed significantly when I moved away to go to NYU in the late nineties. Not only was I no longer in my house, I was attending a school that didn't really have a campus. As many often note, when you go to school in New York the city becomes your campus, your home. I was unmoored, but I surprised even myself by how much I took to it—so many tactile, intellectual, interpersonal possibilities. As aggravating, as crushingly indifferent, as it can be, New York envelops you in its imaginary walls, and by the end of my first semester I already felt like I had a new home, and it existed well outside the perimeters of the transitory freshman-year dorm room I shared with two others.

I also feel lucky to have had my cousin Karen to visit in the city. She and her husband, Sam, lived on New York's Upper West Side, and their enviable, fifth-floor apartment—bought in the early seventies before the neighborhood became desirable—is brimming with old-school New York charm. It became a homey refuge for a bewildered teenager living in a vast metropolis for the first time. Karen and Sam immediately made me feel at home, bringing me to opening night of the 1997 New York Film Festival. This would have been a magical event for any movie-loving kid's first month in New York, but the opening night selection that year couldn't have been more apt: Ang Lee's *The Ice Storm*, which was set, of course, in suburban New England. It's a depiction of home that's considerably more austere and critical than what I was used to in my own life. It was set in the distant 1970s, but the movie became an obsession for me and many of my fellow NYU film students that year, a portrait of disaffected kids and their even more disaffected parents that created a bridge for us between youth and the adult world.

Even at age eighteen, I distinctly remember feeling that childhood already seemed like a distant land. This made each four-hour trip home feel both momentous and melancholy. The profound comfort of being back in Massachusetts became so acute as to be almost unbearable. Even years before my father got sick, I suddenly began to feel the impermanence of everything. Yes, there are the moments when your childhood bed is replaced by a futon and your *Jurassic Park* and *Batman Returns* posters are rolled up and put in the basement where lost things go. The feeling can strike without warning; it's something intangible, a sense of time moving on, inexorably.

This is now the house where my mother lives. She's been widowed for less than a decade, but it seems like it's been like this forever. This is, after all, the same house my dad would come home to every night at dinnertime, tired from a day on the road, throw down his carrying cases full of eyeglass frames, and jokingly say to my mom, "Death of a salesman, Leslie."

My mom told me recently, "Your dad was a great wallpaper. He could have gotten paid for it." I didn't think I realized that he had papered the walls of the house himself. I can barely paint a wall without spattering the floor.

I recently touched a wall in the dining room. For all the years I've wandered through that room, eaten dinners and lunches in that room, had conversations with my mother about movies in that room, grabbed serving platters out of the china cabinet for special occasions, hidden under the table as a child, or watched the way the lights dance in exquisite patterns on the wall if you dare rotate the chandelier on its chain, I don't think I had ever really *touched* the wall. It felt strong, like a heartbeat.

"I'm thankful all the time for this house," my mother said to me. She was thinking back to her childhood, when the idea of having her own full house seemed like an impossible dream. "I got what I wanted, not everything is an illusion."

I still call it "my house." Of course, at this point, I know it belongs, most literally, to my mother. But does a family house ever really "belong" to just one person? When I call and my mother doesn't pick up, I still get an answering machine. It's my mother's voice, saying, "You have reached the Koreskys. Please leave a message." The Koreskys. Plural. It's the same message that's been there from before my father died, like the last remnants of some unknown dynasty, frozen in time. I have never asked if she plans on changing that message. Maybe it's because I don't want her to.

1985: Garden

"How's this book?"

It was early fall, and I'd nonchalantly picked up a heavy tome that was sitting on the ottoman where my mother had left it beside a pile of dispersed sections of the *Boston Globe*. It's a common question I ask whenever I'm home visiting, as I'm curious about the latest literary journey she's embarked upon. In this case it was an 880-page hardcover of Ron Chernow's *The Warburgs*, which boasts the fittingly substantial subtitle *The Twentieth-Century Odyssey of a Remarkable Jewish Family*.

My question had been a simple one, but the answer turned out to be anything but. When it comes to books, you'll never get a one-sentence response from Leslie. I should have known better than to ask her about *The Warburgs* at that moment: following my heavily trafficked, lengthy trip from New York, I was famished and trying to patiently await a promised lunch. A grown man who had been making his own sandwiches for decades, I was nevertheless desperately eyeing the package of bread that she had opened but which was now sitting on the kitchen counter untouched. She became so invested in her sudden five-minute dissertation on the gradual rise of the German Jewish Warburg dynasty, and Kaiser Wilhelm's particular brand of anti-Semitism in the years leading up to World War I, that she neglected to put the bread in the toaster, instead using it as a prop for gesticulation.

It seemed fitting that my mother was so emotionally and intellectually engaged by what she was reading—or rather by the *thought* of what she was reading—that she nearly forgot about lunch. After all, books are perhaps her primary source of nourishment. Out of all the elements of the house on Walnut Road for which I can provide nostalgic encomiums, perhaps none are as essential to its life's blood as its walls of books. The far left side of the house is made up entirely of built-in bookshelves, which span across two separated rooms: the hardcovers are in the living room, which with its upright piano, comfortable-as-a-cloud couch, and oversized podium-perched dictionary, has the feel of a tiny library; the paperbacks are in the guest bedroom/office.

Both rooms are defined by the books crammed into that same far wall; there are probably thousands of them, and each and every one belongs to my mother. For my father, who we have come to suspect may have had some kind of undiagnosed learning disability, books were anathema. They seemed to provoke anxiety for him; when he would drive me to the local library on the weekends, he would adamantly stay in the car. Because of this, I grew up thinking about books in a gendered way: women read, men do not, except perhaps for the newspaper and car magazines. It was my mother who was attuned to history and the never-ending process of self-education.

Some people tend to gardens, bearing witness to their growth year after year with pride—pride that they've nurtured something into being and sustained its life. My mother's book collection is like a garden in this way, and I've been watching the ongoing process of its growth since I was a little boy. Instead of water or plant food, the essential nutrient is emotional and intellectual curiosity, which is, after all, a form of love. Over the decades, I've seen the number of books grow larger, the heights of shelves get taller like beanstalks. It's very rare that any trimming occurs, though there have been a few occasions over the years when she's pruned a bit, donating handfuls to book fairs, secondhand stores, or libraries. Mostly, it just gets bigger, with new tendrils created by rediscovered essentials, heavy-duty history books, or, occasionally, even an intriguing bestseller. There isn't much genre discrimination here: fiction and non, novels and short story collections, histories and biographies, contemporary and classic. Pluck a book off any shelf and you're bound to find something worthwhile, whether you're ready to dig into Thomas Mann's *The Magic Mountain* or Colson Whitehead's *The Underground Railroad*, Stacy Schiff's *The Witches* or Virginia Woolf's *The Waves*, Neal Gabler's Barbra Streisand biography or one of the daunting array of books about Hitler and Stalin.

When I was a kid, the sheer number of books did not inspire awe or admiration. Honestly, it terrified me. There were far more books in the house than VHS tapes. And VHS tapes only took about two hours to watch. Giving the book collection the kind of undivided, deep attention that only a child can—memorizing, cataloging, sometimes organizing them—I became fixated on the idea that every book *needed* to be read, and that my mother would certainly never be able to read all of them. Life simply wasn't long enough. I would calculate in my head how long it took her to read each book, and then how many books were potentially readable in one year. It became clear that the odds were against her. No matter how many books she would be able to plow through— or *savor*, to be more accurate for the unrushed way she reads—it would not be enough. The bookshelves, for all the beauty and life and joy they possess and all the wonder required in their cultivation, also became unresponsive monoliths, looming reminders of mortality.

Finding oneself in one's childhood home allows for a measure of uncanny experiences, not least of which is being encased in time. Simply standing in a room pregnant with so much personal history can make one feel at once young and old, precious and expendable. So many objects and pieces of furniture have come and gone in the decades since I was a child that few things remain that were there when I was very young: couches, chairs, lamps, carpets and rugs, countertops, windows, even the stairway bannister—all have gone through their own changes and evolutions. However, I can still touch the exact same hardcovers of Nabokov's *Lolita* and *Speak, Memory* that I puzzled over as a kid; I can still clutch my mother's high school and college copies of *The Grapes of Wrath* and *East of Eden*, the same copies I read during my own tender years; I can still feel the massive weight of William Shirer's *The Rise and Fall of the Third Reich* and Richard Rhodes's *The Making of the Atomic Bomb*, books that once seemed so outside of my childhood understanding that I still feel residual intimidation even looking at them.

Many of these books predate my existence and, barring some unforeseen catastrophe, will likely outlive me. Leslie's love of reading didn't start from childhood. Her mother, not a huge reader, didn't take her to the library when she was little. She discovered the classics when she was older. As a high school student, she started reading Camus and Steinbeck, whom she credits with transforming her relationship to books. As a teenager, she saved her allowance to enroll in the Book of the Month Club, which at that time would offer beckoning introductory offers— "four hardcover books for something like a buck," she remembers. Soon enough she was a collector. Some of the books she got from Book of the Month Club way back in the late sixties and early seventies still perch on her shelves: *Mary Queen of Scots* by Antonia Fraser, *Jennie: The Life of Lady Randolph Churchill* by Ralph Martin, *Before the Deluge* by Otto Friedrich.

I've always seen them sitting there; they're a part of the house,

as much as any of its photographs, objects, furniture, or living memories. And with the ever-looming transition to a digital ether-sphere, and ongoing debates over where information
should actually live (libraries themselves feel like endangered
species), books now take up a different kind of space. To some,
they are heavy burdens; to others, like my mother and me, they
are more precious than ever, reminders that every home is more
than just a memory palace—it's an archive.

When she finally got the bread into the toaster, my mother
momentarily broke the spell *The Warburgs* had cast over her. Her
inevitable follow-up question: "And what are *you* reading?" Taking after my mom, I am never without a book, and too often
I'm juggling multiple books at once, evidence that my life could
use some streamlining. At this point, I was embroiled in three
very different ones: Suketu Mehta's *This Land Is Our Land: An
Immigrant's Manifesto*, a humane yet harrowing account of the
lives and paths of various migrants across the planet and the xe-
nophobic policies and colonialist histories that make their voyages so fraught and dangerous; the ghost stories of M. R. James,
because fall was approaching and the sun had begun to set earlier; and Larry McMurtry's *Terms of Endearment*, largely for research purposes of the very book you're holding in your hands.
    While I can't say I enjoyed reading much of McMurtry's
book, which seemed to me burdened with endless pages of long-
winded dialogue and a strange lopsided structure that's heavily
weighted toward the mother Aurora's character and her many
suitors at the dramatic expense of the daughter Emma, I admit
that discovering just how significantly different it is from James
L. Brooks's film adaptation created its own sense of fascination.
This is a book, after all, featuring a lengthy scene in which a
character drives a truck straight through the walls of a dive bar
in an attempt to murder someone, and another that revolves
around a bloody machete attack. It's true. While the novel co-

alesces around its expected parent-child emotional center in its final movement, the original *Terms of Endearment* is certainly not your mother's *Terms of Endearment*.

Reading McMurtry's book for the first time, however, gave me newfound appreciation for the film Brooks wrenched out of it, and made me think about the process of adaptation from page to screen, and how we too often prize something for being "faithful" to its source rather than an entirely new creation of its own.

It just so happened that the film on the docket for this month's visit was another novel-to-screen adaptation, and one that I vividly remember being aware of at an early age. In fact, Steven Spielberg's 1985 film of *The Color Purple*, which I watched with my mother when I was seven, was likely the first movie I ever was aware of as having been based on a book. I knew this because she had Alice Walker's Pulitzer Prize–winning 1982 novel on the shelf in our house, and I distinctly remember her reading it. The version she had was a reissue whose cover was adorned with the movie's poster, an image that itself evoked the process of reading: a woman in silhouette, perched on a rocking chair before a large window revealing a setting sun, her neck craned down a bit to look at something she gripped in her hands: A book? No—a letter? I had no idea what *The Color Purple* was about, but I knew she held the book in high esteem, and often spoke with great anticipation of seeing the movie version. Books could *become* movies? What sort of alchemy made that possible?

Though movies ought to stand up and be judged on their own merits, it's fascinating and perhaps essential to discuss *The Color Purple* in terms of adaptation, for a host of irreconcilable reasons. Steven Spielberg was certainly a surprising choice—to put it mildly—to direct the film. One reason was that the source material seemed so completely out of his comfort zone: at this point in his already legendary career, the thirty-eight-year-old wunderkind had basically taken over Hollywood and, along with fellow "movie brat" friends like George Lucas, Francis Ford Coppola, and Brian De Palma, had rewritten the rules of the game. Starting in 1975, Spielberg directed a line of decade-defining, culture-shaking blockbusters, including *Jaws*, *Close Encounters of the Third Kind*, *Raiders of the Lost Ark*, and *E.T. the Extra-Terrestrial*. It was an unparalleled track record of largely un-impeded success, save the misstep of the farcical *1941*, a mam-moth bomb set in LA on the day of the Pearl Harbor attacks whose poor returns obscured a nevertheless fascinatingly bra-zen look at home-front wartime hysteria. Each of these films centered on male characters, from the *Jaws* trio of shark hunt-ers; to *Close Encounters*' family man Roy Neary, who ultimately leaves his wife and children behind to explore the galaxy; to *E.T.*'s Elliott, who connects with an otherworldly being in the absence of a missing father; to Indiana Jones, the ultimate little lost boy, refusing any kind of domestic partnership in favor of globe-trotting adventure.

All these films were testaments to Spielberg's ability to create images of symbolic intensity and emotionally acute narratives that appealed to wide swaths of viewers, yet many viewers re-mained unconvinced that he could direct completely earthbound dramas whose only effects were the emotional bonds between adult human beings. This was just the first reason that the news he'd be adapting Alice Walker's widely adored novel—which had been brought to him with enthusiasm by his producer Kathleen Kennedy—was met with a great deal of skepticism.

The second reason—and one still debated to this day—is that this white, Ohio-born, Jewish, heterosexual male simply seemed like the wrong person in every way to visually realize the Pu-litzer Prize–winning book by a Black female writer about the emotional journey of a Black woman discovering dignity, self-love, and her own lesbian desires in the post-Reconstruction American South. Walker's epistolary novel, written as letters to God, has proven to be an extraordinarily regenerative text, its centrality in our culture reflected in two Broadway musical productions, and, as of this writing, a planned second movie version, this time based on the stage adaptation. Couched in a culturally, racially, and economically specific reality, *The Color Purple* is by now iconic, a kind of anti–Horatio Alger story: the name of its protagonist, Celie, has become shorthand for Black American female marginalization and for the possibility of triumphing over one's poverty and misfortune through self-acceptance and self-actualization rather than material or financial gain. As Celie says in one of the film's most powerful lines, which is paraphrased from the book and returns in the musical as a climactic number: "I'm poor, Black, I may even be ugly—but dear God, I'm here."

If there was continued doubt that Spielberg was the right person in 1985 Hollywood to bring Celie to life, even after the film opened to mostly positive reviews and exceptionally hearty box office (the movie grossed $140 million), few questioned that Whoopi Goldberg had been the right choice to play the protagonist. Watching Goldberg's miraculously nuanced performance—a quiet symphony of internal torment made external—is to be rightly astonished that this was her screen debut at age twenty-nine after years of stand-up comedy and avant-garde theater work. Goldberg wears Celie's pain and trauma on every part of her face and body: her tightening jowls, her stooped posture, her downward glance, the way she covers her smile with her ashamed hands. Convincingly aging from her twenties to her fifties over the course of a decades-spanning narrative set in rural Georgia at the early part of the 20th century, the actress is wholly unrecognizable from her strutting, confident stage presence, which she had been fostering in such theater work as her one-woman show *Whoopi Goldberg*—originally titled *The Spook Show* before it went to Broadway—a performance that had convinced Spielberg she'd be right for the part.

Goldberg was offered the role in a rather fortuitous manner. After hearing Alice Walker read part of *The Color Purple* on the radio, she instantly wrote the author a letter, telling her she'd love to be involved if they ever made a movie version, and would willingly play any part. A shot in the dark, she thought, but Walker wrote back, telling Goldberg that she was a fan of hers as well and that she already had passed along her name to Spielberg. She was shocked to learn that the director then wanted her for Celie, partly because she had never acted for the camera before. Only one year later, after the film's release, the influential critic Roger Ebert was writing that she "gives one of the best screen performances I've ever seen."

I feel the same way. It's clear early in the film that no one could have better embodied Celie Johnson than Caryn Johnson—Whoopi Goldberg's birth name. Perhaps it's the sense of an otherwise extroverted performer harnessing herself so tightly, of constantly sucking in breath and curtailing her feelings, that makes the character so profoundly moving. Goldberg told Ebert that rather than work from the inside out, she maintained a distance from the character: "The way I played Celie was to stand back from her." Indeed, Goldberg is often shown standing away from or behind other characters, hovering in doorways or shadows, taking tentative steps and then immediately retracting. Life is one trial after another for Celie, who was raped as a teenager by her father; helplessly pleaded as her children were taken from her and given away; and marries a cruel, abusive man she only calls Mister (Danny Glover), who viciously cuts off all communication between her and her beloved sister, Nettie. The horrors she suffers as a woman are compounded by the racism experienced overall by her community in the Jim Crow south. I'm not sure I've ever seen someone so fully command the center of the screen while trying to become invisible within it.

Celie's first step toward finding a semblance of dignity comes in the form of Shug Avery, a glamorous, Billie Holiday–inspired blues singer with whom Mister is infatuated. Played by Margaret Avery, who deceptively wields confidence, Shug is a performer outrunning her own demons; she truly begins to shake things up for Celie when Mister brings her home to recuperate after a drunken sickness. Though initially the two women share a seething mutual distrust and jealousy, they soon connect, creating both a replacement sisterhood for the deprived Celie and, finally, an erotic bond. In the book, Celie calls Shug "the most beautiful woman I ever saw," and writes in one of her letters to God, "Now when I dream, I dream of Shug Avery." In the movie, after Shug dedicates a heartfelt song to her at the local juke joint titled "Miss Celie's Blues," the two women end up back in Shug's bedroom. Shug encourages Celie to uncover her smile. She tells her that she thinks she's beautiful, the first time anyone has said that to her. Their hands clasp tenderly, they caress each other's shoulders, and then, finally, Shug sweetly kisses Celie—first on the cheek, then the forehead, then, in an insistent and unambiguously sexual gesture, on the lips. Using classical Hollywood visual grammar, the camera pans over the window, where a delicately breezing wind chime indicates something more explicit that we are not privileged to see. The obfuscation may have worked in some cases—as a child watching *The Color Purple*, I wasn't entirely sure what may have been going on between these two women.

This scene was criticized in its day and remains, for many, a symbol of Spielberg's apparent inaptness for the material. In Walker's book, there's no doubt that the two women share multiple sexual encounters, and also that Shug opens Celie up to the realization of her own body, describing to her the pleasures of masturbation and helping her to not be ashamed of her genitalia: "Listen, she say, right down there in your pussy is a little button that gits real hot when you do you know what with somebody. It git hotter and hotter and then it melt." Spielberg himself has admitted that he pulled punches in his representation of this aspect of Celie's life; in a 2011 interview in *Entertainment Weekly*, he said, "I was shy about it. In that sense, perhaps I was the wrong director to acquit some of the more sexually honest encounters between Shug and Celie, because I did soften those. I basically took something that was extremely erotic and very intentional, and I reduced it to a simple kiss."

Aside from the fact that it would have been highly unlikely to visualize an honest same-sex encounter in a big-budget 1985 Hollywood film, when homosexuality was still largely a verboten topic, it's arguable whether the film would have benefitted at all from a more raw depiction of sex. The fragility and tenderness on display in the bedroom scene between Shug and Celie, however timid, is so immensely satisfying in how it contrasts with the film's one previous sex scene, a mercifully brief, grotesque wedding-night encounter between Celie and Mister in which the camera remains focused only on the head and shoulders of young Celie—the excellent fourteen-year-old actress Desreta Jackson—as she's thoughtlessly pounded against the creaking bed's headboard.

What's more apposite, it seems to me, is to acknowledge the remarkable words spoken in the love scene between Shug and Celie rather than fixate on what was or wasn't explicitly shown. In talking about their respective instances of sex with Mister, Celie reveals that she detests doing the deed, to which Shug responds, "You make it sound like he going to the toilet on you."

"That's what it feel like," Celie admits. It's Shug's response that's the revelation: "Why, Miss Celie, that means you're still a virgin." Taken directly from Walker's book, the line on-screen feels groundbreaking for a Hollywood movie, and essential for its audience to hear. In telling Celie—whose own father impregnated her, and whose husband fucks her without acknowledging her presence—that she's a virgin, Shug is recalibrating for her the idea of what sex is. Rape is not sex. Sex should be about pleasure, and women deserve the pleasure they are so frequently denied.

After we had finished rewatching the film—and had disposed

of the many piles of teary Kleenexes it caused—my mother and I talked a lot about the tenderness of this scene, in particular, and the nuances of adaptation in general. Of course, one would be hard-pressed to remember details about a book they read more than thirty-five years ago, but my mother maintained that Spielberg's film of *The Color Purple* was among the most "faithful" movie adaptations she had ever seen. I pointed out that many people would vociferously disagree with this assessment, though this also reminded me that evaluative words like *faithful* are largely in the eye of the beholder when examining art.

She's not wrong in pointing out that Menno Meyjes's script largely adheres to the cause-and-effect structure of Walker's book: most of the things that happen on the page occur on-screen and generally in the same order. I maintain, however, that the experiences are utterly different in tone and perspective, which is unavoidable with artists such as Steven Spielberg and Alice Walker, who have their own distinct styles. Walker writes in a specific verbal cadence, and in a completely subjective style that's entirely about getting into the head of her beaten-down, resilient protagonist; we see and hear what Celie sees and hears. Spielberg takes a maximalist, classical Hollywood approach, framing Celie's story as the stuff of grand, picturesque melodrama, granting Celie dignity through the conventions of American movie grammar: low-angle camerawork, the caressing glow of empathetic lighting, and a soaring musical score—written by the great Quincy Jones, who also produced and helped get the project off the ground.

Despite recurring accusations that Spielberg's aesthetic—which is, after all, influenced by white male paragons of the medium like John Ford and David Lean—sugarcoats Walker's raw text, *The Color Purple* has proven to be durable and beloved by a great deal of Black viewers, especially women, who have so rarely been represented on movie screens in this country, outside of historically hard-to-see independent features like Kathleen

Collins's excellent *Losing Ground* (1992), Julie Dash's *Daughters of the Dust* (1991), and Cheryl Dunye's *The Watermelon Woman* (1996), all of which have made resurgences in art-film circles in recent years but were never given the chance of a broader platform that a studio like *The Color Purple*'s Warner Bros. would afford.

A minor brouhaha occurred in 2017 when, while giving a speech at an awards brunch hosted by the organization Women in Film, the white actor and director Elizabeth Banks said that Spielberg "has never made a movie with a female lead." Banks, while technically incorrect, makes a fair general point: the percentage of women protagonists in Spielberg-directed films over the years is suspiciously low, and in addition to Goldberg only includes Goldie Hawn in *The Sugarland Express* (1974), Holly Hunter in the underappreciated *Always* (1989), preteen Ruby Barnhill in *The BFG* (2016), and Meryl Streep as Katharine Graham in *The Post*, which was released six months after Banks made her statement; arguably, one should also include Jobeth Williams's inspiring, top-billed performance in *Poltergeist* (1982), a film written, produced, and—according to many still-controversial on-set reports—codirected by Spielberg. Nevertheless, it was Banks's omission of *The Color Purple*, specifically, that prompted an almost instant response, both in the audience during the awards speech, when Shari Belafonte—landmark African-American actor and singer Harry Belafonte's daughter—shouted out the forgotten movie's title, and on social media, where an outpouring of tweets and other posts from Black admirers of the film related their displeasure.

The Black American journalist Ira Madison III wrote an article reporting on the incident in *The Daily Beast* that used the *Color Purple* omission to further criticize Banks: "The speech blatantly ignored that gay people and people of color might include women, and those types of women generally make less money and have more hardships not only in the industry, but in America. So it's not hard to see why Belafonte's interjection during Banks's speech being dismissed drew people to fiercely defend her and *The Color Purple*. After all, while the film was nominated for eleven Oscars, it won none of them. There's a pattern of *The Color Purple* being ignored." Days later, Banks had been dragged enough online that she felt compelled to issue a public apology, writing on Twitter: "I take full responsibility for what I said and I'm sorry... It was not my intention to dismiss the import of #TheColorPurple."

However a minor blip in the scheme of Hollywood scandals, the incident is instructive for how it illustrates something essential about *The Color Purple*'s cultural impact, despite continued and valid misgivings over its provenance as the production of a white, male Hollywood player. Undoubtedly an even greater influence than Whoopi Goldberg, however, on its continued cultural standing is another entertainment figure who is arguably more influential and powerful than Spielberg himself. The film also marked the screen debut of Oprah Winfrey, at a moment that coincided with her ascendance as a nationwide syndicated talk show host, a role that would make her one of the true American icons of the eighties. "One of the fundamental turning points in my life was *The Color Purple*," Winfrey said in an interview for her video series *Oprah's Master Class* decades later. "Nothing has had a greater impact on me, spiritually, emotionally, psychologically, in determining my path."

She has told the story many times. In the early eighties, Winfrey, who had overcome a childhood of abuse and adversity in rural Mississippi, was hit by Walker's book like a thunderbolt. Reading the novel, she felt seen for the first time in her life: "That is my story. Oh my God, somebody else *has* this story?" *The Color Purple* became an obsession; she claims to have bought all the copies from her local bookstore in Chicago and then began handing them out to friends like Christmas cards. At this early point in her career, Winfrey was in her late twenties. She had already gone from a part-time radio news gig in Berry Hill,

Tennessee, to being the first Black female TV news anchor at a Nashville affiliate, to being the host of a morning talk show in Chicago. The rapid rise in popularity of *AM Chicago*, which debuted in 1984, was attributed entirely to her unlikely presence and effortlessly warm, witty, and fearless personality, which helped offset some of the more sensational, tabloid-esque subjects of the episodes; it would only be two years before the program was renamed *The Oprah Winfrey Show* and went national.

At the same time that her star was ascending, and that she was going through her *Color Purple* superfandom, a casting agent called her out of the blue and asked if she would be interested in auditioning for something called "Moon Song." As she tells it in her *Master Class,* Winfrey, who had heard that Spielberg and Quincy Jones were commencing casting and preproduction on an adaptation of Walker's book, suspected the title was a decoy. So despite the day's freezing Chicago weather and the fact that she was harboring a cold and sore throat, Winfrey went to the audition. Indeed, she would be reading for the part of Sofia, the boisterous and brawny take-no-shit woman who marries Celie's son-in-law, Harpo, and who brilliantly functions as a foil to Celie: she begins as fiercely independent and seemingly unbreakable, before being demeaned and demoralized by a racist, patriarchal world that has no interest in her individuality or humanity.

The fortuitousness of the situation led Winfrey to believe that the planets were aligning for her to play this rich and challenging supporting role and therefore be involved in a landmark movie production of her favorite book: after all, even the character name Harpo was Oprah spelled backward, which she took as a sign (she'd eventually name her production company after the character). When months had gone by and she didn't hear anything, she called the casting agent to inquire, only to be firmly reprimanded that there were "real actresses" auditioning for the part, among them Alfre Woodard. According to Winfrey, some weeks later she was in the midst of a rigorous exercise routine, praying to God and singing the inspirational "I Surrender All" to herself, when she was interrupted and informed that Spielberg was on the phone.

Winfrey's involvement in *The Color Purple* is key to a broader understanding of the story's import, as a narrative that has meaning for readers and viewers beyond the page or the screen. Our entertainment landscape is so motivated by racial and gender bias, not to mention an overall juvenilia, that it's easy to forget that for many people Celie, Shug Avery, Sofia, and Harpo are as instantly iconic as Luke, Leia, Han Solo, and Chewbacca—and infinitely more significant. Spielberg's film doesn't require a multifilm franchise to accrue meaning over multiple generations. With Winfrey—a one-woman industry unto herself with a net worth of over two billion dollars—as its tireless champion, even decades after its release, *The Color Purple* stands as something greater than itself, a narrative of Black female empowerment and actualization.

The cultural specificity of *The Color Purple* was no barrier to our love for the film back when it was a Koresky household staple in the eighties. Of all the films we've revisited in the book, *The Color Purple* is the one I've undoubtedly seen the most often, to the point of being able to recite large portions of its dialogue along with the screen. Even when I was young, the film had a kind of incantatory quality for me, that it was speaking a different kind of truth from other movies, and it brought out a particularly deep well of empathy from me as a viewer. To this day, there is no other movie that makes me cry more profusely and often; there are multiple scenes that function as efficiently as buttons—one push and it's waterworks. It's almost Pavlovian at this point: all I need to hear is a few strains of Jones's score and I'm a puddle, even putting aside its grandly satisfying climax, a tears-of-joy reunion between Celie and Nettie that transcends time and continents.

Some might chalk up the film's emotional overload to Spielberg's abilities as a grand emotional "manipulator"—after all, I have similarly tearful responses to Spielberg films as varied as *E.T. the Extra-Terrestrial*, *Schindler's List*, and *A.I. Artificial Intelligence*. But I believe there's something greater going on here, an emotional impact that comes from watching another human being find dignity. The way the film treats its central female characters—protects, embraces, loves them, despite the world's unimaginable hardships—feels almost divine. Near the end, while she and Celie are walking through a splendid field of violets, Shug speaks the line, paraphrased from Walker's book, that refers to the film's title: "I think it pisses God off when you walk by the color purple in a field of green and don't notice it." His movie is a testament to this idea, a work of popular cinema that imbues humanity with an ascendant beauty, while at the same time never forgetting the pain and horror that can sometimes obscure it.

It's fitting that, for me, *The Color Purple* began as just another curious-looking book on my mother's shelf, as the movie itself is so much about the power of reading. Among its most indelible images is a shot of Celie and Nettie standing side by side on a wooden swing, rocking back and forth while reading aloud from an oversized hardcover of Charles Dickens's *Oliver Twist*. As in Walker's book, Nettie teaches Celie how to read, but the choice of Dickens is an invention of the movie. Spielberg, who has said that he found Walker's novel "Dickensian," creates an implicit corollary between the young American woman and the abused, neglected British orphan, and connects Celie's unsentimental education to a strain of classical literature. After Nettie rejects Mister's violent sexual advances and he casts her out of their home forever, reading becomes Celie's way to stay in touch with Nettie. However, decades pass before Celie discovers that Nettie has been writing at all, her letters intercepted by

Mister and hoarded away in a secret box under the floorboards, an astonishing cruelty that leads Celie to believe her sister's silence equaled her death.

In what is perhaps cinema's greatest visualization of the essential power of reading, Celie, unbeknownst to Mister, absconds with her letters and secretly reads decades' worth of them in order of their postmarks. Thus, Celie takes in Nettie's story like a grand novel, which seems almost too impossibly wonderful and exotic to be true: Nettie has been raising Celie's children, Adam and Olivia, presumed lost to strangers after childbirth, in Africa, where she has been living and working with other Black American missionaries.

Reading about Nettie's life becomes a way for Celie to gain knowledge about her long-missing family but also to connect her to her ancestry. The letters from Nettie—and Celie's letters in response—form a grander, lengthier backbone to the novel, while in Spielberg's film they're more of a nested set piece. Yet this extended sequence transforms and defines the movie, giving Celie and the audience a sense of escape from her years of deprivation, setting in motion the possibility for Celie to overcome, which she does in one satisfying emotional triumph after another: cursing and leaving the abusive Mister, reuniting with Shug, inheriting her dead stepfather's property, opening her own tailoring and pants-making shop, and, finally, experiencing an unexpected reunion with her sister and grown children.

The metatextual aspect of Walker's story—it's a book about reading, and how living might not be possible without it—is undoubtedly part of its appeal for my mother. Celie clutches her letters like they're lifelines, not merely papers with words on them. For someone who owns and maintains an ever-sprouting garden of books, my mother is, unsurprisingly, fond of books in part for their tactility. You won't see her holding a sleek Kindle or iPad. A book has to have literal weight and heft to fully contain the knowledge, the depth, the characters, the history therein.

None of this felt incidental or beside the point to me when I was rewatching *The Color Purple* and thinking about its multiple meanings—as book, as movie, as cultural object. I would only really begin to consider as an adult how Alice Walker's novel, which meant so very much to us, was not written with someone like my mother—a white, Jewish Bostonian who grew up in the fifties and sixties—in mind as a reader.

Her appreciation of its astonishing humanity—an appreciation she passed down to me—was inherently that of an outsider. But reading is, after all, one of the best ways to step outside of one's self, to build empathy and understanding across difference. To her credit, my mother has been spreading the gospel of empathy and historical awareness for decades, impressing upon me the importance of reading about and understanding the realities and personal stories left out of American school curriculum, in addition to Walker and Toni Morrison, all but demanding that I read *The Known World* by Edward P. Jones and Isabel Wilkerson's *The Warmth of Other Sons* and Solomon Northup's *Twelve Years a Slave* years before there was ever a movie adaptation.

Despite her curiosity and worldly aspect, my mother has not had the opportunity to travel very much and has indeed only once ventured outside the United States, on a much-anticipated trip to Paris with friends that she had taken in her sixties after my father died. Otherwise, she experiences the world through words, and it's a constant, voracious journey.

I once recommended to her some short stories by Shirley Jackson; a few months later, she had bought a massive Shirley Jackson collection featuring every story, novel, and essay she had ever written and read the *entire thing*. I'm not just admiring of her stamina and unceasing curiosity, I'm envious of it. Even when she was working full-time, she found hours in the day to read, either while in her cozy armchair clutching a late-afternoon cup of tea or in bed before lights out.

She's good at weeding out the stuff that might otherwise rot her garden: I recently gave her a copy of Cormac McCarthy's violent *Blood Meridian*, which she promptly gave back and told me, when I got around to reading it myself, to "have a barf bag ready"; she famously hated the inertia of Annie Proulx's *The Shipping News*; and she has no time for historical romance novels. Yet the great discoveries have far outweighed the duds, and the list is ever-growing. It was only during the writing of this book that she first read, upon my recommendation, John Kennedy Toole's *A Confederacy of Dunces*, one of the few books that ever made me laugh out loud. My mother, on the other hand, laughs out loud quite a lot, but *Confederacy* had her convulsing. I found inspiring but also poignant the delight and amazement with which my mother discovered Toole's Ignatius J. Reilly, a singularly dyspeptic character in American literature, and her sadness upon discovering Toole's tragic personal story: the Pulitzer Prize–winning book wasn't published until more than a decade after the author committed suicide, following years of rejection.

"Did you ever want to be a writer?" I inquired over pizza and salad, the profound humanity of *The Color Purple* still buzzing in our heads. I ask her this knowing full well that she is one. Not only did she once write regular opinion columns for the town newspaper, the *Chelmsford Independent*—the perfect forum for a real "loudmouth"—she also wrote a young adult novel. She conceived and wrote *Audrey's Garden* in her fifties, while my father was sick. A four-year process, she finally finished it after his death, publishing it with a local Massachusetts press in 2014. The emotions of those years is plainly displayed on every page for me; for the general preteen reader it's simply relatable, a vividly drawn tale of a middle-schooler dealing with the effects of bullying. The evocative writing and palpable empathy of *Audrey's Garden* draws upon the frustrations of her own, occasionally lonely childhood, and is evidence of yet another different career path Leslie's life could have taken.

"I never thought of myself as a writer—or a singer for that matter," she answered my question after hesitating. "That doesn't mean I don't think I can sing or write, but I've always shied away from labels."

She reports to me that people around town still come up to her and tell her they're sorry she doesn't write for the newspaper anymore. That might have been different if the *Chelmsford Independent*, like so many local town papers, hadn't been bought by a syndicate that homogenized their articles into anonymous "content." For years I had suggested that she start her own blog, and perhaps build up an audience for her ripe observations about daily suburban domestic life and her occasional political takedowns. She's always rejected the idea, both out of disinterest in the technological demands and the give-and-take community-building it would require.

During this conversation, it's not lost on me that at this point we're halfway through our book project, and that, although I consider it a collaboration, I am the one writing it. I am the one whose name will be on the cover. This despite the fact that none of it would be remotely possible without her—without the love of writing she passed down to me and, of course, the passion for film. As writers, we must acknowledge those who have helped shape our views and taste as much as whatever illustrious artists influenced us. Too often we don't acknowledge those who have inspired us to love, to think, to act, how to move in this world; the bylines of books should be much longer than just one name.

My mother wishes that more people—specifically young women—had read *Audrey's Garden*. I always tell her that she should be proud of the accomplishment, of having written something so formidable and moving, and that when writing is out there in the world, people find it. Eventually, one way or another, they find it. The book will be sitting on someone's shelf, maybe for decades, maybe more. It will be in libraries. Some child somewhere will pick it up, out of curiosity. She'll begin reading, and find herself engrossed. And maybe, without being able to articulate it, she'll realize that she has been somehow seen by this book; that this woman from Massachusetts, wherever that is, whoever she is, understood her.

1986: Monsters

I was in my bedroom, but it wasn't my bedroom. It was narrower and longer than my actual room on the second floor of the house on Walnut Road. Because the room felt as though it had been stretched like taffy, the window, the one that looked out onto the front lawn, seemed so far away, like it was at the end of a shadowy tunnel. A rumble of thunder outside…a storm was coming.

In the nightmare, I had come into the possession of a heaping pile of stuffed animals, the gifts of a great-aunt and -uncle, now long dead. I wanted to run to the toys, to sort through them and find something plush and pleasing to hug, but the lights were off and I could only make out an indistinct mass. As I glanced at the treasure, so close yet so far, a flash of lightning lit up the darkness, revealing something at the window that chilled my blood: a face, immobile, with cold, unblinking pupils and streaked with red veins, staring back at me. Then it was gone. But with every new lightning strike, there it was again. Was it looking at me? Trying to get in? Frozen in bed, I could never reach the toys.

My mom's nightmare went like this: while in her bedroom, also upstairs, she hears odd shuffling and grunting sounds coming from the front lawn. She peers through the window shade, and sees a sight that's no less disturbing for being absurd. It's a strange figure, perhaps a giant, but more like a disproportionate man with terribly long legs, as though he's walking on stilts. The unwanted man—or is it a monster?—lopes around the front yard in a swerving, unfocused, perhaps drunken state. There's a menacing quality to his gait, and the truly awful thing is his height: he's tall enough to peek in through the second-floor windows.

She told me about this when I was young; I can see it so vividly in my mind's eye that it seems like I dreamed it myself. It has stuck with me all these years for many reasons, one of which is the dream's similarity to mine, the horror that something outside is trying to get in, trying to breach the fragile fortress of our little suburban home, and for reasons we cannot comprehend. We seem to share a fear about the penetrability of our presumed safe zones. Another reason I remember it so vividly is because it gave me a little peek into her particular anxieties, of a woman who for years was taking care of two young children while her husband was often traveling on business, and of being a five-foot-one woman in a world of taller, aggressive men.

Other than these dreams, and the specific dread they infer through their pictorial—one might say *cinematic*—imagery, my mother and I haven't often discussed our fears. What my most memorable nightmares say about me, I leave up to someone else's interpretation. It's through films that I've most learned about what really scares me and, through my discussions with my mother, about what really scares her.

I came home for a few days in October, my favorite month of the year. I was visiting Chelmsford the weekend before Halloween—which this year fell on a disappointing Thursday, meaning I'd have to be back in New York. Halloween in the city has long had its considerable charms—the dauntingly elaborate Greenwich Village Halloween Parade; late-night monster movie marathons; and more trick-or-treaters per block than you can shake a wand at—but nothing for me can compare to the uncanny experience of Halloween in the New England suburbs. Here, normally quiet streets become nocturnal playgrounds for children in disguise, crunching on dead leaves as they run amok, shrieking with anticipation for candy, pounding on your door with demands for treats. Homes become alternate versions of themselves, festooned with demonic faces and carved gourds, which were traditionally intended to ward off evil spirits but now simply serve as annual seasonal markers.

As a child, I loved Halloween so much that I would start thinking about my costume months in advance, as if I wouldn't end up just wearing something my mother bought from the store, usually plastic: one year it was E.T., another year I was Gizmo, the cute Mogwai from *Gremlins*. And then there was the year I was very simply a ghost, meaning that I wore a white sheet with some eye holes I could barely see through as I tripped my way from doorbell to doorbell. I fervently anticipated the television special *It's the Great Pumpkin, Charlie Brown*; when it ended, with Charlie and Linus leaning bereft on a brick wall the morning after their ruined holiday, I would feel a pit-of-the-stomach sadness. No, it can't be over; we can't go back to the normal world. The existential agony of the Great Pumpkin's annual absence sent a chill through my bones, and that disappointment was superseded only by my realization that I'd have to wait another year before he once again didn't arrive. Even my stash of hard-earned Reese's Peanut Butter Cups and Milky Ways, to be measured out over the next month, couldn't quell the sadness.

Halloween, for me, remains a state of mind. The unofficial kickoff to the American holiday season, which unspools breathlessly one milestone at a time through New Year's Day,

Halloween is often treated as though it's the unserious one, an event strictly for children that we would all do better to outgrow. I've always found it to be more essential than this, a moment in the calendar year that hearkens an extended period of reflection. Aside from the costuming aspect of Halloween, it's a time of quite literal transformation: the days grow shorter, the air gets colder, the leaves change color. And without the distractions of jubilant—or dreaded—family get-togethers, Halloween feels rather lonely, pagan and untethered. Unlike Thanksgiving, there are no propagandistic national myths meant to inspire; unlike Christmas, there is no rite of passage, no promise of ecstatic religious rebirth. It's a time of year for contemplation, for acknowledging the encroaching darkness.

What this meant for my mother and me was obvious: we'd have to watch a horror movie. It would be the first and only one of this genre in our ongoing project. This wouldn't be as out of the ordinary as it might seem. We both love horror movies, and we love talking about them almost as much as we love watching them. Over the years, my mother and I have often queried one another: "What do you think is *the* scariest movie?" We have yet to come up with a definitive answer, and we likely never will. Alongside that question is a deeper one, and an even harder one to answer: *Why* do we like being scared?

It's a philosophical query as much as a personal one. All the other genres in which my mother and I willingly partake time and again grant us more of an obvious catharsis: comedies make us laugh together, musicals scratch our itch for collective harmony and spectacle, melodramas allow us to feel a kind of shared humanity through tears. Horror movies, on the other hand, repulse and chill. Like so many people who consider themselves scary-story aficionados, we embrace a central paradox: we willingly invite fear, an unpleasant feeling by any biological, instinctual standard.

Why do we voluntarily go to that dark place? In writing about the effects of Henry James's classic ghost story "The Turn of the Screw," Virginia Woolf argued that its scares aren't external, but rather reflect that "we are afraid of something, perhaps, in ourselves." Noel Carroll wrote an entire book, *The Philosophy of Horror*, trying to figure out the contradiction of why we enjoy something that disgusts us, identifying it in part as a kind of wish fulfillment, a return of suppressed, forbidden desires. After much consideration, my mom came to as good a conclusion as any of them: "They're comforting." An ironic answer for a genre that intends to provoke, upset, and alarm.

Is it that we can easily turn on the light and go back to reality? I think, for my mother, it's something more than that, something more abstract. She's always been more attuned with a spiritual world than I have been. My skepticism only comes from my lack of experience: I have never seen or felt the presence of a ghost, and so have never given myself the opportunity to seriously consider the possibility. My adoration of ghost stories, especially those by the greats, like M. R. James, Algernon Blackwood, and Shirley Jackson, makes me endlessly curious, but my belief systems tend to stay within the boundaries of the page. It's different for my mother, who holds a certain faith in an invisible alternate reality, which might partly come from a traditionally American connection to superstition.

Considering Leslie's belief in ghosts, and the general free-floating presence my father still seems to have throughout her home on Walnut Road, the inevitable question arises: Is this a haunted house? As I often feel like the house has a life of its own, who's to say that life isn't partly a conglomeration of spirits?

At my mother's request, I had taken down the wind chimes, so now and for the rest of the season the breeze only sounds like breeze. This time of year, the house on Walnut Road is always subtly decorated, inside and out, with tokens of the season: ceramic ghost and bat figurines perched on the piano; the trio of

mini wooden pumpkins that have been a part of the family almost as long as I have; a smiling, fabric scarecrow hanging on the
front door; electric jack-o'-lanterns that she never forgets to plug
in at night, their ghoulish faces peeking out from those upstairs
bedroom windows that have featured in our dreams. My mother
continues to decorate the house, for herself, for the neighborhood kids, for the memory of the family that once lived there.

The tall, imposing oaks that surround and dwarf the home
appear more menacing than they do in the summer, not yet entirely shed of their leaves and creating a thick, shadowy canopy
over the neighborhood as soon as the sun sets. Here, in the quiet
house, surrounded by the dark October night outside, my mother
and I sat in the dining room, munching on a particularly delicious frozen pizza she had just discovered. We were in astonished
agreement: the pie tasted almost exactly like the legendary—in
our house at least—Town Spa pizza from Stoughton, MA, that
my father was known to *kvell* over. The crust wasn't as delectably
crispy, perhaps, but the cheese had that sharp, rich, cheddary flavor that instantly shuttles my mind back to childhood, and to my
dad's delighted lip smacking. It was pizza as madeleine, and the
nostalgic feelings it stirred up were only made richer and more
comforting from the red wine we were imbibing and from the
pleasant sounds of Game Four of the Astros-Nationals World Series that were drifting in from the television, left on in the family
room in case something exciting happened.

The warmth of that moment was much appreciated. All
month, my mother was experiencing a series of general anxieties. Some were about money: an important new heating system
had been installed, and it had cost much more than expected,
as had a series of big vet bills for her little kitty, Daisy, who was
plagued by ongoing health problems and was looking more haggard than ever. Others were medical: new pills she had been
prescribed for her myeloproliferative blood disorder—the vagaries of which were still a matter of anxiety for me as well—had

been giving her painful migraines and so she was waiting impatiently for her doctor to adjust the medication. All these worries were clearly taking an emotional toll; their confluence seemed to put her in a state of higher stress than usual, mostly manifest in her obsessive monitoring of whether the cat was eating or not.

Amid all these real-world fears—fears of pain, of sickness, of aging, of financial uncertainty—we seemed all too happy to retreat into a world of movie fears. In between bites of pizza, we again posed the question of what was "the scariest movie ever." Is it, I wondered, the 1982 ghost home-invasion mainstay *Poltergeist*, which I saw way too young and which has never really left me, like fears of the dark, of the woods, of strangers and bullies and mean schoolteachers? Is it, she asked, MGM's sinister 1945 version of *The Picture of Dorian Gray*, which leans into Oscar Wilde's timeless supernatural conceit, making the author's classic morality tale—about a man who never ages while a painting of his likeness grows old and vile—into a work of chiaroscuro horror? Or perhaps, she supposed, it's *Rosemary's Baby*, which offers up the terrifyingly perfect idea of a woman's unborn child being sold to the devil by her narcissistic actor husband in order to further his own career. Or maybe, I added, it's Kubrick's adaptation of Stephen King's *The Shining*, in which, isolated by snow in a hotel for the winter, an ostensible American everydad gives in to his demons and turns on his own family with an ax. In terms of sheer visceral fright, my mother's single worst moment came just a few months after I was born, when the November 1979 TV miniseries *Salem's Lot*, adapted from King's best-selling novel, aired. So shocked by the initial appearance of the snaggle-fanged, Nosferatu-like vampire "Mr. Barlow," she let out a bloodcurdling scream, threw aside the laundry she was folding, and lunged toward the television's off button. My father was away on a business trip; my brother and I must have been sleeping upstairs. She never finished watching *Salem's Lot*.

My mother's appreciation of the genre is not unrelated to

her being part of the first generation raised on television. She has many times eagerly told me about those childhood frights beamed directly into her living room: Disney's animated *The Legend of Sleepy Hollow*, featuring the Halloween midnight ride of Ichabod Crane and the Headless Horseman; the devilish "Howling Man" episode of *The Twilight Zone*, in which Beelzebub himself is caught but slyly tricks his jailers into releasing him from prison; "An Unlocked Window," an episode of *Alfred Hitchcock Presents* in which a trio of overnight nurses are stalked by an escaped maniac. Both on the small and large screens, the postwar fifties were riddled with teenage werewolves and outer-space invaders, responses to a whole new set of terrors: nuclear catastrophe, the cold war with Russia, suburban conformity. It's certainly no coincidence that a generation of kids raised on a steady diet of chillers and creature features would end up becoming purveyors and consumers of the next big horror wave; after all, my mother was born only two years after Steven Spielberg and one year after Stephen King. There was no way she wasn't going to read *The Exorcist* when it hit the bestseller list in 1971. As she has often said, the book had her quite literally looking under her bed before tucking in for the night.

Thinking about my mother's push-pull, fascination-repulsion relationship with horror, I began to realize just how many films in the genre are female-driven. Yes, there is the much discussed "final girl" in so much horror—in which a female character, usually young, is the last character left alive to fight the villain, often requiring her to summon superhuman powers to do so; this is almost always the conceit of thrillers and slasher films, such as *The Texas Chainsaw Massacre*, *Halloween*, *Friday the 13th*, *A Nightmare on Elm Street*, etc. Yet on a deeper level, a great many horror movies are about women's bodies, as related to sex and motherhood.

Unsurprisingly, many of these films are my mother's particular favorites, not only the grimly entertaining *Rosemary's*

Baby—which both of us, at this point, surely have memorized—but also *Poltergeist*, which features such hard-to-miss imagery as a mother rescuing her daughter from ghost kidnappers by reemerging through an ectoplasmic womblike rebirth canal; the elegantly creepy 1942 classic *Cat People*, in which a woman turns into a killer panther when sexually aroused; and *Cujo*, in which a fed-up mom has to fight a rabid Saint Bernard to the death to protect her little boy. Even more recent horror phenomena, like Jennifer Kent's *The Babadook* and Ari Aster's *Hereditary*, have captured her imagination. Never mind that in the former a mother tries to stab her hyperactive little boy with a butcher knife and that in the latter a grieving mother tells her teenage son, "I never wanted to be your mother"—these are gut-wrenchers we've both enjoyed, sadistically.

With every last crumb of the pizza scarfed down, we filled up the dishwasher, turned off the lights, and settled in for our 1986 selection, a perfectly apt one for October: James Cameron's horror epic *Aliens*. "I don't think I've seen this since it first came out," my mother marveled. Unlike with *Terms of Endearment*, she seemed to be looking forward to the movie with excitement rather than dread—despite the fact that it would contain exploding chests, flying viscera, and hideous, ravenous extraterrestrials.

In a decade in which sequels and franchises were becoming the test-marketed norm for a Hollywood ever more cognizant of the bottom line, Cameron's much-hyped follow-up to Ridley Scott's 1979 hit *Alien* was an unusual event: a film that was widely considered to have at least equaled its original in quality, and in many ways surpassed it. It is, however, quite a different film in tone and scope. Whereas Scott's original was a slow-build "who goes there?" work of horror, a classical haunted house story that just happened to be set on a spaceship, Cameron's pluralized sequel was something grander, more amped-up: a search-and-destroy mission that reflected—and critiqued—

the Reagan eighties' obsession with militarism and hypermasculinized American warfare. One thing they had in common was Swiss artist H. R. Giger's exquisitely repugnant alien design, brought to fleshy, organic life by special effects guru Carlo Rambaldi: a biomechanical, acid-blooded hybrid that looked like both machine and monster, whose pièce de résistance was a retractable set of snapping teeth within teeth within teeth. Another thing they had in common was Sigourney Weaver.

A staple of my movie-watching youth, Weaver fascinated me for her ability to show versatility while always remaining her unique, statuesque self. Bill Murray's no-nonsense love interest in *Ghostbusters*, her passive-aggressive viper of a boss in *Working Girl*, the maniacally driven conservationist and animal activist in *Gorillas in the Mist*—these were clearly all the same woman but with subtle variations of distinction. Weaver is undoubtedly best known for her *Alien* character Ellen Ripley, eventually the figurehead of a franchise. Her character is a miraculously resourceful, unkillable action star, yet watching *Aliens* again I was reminded that she's no superwoman. If Ripley hadn't been so relatable as the emotional center of these dark, bloody monster movies, it's unlikely she would have so fully captured the moviegoing public's imagination. Like the greatest movie heroes, Ripley is vulnerable. She is haunted, and reticent to fight. Yet when she must gear up for battle, she does so without hesitation. And in *Aliens*, she does so repeatedly, to protect others, most vigorously a little orphan girl for whom she becomes a surrogate mother figure. For all its testosterone, artillery, and bordering-on-camp military machismo, *Aliens* is first and foremost about the maternal instinct.

This is a prime reason why the film so appealed to my mother, and it would prove to be one of the elements that would most connect her to the film upon this rewatch. I remember she and my father going to the movies one night to see it while my brother and I were left with the babysitter. The film intrigued me from some forbidden-looking clips and trailers my brother and I had seen on television, but I assumed that I probably wouldn't be allowed to see this R-rated nightmare: not long before, upon perusing the horror section of our town's Video Paradise, I had eyed the box for the original *Alien*, featuring nothing more than an image of a weird, green, egg-shaped object, and inquired about it. My mother had summarily informed me that I would not be seeing that movie, claiming it was "the scariest movie ever made." (I reminded her of this, and she doesn't remember saying it; a child never forgets.)

It was only years later, upon learning *Alien*'s theatrical release date, I realized that she must have been seven months pregnant with me when she saw it: probably not the optimal condition to see a movie in which an extraterrestrial creature bursts through a man's chest and kills him after gestating inside his stomach— cinema's most famous image of a fatal childbirth.

For some reason, my mother found it acceptable for my brother and me to watch *Aliens* upon its home video release, even though I still hadn't been allowed to see *Alien*. The night we all watched it as a family, I must have been eight years old, and I remember being nervous and queasy as it began, though my fear eventually gave way to exhilaration. Without any foreknowledge of the first film's plot or imagery, I had a constant sense of discovery and even a pleasing kind of nausea. The beasts themselves were undeniably terrifying, but they were also aweinducing, and I was aware that they were the result of some kind of magic puppetry. At the time, I was quite keenly obsessed with the 1986 movie version of the camp musical *Little Shop of Horrors*, seeing it twice in the theater, owning the soundtrack, trading cards, and a comic book version; and in some way, I found a kinship between that film's bloodthirsty singing plant, its Venus flytrap mouth and slithering vines made possible by Jim Henson's workshop, and the toothy, gooey, tentacle monsters of *Aliens*, brought to life by the late effects guru Stan Winston.

They were both, after all, to paraphrase *Little Shop*'s climactic song, mean, green—or metallic black—*mothers* from outer space.

It makes perfect sense for a film dripping with images of wombs, amniotic fluid, and phalluses (the aliens' heads are positively penile) to be preoccupied with motherhood. In the original *Alien*, Weaver's Ripley was purposefully without backstory, one of many somewhat anonymous working-class crewmembers who find their ship, the *Nostromo*, besieged by a malicious foreign entity it had picked up while investigating the planet LV-426 on company orders. She was the only one—along with orange tabby cat Jones—to survive the ensuing massacre. She had done so by setting the *Nostromo* to self-destruct and escaping in a shuttle. *Aliens* picks up with this unlikely hero's story fifty-seven years later, after her shuttle is discovered floating in space. Ripley has been frozen in hypersleep the entire time, meaning that she hasn't aged even as the decades have passed. Upon being reawakened, she is hospitalized and interrogated by the Weyland-Yutani Corporation overlords who revoke her pilot license and inform her that her daughter has died—at age sixty-six. A mournful Ripley replies, "I told her I'd be home for her eleventh birthday."

This crucial detail—which had been reinserted into the film's later, lauded director's cut, the version we are watching—appears to move my mother deeply. She lets a quiet "wow" escape from her lips; it's a moment of awe and sadness only possible via science-fiction—great fantasy horror functioning as melodrama. Weaver's response in this moment, and her overall aching evocation of Ripley's all-consuming melancholy, is what truly fuels Cameron's film, perhaps even more than its various gripping action sequences and creature attacks. As in his breakthrough, *The Terminator*, released just two years earlier, the film's terror is impossible to separate from its foreboding. In that film, the underlying theme was imminent apocalypse; in *Aliens*, there's a similar sense of futility and mortality. Absent her daughter and any connection to anything or anyone she ever knew, Ripley would seem to have nothing left to lose. Thus it's perhaps not entirely shocking when she is convinced, against her better judgment, to return to LV-426, where her crew first encountered the alien pods, whose tentacled, spiderlike face-huggers would plant the seeds of destruction for the *Nostromo*'s human crew.

Ripley is horrified to find out that American colonists have been living on the once uninhabitable planet for years, setting up the communal outpost "Hadley's Hope," financed by Weyland-Yutani with a population of 158. When the company loses contact with the colonists, Weyland-Yutani representative Carter Burke—an effortlessly slimy Paul Reiser—offers to reinstate her flight officer status if she goes with them, claiming her expertise essential. Ripley agrees only on the condition that they destroy the creatures, rather than bring them back for study. Crucially, a troop of hard-ass marines is coming along on the mission, led by the green Lieutenant Gorman. "I can guarantee your safety," he promises Ripley, who seems understandably unconvinced. As *Aliens* goes on to demonstrate, all the chest-pumping machismo in the world cannot compare to a mother's fortitude.

Bluster and bravado is not strictly the purview of males; in Cameron's progressive vision of this future American military, women serve alongside the men, most memorably the proto–G.I. Jane character Vasquez (Jenette Goldstein), first introduced brandishing muscled biceps as she shows off her pull-up skills. When a male marine taunts her, "Ever been mistaken for a man?" she quickly replies, "No, have you?" Outside of this brief moment, Vasquez's difference isn't noted; gender equality seems to be just a matter of course. This also extends to Ripley, whose outsider status isn't based on her gender so much as her lack of military training and knowledge of weaponry. She learns how to handle semiautomatic rifles, shotguns, and flame-throwers, under the tutelage of sensitive, boyish Corporal Hicks—played by my once undetected crush object Michael Biehn. It's to the

film's credit that the obvious attraction between Ripley and
Hicks never blossoms into a real affair, leaving it a tantalizing
what-if for the romantics in the audience.

It's to Weaver's credit that she has spoken on the record many
times, including upon the film's release, that she was greatly put
off by taking part in a movie with so much gun violence. "It's
hard for me morally to justify being in a film with so many guns;
I just find it very upsetting," she said in a 1986 television interview shot on the film's set, claiming to have not realized while
looking at the script just how prevalent the artillery would be,
and adding that she had and would continue to donate to anti-
gun legislation.

Considering the amount of warfare depicted on-screen, it's
worth pointing out that *Aliens* does have an ambivalent, or at
least complex, relationship to its images of military violence.
This is, after all, a film in which a group of human colonizers
are technically the aggressors, landing on a planet with the sole
purpose of wiping out a species that got there first. While it
doesn't take this concept as far as, say, Paul Verhoeven's explicitly
satirical *Starship Troopers* would a decade later, *Aliens* constantly
reminds the viewer that this "bug hunt," as Bill Paxton's blovi-
ating Corporal Hudson puts it, never would have happened if
humans hadn't meddled in the living biosphere of another planet
in the first place. *Aliens* is, in essence, the story of American soldiers being shipped off to fight a war—under the auspices of a
rescue mission—that was never theirs to fight, and thus they are
essentially sent to the slaughter one by one.

The scars of Vietnam remained fresh during this period, with
the war having ended little more than a decade earlier. *Platoon*,
Oliver Stone's emotional reckoning with his personal experiences
in Vietnam, would be released that same year, winning the Best
Picture Oscar, and just one year later, Kubrick unleashed *Full
Metal Jacket*, which used Vietnam as the backdrop for a dramatization of the military's dehumanization and the mechanization of

soldiers in preparation for combat. These popular films weren't backward-looking period pieces, but pointed responses to President Reagan. One of Reagan's mantras was "peace through strength," and his time in office was in part defined by a major resurgence in the military, Cold War escalation, and a huge increase in defense spending, including a wildly expensive, proposed defense shield to protect the US from nuclear missiles; nicknamed "Star Wars" by detractors, it was an instance of real politics imitating the outlandishness of science-fiction movies.

At the same time, Reagan's eighties were defined by the rise of unchecked corporate interests, made possible by his insistent economic deregulations. This also surfaces as one of *Aliens*' main themes, largely through Reiser's anything-for-a-buck company man Burke. Despite its being an obvious product of—and response to—the era of Reagan military machismo, *Aliens* is spiritually more akin to *Country* than *Rambo*. Jessica Lange's Jewell Ivy, protecting her family against soulless corporate interests, finds correlation in Sigourney Weaver's Ripley, whose personal connection to this fight—and possible suicide mission—takes an emotional turn when she discovers a little girl, Rebecca, nicknamed Newt (Carrie Henn), the sole survivor of the Hadley's Hope colony.

Newt is introduced as a feral, mud-covered wild child who has somehow stayed alive by scurrying through vents and aqueducts. We come to realize the girl is in shock from having seen her entire family and community killed or else kidnapped for the aliens' grotesque incubation process. Skeptical of the marines' ability to protect her or themselves from the looming menace, Newt gradually grows attached to Ripley, for whom she becomes a surrogate daughter and, ultimately, a reason to keep fighting. Weaver says that getting to work with then nine-year-old Henn was one of the prime appeals of making *Aliens*. Though at this point the regal, six-foot actress had been headlining Hollywood movies for seven years, she had forged a career playing mostly single career women and diplomats, in movies like *Eyewitness*, *The Year of Living Dangerously*, and *Ghostbusters*. As her career advanced, Weaver has continued to avoid being cast in stereotypically feminine or maternal roles.

Four years after the release of *Aliens*, Weaver gave birth to her first and only child, Charlotte, when she was forty, but this didn't have a noticeable effect on the roles she took. Ellen Mitchell, her First Lady in Ivan Reitman's 1993 presidential satire *Dave*, is notably childless; even in her most memorable role as a parent, in Ang Lee's 1997 *The Ice Storm*, it's made clear that her character, a depressed, philandering Connecticut housewife who can't get through to her equally unhappy kids, probably was never cut out to be a parent in the first place. Ironically, perhaps, Ellen Ripley is the most relatable, emotionally accessible, and maternal character of her career. The first thing my mother said to me when we finished the movie was: "Strength has nothing to do with machismo."

"My mommy always said that there are no monsters, no real ones," says Newt. "Why do they tell little kids that?"

"Most of the time it's true" is Ripley's brilliantly matter-of-fact response. *Most of the time.* It's stayed with me all these years, and it's an especially frightening statement for a child to hear. Yes, there are monsters, and it can't be denied: creatures who disrupt and endanger our lives, out of bloodlust or greed or monomaniacal thirst for power. Whether primitive reptiles, angry ghosts, or self-interested politicians, monsters are out there; it's just that most of the time we're protected from them, safe in our own homes, cowering from behind our bedsheets as the lightning illuminates their toothy, drooling faces at the window.

Aliens tells us that only mothers can protect us. Yet in the film's complex equation, even monsters have mothers to protect them, too. In the crowd-pleasing climax, Ripley must rescue a kidnapped Newt from the clutches of the aliens, who have immobilized and prepped her for their disgusting brand of oral impregnation. Carrying two guns duct-taped together in one arm, a flame-thrower slung over the other, she descends into the aliens' lair, where the eggs are laid. Finally, after freeing Newt from her prison of supergoo and carrying her to seeming safety, Ripley comes face-to-face with the alien queen herself. She is dinosaur-huge, a hulking arachnid with a mouth bigger than Ripley's entire head. When Ripley lays waste to rows of Mama's pods, the beast lets out a shriek of agony and anger that *almost* makes one feel sympathy. She'll do anything to protect her children. Both creatures remind me of Shirley MacLaine's Aurora shrieking for the nurse to give her daughter the morphine shot in *Terms of Endearment*, a very different kind of horror.

The final battle of *Aliens* is so rousing in such a pure, rah-rah action-movie way that one forgets we're watching something that's in essence rather melancholy: two beings who have lost children and who have very little left, duking it out to the death. To be on more equal weight and footing, Ripley has put herself into a burdensome yet intimidating exo-suit, which she had learned how to operate while working on the space station's cargo docks; encasing her in metal, it makes her into a human forklift, as though she's half woman, half machine. From behind her robo-skeleton, she manages to bully the queen mother away from a terrified Newt, uttering the film's killer line: "Get away from her, you *bitch*!" In an intense dramatization of the long-believed phenomenon that a mother can summon enough delirious, protective strength to, say, lift an entire car off her trapped child, Ripley wrestles the monster all the way to the ship's emergency airlock, through which she manages to blow it into space. Safe at last, Newt runs into Ripley's arms and, muffled with tears, cries, for the first time: "Mommy."

Aliens is remarkably empowering, especially for being part of a genre that so often hinges on female vulnerability. Even when they find courage and fortitude, women in horror movies see their bodies stalked and victimized (*Halloween*), owned (*Rose-*

mary's Baby), or possessed (*The Exorcist*); even when they're given special powers, like Sissy Spacek's teenage Carrie, whose telekinesis is signaled by her first menstruation, they can lose control of those powers and wreak havoc. Ripley is different, an emotionally complex hero whose strengths are uncomplicated. The vulnerability that Weaver brings to the role only makes Ripley stronger; she's flesh and blood yet even a creature with a defense mechanism so advanced that it spurts acid when injured is no match for her protective instinct. Perhaps only Ripley can conquer the queen, one mother to another, because, having given birth herself, she's the only human who can understand her.

She had recently given birth to her first child, my older brother. It's the middle of the night, and she gets out of bed and crosses the landing to enter the bedroom where the child sleeps. She approaches to peek inside the shadowy crib to check on the infant, who's not making a sound. The crib is empty. Before she has a chance to panic, she turns her head to the right. There he is, in a white chair, sitting up, unnaturally stock-still. He's not moving or crying. He's just staring back at her with an eerie, expressionless serenity.

It was enough to jolt her out of slumber, and all these years later she still can feel the pit-of-stomach dread it induced. My mother has frequently told me about this one over the years, memorable for its hair-raising subtlety. Nothing overtly horrific or supernatural happened in the dream: the baby wasn't dead, the baby wasn't talking in full sentences, the baby wasn't attacking her with a pair of scissors. The baby was simply not in its right place.

The new-parent anxiety of the dream is clear enough, and far more thematically readable than even my most memorable nightmares, such as the one I had as a college freshman in which I accidentally sank my teeth into the guts of a huge writhing, squealing worm hidden under a stack of delicious pancakes.

Whatever that dream was conveying about my emotional situation at the time—some corporeal truth concealed under the veneer of normality—is less obvious than what my mother's dream was representing about her anxieties. After all, I was only wrongly ingesting something into my body; she was envisioning that something was askew about this strange new being that came *out* of her.

It's strange to think that I was once a monster, writhing, squealing, gasping for air in a new world. I'll never know what it feels like to be on the other side of that equation, a fact that keeps me at a fairly consequential distance from my mother's experience. As the next movie we shared would attest—in a far lighter, less bloody manner than *Aliens*—being a parent doesn't have to originate from birth and viscera, but it does come from a certain biological imperative nonetheless, an urge to keep humanity going no matter what horrors we perpetuate as a species. On a dying planet, that's a scary thought.

1987: Kids

With Halloween safely in the rearview mirror, a far more frightening holiday was looming on the horizon. Chris and I had agreed to host Thanksgiving for ten in our small Brooklyn apartment. It boasts a kitchen as narrow as a library aisle, offers no counter space, and can barely fit two grown male husbands at once. But with Chris's exhausting new work schedule, which required frequent travel, we decided not to schlep all the way to Chelmsford for the holiday, as we normally would, and instead invited family and friends to come to us, including, of course, mom. We had accomplished such a dinner, with its requisite stuffed turkey and bounty of sides and desserts, in this dauntingly tiny room four years earlier, though not without our share of the kinds of harrowing fights that only small New York apartments can encourage.

Initially I thought we might be able to continue our trip down movie memory lane during her visit, but the overwhelming stresses and anxieties of the week made that impossible. In addition to the hosting, the shopping, the cleaning, the prepping, the cooking, the serving, the cleaning again, and, finally, the collapsing, a low-budget labor-of-love movie that I had written and codirected with my dear friends and artistic collaborators, Jeff and Farihah, was opening that week in New York, occasioning my appearance at a series of Q&As. The timing for the holiday-themed film couldn't have been better: titled *Feast of the Epiphany*, it's a fiction-documentary hybrid that combines a story about a dinner among friends in Brooklyn and an observational portrait of life and work on an upstate farm, where the food comes from. Yet I was left exhausted by all the running around, and didn't have the emotional space to delve into the next movie selection. This Thanksgiving, we wouldn't have time to watch anything.

A holiday without movies is like sleeping without dreams. Did it even happen? Often my mother and I will watch films that have been specifically designated for holidays, loving, perhaps requiring, the comfort brought by tradition—we take annual pilgrimages back to them, reveling in familiar lines of dialogue, and delighting in how they're delivered by beloved actors. With Thanksgiving comes Jodie Foster's rollicking yet poignant *Home for the Holidays*, an annual standby in the Koresky household ever since we first saw it in theaters in 1995 (it was also the first film I ever reviewed for the *Chelmsford Independent*, as a precocious high-schooler), or perhaps the original 1947 *Miracle on 34th Street*, which, though a comedy about an apple-cheeked, geriatric New Yorker who claims to be the real Santa Claus, kicks off the season by starting with an extended sequence set during the Macy's Thanksgiving Day Parade.

There's an even more personal turkey-day movie for me: Barry Levinson's 1990 *Avalon*, extraordinarily close to my heart for how it uncannily evokes so much of my family history on-screen. For me *Avalon* is the ultimate example of how movies can inadvertently function as mirrors. Set in 1950s suburban Baltimore, the film concerns a secular Jewish family of Eastern-

European descent named Krichinsky. Elijah Wood, with piercing blue eyes, enormous like a Keane painting, plays little Michael K. (my identifying moniker all through elementary school to differentiate me from the surplus of Michaels), and the film centers on his relationship with his traveling salesman father (sound familiar?), his kindly grandfather, a musician and jazz-enthusiast (my dad's jazz-enthusiast father was a professional clarinetist and saxophonist), and his withering, take-no-prisoners grandmother (no comment). A major family controversy is that one subset of the family changes its last name to Kay to better assimilate into non–Jewish American life; this happened in our family as well, when my great-uncle's clan branched off and changed its last name to Kent upon moving to California in the fifties. But the biggest conflict arrives when, one Thanksgiving, the extended family begins the meal before the eternally whining, always late Uncle Leo—a real *alta kaka* ("an old shit"), as my parents would say—arrives. "You cut the *toikey* widdout me??" Uncle Leo exclaims, his astonishment ascending to apoplexy before he and his wife storm out. What initially seems like an amusing anecdote ratchets up into a lifelong festering resentment.

Avalon is worth briefly invoking because of how much it means to me as I age. Though initially steeped in nostalgia for the fifties, Levinson's film subtly reveals itself to be about what's lost as time progresses, as people age, as the customs and languages of immigrant life are absorbed into the mainstream. By the end of the film, the family, once big and bustling with aunts and uncles and cousins, all of whom could barely fit around multiple, leaf-extended tables, has shrunk to a handful of people who barely see each other anymore. Frozen dinners are eaten by frozen people in front of carelessly left-on television sets. Michael's grandfather is alone in a nursing home, still regaling whoever will listen to his stories of coming to America in 1914.

Families change. Sometimes they expand. Children grow up to have children; brothers and sisters become aunts and uncles, cousins are born. My family, however, has grown smaller. It's been on my mind a lot as I've transitioned into the confusing life of a forty-something. I felt it acutely at my Thanksgiving dinner this year. While it was wonderful to have so many loving, lovely, loved ones around the table, it has only become more striking with the passing years that there are no children around. My dear cousins Karen and Sam, now in their late seventies, never had children. As of this writing, my three first cousins do not have children. Neither do my brother and his wife, nor do Chris and I. It feels most conspicuous at Christmas. Whereas Chris's nephews and niece have ensured for years that Christmas in Milwaukee is full of sugar-fueled excitement over unwrapping presents and a general bursting-at-the-seams togetherness, for the Koresky clan the holidays are now a grown-up affair, evoking the rich, full loneliness that can be a hallmark of this time of year. With no youngsters crowding my peripheral vision, the holidays have become for me poignant affairs—they're steeped in traditions I love, but that I'm unable to pass down.

I can't help but notice the ways in which the parent becomes like the child, and vice versa. Back in Chelmsford, my mother is clearly, efficiently master of her domain; when visiting New York, out of her element, she's more dependent on my guidance. Maybe it's because of her diminutive height and persistent ignorance of the city's layout—and because of my tendency to walk way too fast, dodging slow pedestrians and scuttling across streets to beat Don't Walk signals—that I often feel like she's the vulnerable one who requires tending to. For those of us without cars, getting around New York feels more arduous when you're with an outsider; and the feeling of overprotectiveness becomes overwhelming when you're guiding around your mother.

This feeling was especially acute during a strange moment the Saturday after Thanksgiving, as I brought Leslie to the bus that would take her home. I had already spent the previous night on the phone moving her ticket up a day to avoid a snowstorm that promised to blast the Northeast. Leslie and I sat for nearly an hour at the eternally charmless Port Authority Bus Terminal waiting for her transportation back to Massachusetts, watching sour-faced city denizens, tired travelers, and occasional belligerent drunks pass by. So much has changed in New York, but the Port Authority stays the same. Chris stayed in Brooklyn at our mercifully becalmed apartment, waiting with a bottle of wine. When we found out that the bus—already a half hour late—needed another forty-five minutes to be cleaned out before loading passengers, my mother shooed me off.

"I'll be fine, just get back home and relax. What's another forty-five minutes?"

"Are you sure?"

She insisted she would be fine. I hugged her goodbye, and told her what a lovely visit it had been and that I'd see her in just a few weeks for Christmas. As I walked away, down the long, clogged, but somehow lonely corridor that connects Port Authority to the subway, its walls dotted with posters of the maniacally smiling Radio City Rockettes promising another Christmas spectacular, I glanced back. Tiny in general, my mother looked downright Lilliputian from a distance.

I ascended the escalator and was fumbling for my wallet to get my Metro Card. Instead, I grabbed my phone and called Chris. I suddenly felt exhausted, partly from the week, partly from guilt at leaving my mother alone in one of the most heavily trafficked and notoriously unpleasant places in New York.

"Go back to her," my wise husband said, matter-of-factly.

I had momentarily let my selfishness get the better of me. I turned around and went right back, weaving in and out of the many holiday travelers and back down to the tail end of the endless hallway where her bus was still being cleaned. As I approached, she looked up and saw me, a relieved smile spreading across her face.

★ ★ ★

In outlining this book, I always arrived at a bit of a quandary by the time I reached 1987. Scanning back through the eighties, I had found it relatively simple to choose a film from every year that fit the criteria: movies my mother introduced to me, featuring women unambiguously cast in leading roles, and which had some kind of shared significance in our lives. If the movie ticked all three boxes, then I assumed it would naturally open up new avenues of thought and inquiry upon our revisiting it together. The problem with 1987 wasn't that there was a paucity of choices—it was that there were too many.

Looking back at this era of American film, it was evident to me that, certainly compared to future decades, the movies were all but overflowing with emotionally rich, adult fare featuring potent female stars in vivid leading roles that avoided clichés of cinematic femininity. Between 1986 and 1987, the era seems to have really hit its sweet spot. For instance, in 1986 alone, thirty-seven-year-old Sissy Spacek, that most unusual of major movie stars, a woman who can easily inhabit an inscrutable outcast or sandy-haired girl next door, was featured in above-the-title leading roles in three studio-financed films: *Crimes of the Heart*, *'night, Mother*, and *Violets Are Blue*. All of them were formidable character pieces about women who live independently of men. Told by producers at the beginning of her career that she'd better lose her Texas accent if she wanted to make it in show business, Spacek instead kept her twang, breaking conventional wisdom and proving that an actor need not be a chameleon to demonstrate her versatility.

Over the course of 1987, we'd see an array of movies headlined by women that would in one way or another become Koresky household staples: Holly Hunter as one of the most idiosyncratic working women of the decade in *Broadcast News*; Debra Winger and Theresa Russell in *Black Widow*, a kind of proto–*Killing Eve*; Jennifer Grey coming of age, morally and sexually, as "Baby" in *Dirty Dancing*; Glenn Close as the tragic one-night-stand-from-hell in Adrian Lyne's slick but essentially misogynist *Fatal Attraction*; Lindsay Crouse as an unflappable grifter-in-training in David Mamet's *House of Games*; Cher, that year's Best Actress Oscar winner, as an inspiringly confident Italian-American widow in *Moonstruck*; Barbra Streisand as a high-priced call girl accused of murder in *Nuts*; Goldie Hawn nearly overcoming the brain-poisoning sexism of *Overboard*; and, the pièce de résistance, Cher, Michelle Pfeiffer, and Susan Sarandon joining forces to outwit Jack Nicholson's chauvinist pig and literal devil in *The Witches of Eastwick*.

For a while, *Eastwick* was my selection; an oft-rewatched favorite since childhood, George Miller's genuinely strange studio film fascinated me for its supernatural fantasy of female empowerment; for how it allowed its three stars to be sexual but not erotic objects; and for how I was honestly spellbound by the film's depiction of friendship—an image of sisterhood, unbound from the masculine codes of boyhood, a kind of presumed paradise that I felt unfairly exiled from. Yet as the autumn wore on, the days got shorter, and the holidays began their inevitable rollout, it started to feel like an impersonal choice, its allegory perhaps too detached from my experience to bear real fruit.

My mind kept returning, instead, to *Baby Boom*. The Diane Keaton star vehicle was on VHS repeat in my house growing up, and it remained a particular favorite of my mother's. Initially I had counted out *Baby Boom* because, as a woman-in-the-workplace comedy, it seemed too similar to *Nine to Five*. But that was only the film's milieu, not its more expansive emotional meaning—a meaning, I would come to realize, my mother felt in an intense and personal way.

Unlike *Nine to Five* before it and *Working Girl* after it, *Baby Boom* is specifically invested in what it means for a woman to juggle work and motherhood, and the unfair sacrifices she is expected to make to negotiate a male-dominated world.

Keaton's high-powered corporate advertising executive J. C. Wiatt had sworn off having children yet finds herself suddenly saddled with a toddler after a distant cousin's sudden death. The premise is screwball absurd, but the questions it raises are anything but. Ultimately, it's a movie about choice. J.C.'s decision to keep and raise the child leads to the exposure of unequal treatment by her formerly chummy male bosses and associates. She's constantly told that a woman "can't have it all," yet she goes on to show that maybe she can—with just a little bit of sacrifice.

Aside from the sheer pleasure it affords, it was the lack of children in my life that ultimately led me to want to reconsider *Baby Boom*. My husband and I have decided not to raise children, and for gay male couples this does indeed increasingly seem, oddly, like a choice. We have not felt a biological urge to procreate, yet the growing number of our gay male friends having children through complicated and expensive surrogacy procedures makes it a recurrent, even expected, topic of conversation. Once upon a time it was an inspiring aberration for same-sex couples to even be asked if they wanted children; today it's regularly inquired of us. Even beyond the query "Do you want kids?" is the occasional assumption "*When* are you going to have kids?" It's a reflection of the positive advancements of our young century that such a presumption is made, though the persistence of people's questioning certainly has made me more sympathetic to my female friends who have chosen not to have children and must deal with the bombardment of social expectation.

Despite the surety I feel about the reasons Chris and I have decided not to have children—personal, political, environmental, economic—I'm acutely aware that this choice has a poignant, ancestral consequence for me at least: I will likely be the end of the family line. While I can rationally acknowledge that such thinking is the most self-involved way one could possibly define the needs for procreation, it can't help but stay on my mind as a kind of personal existential threat. Though it's hubristic of me to think that this matters—that *I* matter—it's a specific, sometimes eerie, almost physical feeling to walk through the world as the last of something.

Sometimes that feeling is empowerment. There's a strain of queer theory that's focused specifically on the temporal experience of gay and lesbian people, about how historically, because we've been left out of the dominant, heteronormative narrative, we feel time differently, we exist in its folds rather than at its forefront. Though there's no true way to quantify time, it's been traditionally understood, studied, and discussed in a basic cause-and-effect, linear way: time marches forward. But forward motion—the sweep of human history—is naturally wedded to the idea of human civilization as a procreative force. Theorist Heather Love wrote of this in her book *Feeling Backward*: "For queers, having been branded as nonmodern or as a drag on the progress of civilization, the desire to be recognized as part of the modern social order is strong." This is why we fight, and this is why we bask in the shared glow of every triumphant move ahead. At the same time, for gay people to suddenly be a part of a narrative they have historically been left out of—to be suddenly assumed as helping push civilization forward—is both a positive development and the beginnings of a potential queer identity crisis.

"There's something truly strange about living in a historical moment in which the conservative anxiety and despair about queers bringing down civilization and its institutions (marriage, most notably) is met by the anxiety and despair so many queers feel about the failure or incapacity of queerness to bring down civilization and its institutions." This is from Maggie Nelson's galvanizing 2015 book *The Argonauts*. I was intensely moved by this lengthy, digressive essay, which goes on to radically explore—in ways so complex I couldn't even begin to fairly summarize here—

our social heteronormative assumptions. Though it's a book that's partly and significantly about the specific experience of a cis queer woman, her trans male partner, and their experience becoming parents together, I found myself often gasping and smiling in unexpected recognition. Nelson's imagery, however—her terrifying but cleansing descriptions of flesh-and-bone viscera—was powerful enough to make me feel as though I was missing out on something I never really wanted.

Though I had read challenging, revelatory ideas by such queer theorists as Love, Lee Edelman, Eve Kosofsky Sedgwick, and Elizabeth Freeman throughout my thirties, it was only upon turning forty that I began to understand their writing as not merely theoretical, but very real, something that could be *felt*. Not having children, and furthermore not having the desire to have children, has begun to instill in me a sense of drift, as though I'm untethered to a world, one that is, after all, in the process of extinction. I increasingly feel like I exist in those in-between moments and spaces of time, and I expect that as I age these feelings will magnify.

The movies I grew up on were filled with images of death and melancholy, but they were also, as often, filled with reassuring stories of families. Of love and birth. Of bustling holiday gatherings and joyous pregnancy announcements. No matter how grim things got, in most of those movies, life would go on. Even scenes of climactic funerals—as in *Terms of Endearment* but also other eighties tearjerkers *Beaches* and *Steel Magnolias*—would often be followed up with cheering images of children or adorable toddlers, evidence of hope for the future.

It's strange—perhaps scary, perhaps liberating—to feel like there's nothing behind you, just a stretch of time to be filled by other people and other people's kids. As Christmas approached, all of this was on my mind. A time of the year that inevitably summons feelings of deep reflection, the holiday is also saturated with images of birth and regeneration. Though I usually manage to steer clear of Jesus, my mother's continued connection to the Unitarian Universalists meant that I would do something quite rare upon my visit home this Christmas Eve: go to church.

My skepticism about my mother's joining the Unitarians already rocked upon my visit back in the spring, I found myself unusually open to attending. Additionally, my mother would be singing in the choir, which sounded about as nice as our common Christmas Eve plans: watching the George C. Scott version of *A Christmas Carol*, maybe ordering Chinese food, maybe stopping by the house across the street, where my mother's longtime neighbor Bonnie would be hosting a small get-together full of warmth and holiday cheer. The next day, as always, we would pack up the car with whatever gifts she had for my brother and his wife and head up the road to New Hampshire and spend it with his Catholic in-laws.

As Jews, we never really solidified any elaborate traditions around Christmas; as a result, for me the holiday grew even more appealing—something mysterious and beautiful that we never had emotional access to. I've found it common in many secular Jewish Americans that the customs of Christmas are so culturally sanctified and omnipresent that they take on outsized, idealized meaning for those left out of it. My most treasured Christmas memory is completely private and more about a feeling than an event: delivering the evening newspaper on Christmas Eve as a teenager, looking in the lighted windows of the other houses in the neighborhood as the people inside were getting ready for whatever evening festivities they had planned. Families gathering, trees lighting up, bundles of presents being carried inside from cars. Other people's lives. Now that I'm grown and married to a man from a Catholic family, I'm annually tickled anew that every December I get to help foist up my own tree in Brooklyn. I am somehow *allowed* to do this—while never having to give two shits about Jesus Christ.

During the Christmas Eve service, if I still wasn't able to

feel like I truly belonged there, I was at least able to bask in the warmth of music, candle-lighting, and a sermon that seemed tailor-made to help me get over my misgivings. The minister reminded us that the holiday allows us to momentarily open our-selves to joy, to be able to sing amid all the brokenness we feel and see around us. "The season is not a time of false cheer," she said. "It's a time of grace." It's a simple sentiment, but it stuck with me, allowed me to breathe a little easier, to not feel guilty about appreciating love, hope, and goodwill, even as I might be a faithless schlub the rest of the year.

Here in the spare, unadorned First Parish, I had to admit I was moved. I was moved by the story of Jesus's birth, by the evocative picture painted by the description of the nativity. I was moved by the minister equating the cold night journey of Joseph and Mary to those of refugees all over the world, seek-ing shelter from the harrowing circumstances they've fled. I was moved by the minister also stating, without political af-filiation, that she was fearful for the health and well-being of a country that felt so irreconcilably divided. I was moved by try-ing to make out my mother's voice as the choir sang the beau-tiful British classic "The Sussex Carol" (the one that goes "On Christmas night all Christians sing/To hear the news the angels bring.") I was moved in joining everyone to sing "Silent Night," holding candles and reverently filing out the pews. And finally, I was moved upon emerging out into the chilly night air, see-ing the Chelmsford town common where I spent so much of my childhood, now decorated in glistening lights, the lawn still covered in a layer of white from the last snowfall. How is it that I've never seen the town from this vantage point? How have I never seen it look so beautiful, so still?

Leslie was still inside, finishing up with her fellow choris-ters, so I was standing here alone. I immediately wished Chris were here to experience this moment with me rather than back in Milwaukee with his more sprawling family. But then I realized that this was mine, my solitary moment. I was of late feeling the pull of the past and the uncertainty of the future, and this somehow made this unostentatious little town—a place I've loved and resented in equal measure—more indescribably beautiful than anyone else could have seen.

As I stood on the church steps, I saw my own breath disperse into the dark night. I turned around and went back inside to find Mom.

Despite the fact that it's not really a Christmas film, *Baby Boom* turned out to be the right selection for the season. It feels somehow celebratory, a movie that never fails to make my mother laugh. But it also moves an emotional part of her that's largely inaccessible to me. While my mother says she cannot specifically relate to the film's supposed dilemma—the forced choice between corporate careerism and motherhood, a decision framed by some in the film as impossible—she says she has always felt a kinship with Diane Keaton's J. C. Wiatt, as though her trajectory both challenged and validated her own.

My mother finds *Baby Boom* cathartic. As a child, I simply found the film funny. It was directed and cowritten by Charles Shyer, but other than from Keaton, the film's true personality stamp undoubtedly comes from its other credited screenwriter, Nancy Meyers. Then partnered with Shyer, Meyers, thirty-eight at the time, has gone on to be a female Hollywood auteur—an unfortunately rare thing—her distinctive brand being seemingly breezy romantic comedies whose glossy exteriors conceal deeper truths about class, age, and gender biases. In the eighties and early nineties, Shyer and Meyers were considered a brand unto themselves, the magic of such films as *Private Benjamin* and *Father of the Bride* a result of their paired alchemy.

After separating from Shyer later in her career, Meyers struck out on her own and went on to write, produce, and direct such films as *Something's Gotta Give* (a major comeback for Keaton in

2003), *It's Complicated* (2009), and *The Intern* (2015), slick Hollywood movies that nevertheless feel imbued with the weight of lived experience and which come with women's perspectives on work and relationships. To underestimate Meyer's work is to ignore the real social realities and legacies they were tapping into. In the 2017 book *Nancy Meyers*, Deborah Jermyn writes of her symbolic significance: "Meyers's film career bridges the period moving from the second and third through to recent professed fourth waves of feminism, and the move to 'postfeminism' since the 1980s. Perhaps only Nora Ephron can be compared, being another woman practitioner who similarly started out in journalism before becoming a Hollywood fixture."

In retrospect, *Baby Boom* seems like a Meyers film to its core, an amusing but not unserious wrestling with genuinely hard-to-reconcile social conditions and expectations foisted upon white, upper-middle-class women. When the film was released in late October 1987, Meyers was the mother of seven-year-old Annie, and twelve-week-old Hallie (who has gone on to become a filmmaker herself, directing the Reese Witherspoon rom-com *Home Again*, released exactly thirty years after *Baby Boom*). So for Meyers, who had been pregnant during the shooting of the film, the concerns of *Baby Boom* were not just political, they were personal. One can see *Baby Boom*'s merciless corporate world as a metaphor for her experiences in Hollywood, a realm that was and remains male-dominated, even today after the long-overdue mainstreaming of discussions around gender inequity in the wake of the #MeToo movement. In a *Sun-Sentinel* interview from that November, Meyers said, "Though I vote for having it all, the pressure to do it all is very hard and very exhausting. Getting past the comedy in *Baby Boom*, this is a pretty serious subject. We dealt with what it's like for women who find there is little child care available and hardly any help from major corporations."

Watching today, *Baby Boom* seems fairly progressive in this way, detailing how J.C.'s flirtation with and eventual devotion to motherhood brings her nothing but grief from her wildly unsupportive male bosses and colleagues. As the film begins, she is being aggressively courted for a partner position in the prestigious New York management consulting firm, a company that grosses $200 million a year and where she's earned a corner office. Dubbed "The Tiger Lady," she moves rapidly through the office, only stopping to say things like "Get me the CEO of IBM ASAP" and letting her assistant know she has to work late and cancel her long-standing plans to go to the ballet. She and her similarly career-driven investment banker partner, Steven (Harold Ramis), fit in three-minute sex sessions before bed like business transactions. She goes to high-priced power lunches, ordering then-exotic-sounding dishes like "free-range chicken with dandelion greens." My mother and I exchanged a knowing glance at this joke, as this is a dish that now sounds fairly common to any farm-to-table restaurant anywhere in the US—or even some NYC fast-food lunch counters.

Fearsome, career-driven J.C. says, with a shrug, that she works "seventy, eighty hours a week." In response, her boss, Fritz (Sam Wanamaker), gives her what he must assume is the ultimate compliment: "Normally I don't think of you as a woman." Keaton's reaction is priceless—a snicker that contains flickers of pride, shame, and bafflement all in about three seconds of screen time.

By the film's midpoint, however, J.C. has been left in the lurch by an unsupportive Steven, demoted and humiliated at work, and finally all but coerced by Fritz into quitting. The only thing that's really changed about her life is that she's become a sudden single mother, creating the perception with her superiors and colleagues that she's now insufficiently dedicated to her job. J.C.'s treatment is reflective of the era: a whopping ninety-five percent of women claimed to have suffered discrimination at work and unequal pay by the close of the decade. Though a clear victim of gender discrimination—with the minimal legal protections of the era—J.C. leaves the company rather than fight, escaping from New York entirely. With the goal of restarting her life with baby Elizabeth, she uses her copious corporate earnings to purchase her Vermont dream home, setting up the film's second section, which follows her daffy, screwball romance with Dr. Cooper, a charming local veterinarian (Sam Shepard, acres away from his desperate alcoholic in *Country*), and the rapid rise of her own gourmet baby food startup.

Much of the humor of the first half of *Baby Boom* comes from J.C.'s befuddled fish-out-of-water response to instant parenthood: carrying the poor tyke sideways under her arm like a briefcase without handles; feeding her linguine with shaved parmesan instead of baby food; astonishment at the complexity of disposable diaper adhesives (this was also a central comic bit in that year's even bigger hit *Three Men and a Baby*, both instilling in me at a young age the idea that applying a diaper to a baby is the world's greatest challenge). In other words, the joke is that she's unnaturally unmaternal, which might feel more subversive if the film didn't then go on to presume that her proclivity to motherhood was always there, it was just lying dormant.

Diane Keaton is marvelous at selling this slightly screwy character, who on the page would seem wildly inconsistent, veering between rigid control and flailing neuroses. Yet the actress also makes you believe that this oscillation between confident self-definition ("I don't want it all," she insists to Fritz at the outset) and hapless bewilderment makes J.C. somehow complete: a multifaceted woman of contradictory impulses rather than a hackneyed rom-com construct. As Meyers once stated, recalling the legacy of screwball comedy: "We write with Roz Russell, Katharine Hepburn, and Carole Lombard in mind." Keaton taps into, yet distinctly modernizes, the age-old Hollywood trope of the working woman.

Throughout her decades-spanning career, the Los Angeles native, whose birth name was Diane Hall, has remained unmarried.

And Keaton had no children at the time she made *Baby Boom*; she would adopt the first of two in the late nineties. The range and span of her career has encompassed wives and mothers (including her breakthrough role in *The Godfather*), but Keaton has always radiated independence. Even in male-female romances such as her Oscar-winning performance in Woody Allen's *Annie Hall*—named after her—and Warren Beatty's *Reds*, to cite two of her most famous parts, her characters remain distinct individuals, self-sufficient units rather than codependent appendages. In these later years, she has become a prolific memoirist, delving into her own family history and professional career to make sense of her life. In *Brother and Sister*, released in 2020, and her third book in less than a decade, she tries to reckon with the irreconcilable past and divergent present of a troubled sibling with care and nuance: it's a reminder that Keaton never defined herself, or tried to identify herself, with any romantic partnerships. Family and self-definition have been paramount; even her oft-remarked-upon "quirky" sense of style—as typified especially in her epochal *Annie Hall* wardrobe—has always seemed less a sop to fashion than an externalization of a genuine individuality, a Hollywood anomaly.

Keaton's distinct selfhood makes J.C.'s treatment at the hands of faux-benevolent men in power all the more stomach-turning. Due to her particular star persona, it's almost preposterous—we surely cannot imagine Keaton herself putting up with this. Perhaps that's where the power of *Baby Boom* lies: that even the strongest fighters—the Diane Keatons of the world—have too long been subject to a system that treats them as subordinates. That's also why the movie's kicker is so satisfying. J.C.'s new made-in-Vermont company, Country Baby, has hit it big across the US, and "The Food Chain," a major client from her old firm, wants to buy it for a hefty sum. She leaves her idyllic New England town for the day, returning to the city in triumph. At a huge conference table at her old office, she's offered a megadeal: three million in cash up front plus a huge salary as its chief operating officer. Fritz, seeing dollar signs of his own, is clearly thrilled to take on her lucrative company, hoping all between them is "water under the bridge." After consideration, and in-stilling her smirking former colleagues with hope, she turns them down. It feels both like revenge and a moment of final self-definition. She vows instead to grow her business herself in Vermont—while also continuing to date Dr. Cooper and, of course, raise Elizabeth.

I've gone through different phases in my feelings about *Baby Boom* and its somewhat fraught political terrain. J.C.'s ultimate decision is undoubtedly an assertion of her independence and go-it-alone business savvy, yet she's also walking away from "the deal of a lifetime" so that she can assume what is a more tradi-tionally feminine role: mother, lover, owner of a warm domestic space. The last shot is of J.C. cuddling her adorable daughter in a rocking chair in the most idyllic pose imaginable: the camera pulls back, sunlight streaming in through gauzy curtains. She is firmly entrenched in an image of motherhood, far away from the urban rat race. Trying to be a good feminist, I have long been troubled by this wrap-up. It seemed to dictate an idea of conservative femininity so pure it was almost propaganda. Even her Country Baby triumph was only possible by synthesizing her creative marketing know-how with her newfound mater-nal self. In other words, the baby was the key to every possible happiness and success.

I have not been alone in this perception. In Susan Faludi's rigorous and incisive 1991 book *Backlash: The Undeclared War Against American Women*, about the reactionary politics of the eighties that insidiously sprang up in every aspect of social and cultural life in response to the strides made by women in the seventies, the author singles out *Baby Boom* for criticism. She writes, "It was a movie that the media repeatedly invoked, as 'evidence' that babies and business don't mix." She condemns the film on multiple fronts: for J.C. leaving the city rather than fighting for her equal rights, for J.C. not using her final board-room speech to more fully chastise the men for their discrimi-natory behavior, and for "its implication that working women must be strong-armed into motherhood" and its "struggle to make motherhood as alluring as possible." Here, Faludi also cites *Three Men and a Baby* and the 1989 Ron Howard movie *Parent-hood*: "well-decorated infants function in these films more as collector's items than people." Faludi is especially hard on Mey-ers directly, taking her to task for capitulating to the conserva-tive expectations of the Hollywood studio system.

While Faludi articulates so many of the discomforts and sus-picions I have long had about *Baby Boom*, watching the movie again with my mother that Christmas also opened my eyes to another perspective. When the film was ending, the image of Diane Keaton rocking Elizabeth back and forth as Bill Con-ti's synth score—which uses childlike "la la la" voices—drifted through the family room, I noticed my mother had tears in her eyes and was reaching for a Kleenex. Both of us often set aside a film's politics for the pleasures of its story. Many times we've watched and enjoyed both *Fatal Attraction* and *Overboard*, movies overtly retrograde about women and their place in the profes-sional and domestic spheres. But *Baby Boom* was different; my mother's wellspring of emotion toward the film spoke to some-thing deeper, and I know it went beyond the film's set design, which she claims inspired her to paint the kitchen cabinets blue and buy blue-and-white gingham curtains. I asked her why she was so moved.

"It kills me every time," she said, blowing her nose.

She was somewhere else. It was clear that *Baby Boom* sent her off into a kind of reverie.

"I liked being home with you kids. I liked our house. I liked our life. I never felt I should be someplace else. I was lucky."

I was taken aback by her consistent use of the past tense.

Clearly she was talking about a time long ago, but is it lost? Isn't this the same house that it once was, or is a house only a home depending on who's in it and when? Does she no longer consider herself lucky? Does luck exist, and, if so, does it run out?

I didn't say anything. I wasn't sure how to respond anyway. She continued: "This character is lucky she found such a nice man. I felt the same way. I never wanted a lot more. I was just really happy to be here with you kids."

Baby Boom is so much a film questioning the concept of "having it all," but of course "having it all" is highly subjective. My mother worked, before, during, and after raising my brother and me, but the work portion of her life might not have had anything to do with "having it all." Leslie has no hesitation in calling herself a feminist, yet she takes little exception to the message of *Baby Boom*, a movie she says "kind of reinforces my particular values." Does that make her conservative? Only if we think in such strict binary terms. Many hold to certain conservative values in one way or another, despite whatever progressive political tendencies we may aspire to. We all want comfort; we all need love.

Upon this rewatch, *Baby Boom* felt like a wise and warm refutation to Fritz's claim that a woman cannot have it all. Even if there's a dubious hint of sanctimony to the way the film frames her happiness—which is ultimately tied to the child she always claimed she didn't want—J.C. has nevertheless found her own way to prove them all wrong. By that final shot, you don't get the sense that she's leaving everything behind to be a housewife, but that she's about to build an empire. And that she didn't have to choose one over the other. In the film's calculus, she was lucky.

We had done our spaghetti dinner's dishes before the movie began, so after it was over we were able to stretch out on the couch and talk. This conversation would end up going well into the night. Usually she tucked in around eleven, but it was approaching midnight and my mother seemed energized.

She admitted to me that though children became an essential part of her life, she really only had us as part of a social assumption. Growing up in the fifties and coming of age in the sixties, she just never thought she wouldn't be a mother. She acknowledges that by 1975, the year she had my older brother, it was "a transitional moment for women…but we were holdovers from an earlier time."

"I wasn't one of these women who more than anything wanted to cuddle a baby," she says, which surprises me, her once oft-cuddled son. "I just saw the big picture. I saw a family in my life, I saw children in my life. Not a lot of thought went into it. It's what I grew up seeing. It was just following a path, a suburban kind of existence. There are women, who, since they're young girls, have a longing to take care of children. I didn't have that."

A child assumes they were always wanted, or at least wants to believe it. Did my father want children? As much as he was a loving parent, I can easily have seen his life going in a different direction than family man. Perhaps he wanted to be a race-car driver. Perhaps an airplane pilot. Perhaps a freewheeling bachelor, in keeping with the clichéd persona of the traveling salesman.

"If I hadn't mentioned kids first, I don't think he would have thought of it. I came up with the idea. And I came up with the idea of getting the house…" She trails off for a second. "In fact, I came up with every idea. Every goddamn thing." She emphasizes *goddamn* not with anger but an almost epiphanic joy. "Replacing the old wooden steps with brick ones. Building the porch. Screening in the deck."

When Leslie found out she was pregnant, she told Bobby that they would have to begin looking for a house; the apartment was simply too small a space to start a family. She also knew that she would stop working her clerical hospital job once the baby was born. No great sacrifice, she says—it was not a career path she aspired to—but stopping work meant they would no longer be putting money away. They were only able to make a down payment on the house because of the extra she was making. She knew that if they didn't buy at this tender moment they might never be able to afford a house, and could get trapped in the apartment for a long time. Thus, Jonathan was born on Walnut Road—a new home bought to cradle him and make him feel loved.

"Being a parent is worry," my mother says. "It starts when you're carrying the baby, and then it never ends."

One of the many, many, many reasons I tell myself I don't want children is that my already-high anxiety would likely reach nuclear alert levels. Worrying whether the dog is getting her proper daily walks already takes up too much space in my mind. My love for the child would grow like a tumor, pressing on my brain, on my ribs, my heart. I would worry about them from breakfast to dinner; I would worry about them in my sleep. Chris and I would disagree on parenting methods, small skirmishes ballooning into larger disputes. I would probably let them get away with murder and resent Chris for being practical, which I would interpret as strict. At the same time, I would be so mortified if they made too much noise or a fuss in public that I would become a harried tyrant dragging them through the city streets while they wailed and screamed and onlookers would have no other choice but to figure I was some evil kidnapper.

Would I be as terrible as I think? Are my anxieties about parenthood too wrapped up in my own paranoia and selfishness? I will never find out—unless of course a distant cousin dies and I inherit a baby.

Our post–*Baby Boom* conversation has been leading to one moment, one question, an uncomfortable truth for both of us. Just as in her twenties she casually expected she would be a mother, did she think that by the time she was in her seventies she would have been a grandmother?

She didn't hesitate, though I think not to be cruel, to me or to herself: "Yes, I always thought I'd be a grandparent."

"You'd be a great grandparent." I nodded.

"I *would* be a great grandparent. I'd be, like, the best."

At this point, no one in the family is likely to grant her the ability to fulfill such a natural role. It seems somehow unfair. Yet she says she's disinterested in pining for grandkids, and claims to not feel jealous of her friends, most of whom are surrounded by their children's children, and are often employed to help raise them. When she sees the responsibilities so many other grandparents have, she's relieved. "I don't want to raise children again. I did that already."

I wonder. I don't doubt she tells me the truth about her feelings, but is she being completely honest, with me or herself? There's a part of me that suspects that when she tells me she doesn't truly desire grandkids, it's because her protective maternal instinct has kicked in. She doesn't want to hurt me.

We all hold so many contradictory truths within us. As much as I don't want children, I cannot deny that I sometimes think about the potential fulfillment they would bring. But is it an illusion of fullness that captures my imagination? Once upon a time, accepting my queerness would have protected me from having to truly consider the option of children. I still think that it does.

I felt troubled by my own questions, my own conceit of certitude.

Christmas morning came.

My mother gave me a strange serving dish tchotchke ("is it for *olives*?"), a few pairs of Happy Socks, and a tea mug that says "My HEART Belongs to My Rescue Dog." I gave her a Judy Collins CD, Sarah Broom's memoir *The Yellow House*, and a couple pounds of dried California apricots, the tart, shriveled ones. The small pile of discarded wrapping paper has in recent years come to look so different—so quiet, so manageable—from the heaving mounds of red and green that would create its own festive carpet on the living room. It used to be fun to throw the colorful paper around, collapse into it, watch the cats paw around in it. Lucy, the rescue dog to whom my heart belongs, wandered in. She sniffed the holiday detritus indifferently, and looked up at us with her sad brown eyes as we started stuffing the remains into a garbage bag.

1988: Lox

The girls looked smashing in their new fall clothes. It was Rosh
Hashanah, and services had ended. Everyone was meeting at
"The Wall." Made of stone, this waist-high structure abutted
the sidewalk on Blue Hill Avenue, separating Franklin Field
from the street. Lined with three- and four-story brick apartment houses, drugstores, and restaurants, Blue Hill Avenue was
the four-mile main drag that went right through Roxbury,
Dorchester, and Mattapan, the Boston neighborhoods that had
been predominantly Jewish since the turn of the century. Leslie would live in all three at different periods throughout her
childhood, so this point of intersection would come to feel like
a kind of nesting place for her.

This highly coveted spot at The Wall provided the hope-
ful young Jewish fashionistas a perfect spot to show off new
duds, many of which had likely been procured at recent sales at
Filene's department store or Jordan Marsh. Leslie felt free from
family here. The redheaded twelve-year-old was still recuper-
ating from the dull High Holy service; she didn't understand a

word of Hebrew, and had to keep stifling a yawn. While she and her friends milled about, hearing the occasional *"Gut yontif"* from passing locals, they talked about what really interested them: cute boys at school; new movies at the Orient; the latest episode of *Dr. Kildare*, starring the dreamy Richard Chamberlain; their recent purchase of Bobby Darin and Frankie Avalon ninety-nine-cent records.

Leslie's whole body felt a little overheated. Though it was mid-September, the day was humid. It often was still summery weather on Rosh Hashanah, but that didn't stop the girls from donning their latest back-to-school fashions. Sacrificing comfort for beauty, Leslie was encased in a smart wool dress—which now didn't feel so smart as it scratched at her sweaty neck. Still, no one questioned it: this was tradition.

The Wall was a rite of passage, a sign of coming-of-age, and a first indication of breaking away from the domestic shackles of childhood. Soon they would have to make their way home and have leftovers from the New Year celebrations of the night before: reheated roast chicken; soup with knaidels; honey cake and challah. Alas, home again, but when she tasted those holiday delights, she would momentarily believe there was nowhere else she'd rather be.

How do I tell my mother's story? But also how do I tell my own?

Often while writing this book I've experienced feelings of mortification. Writing film criticism has largely allowed me to avoid delving much into my own personal life. For years I found the idea of writing anything with even a hint of autobiographical material to be anathema, evidence of a lack of imagination, perhaps. If done indelicately, the incorporation of the self into the critical appraisal of a work of art is worse than egregious—it can be distasteful. In editing other writers, I've consistently encouraged—sometimes forced—them to remove the "I" voice, which I've long thought of as a critical crutch that needs to be earned if used at all. Yet here I am, a hypocrite exposed, starting the penultimate chapter of a book that I've begun to feel is positively demonic in its intimacy. I've likely told you more in these pages than I've told friends. The queer novelist and memoirist Edmund White once wrote, "The most important things in our intimate lives can't be discussed with strangers, except in books."

By foregrounding the self in criticism, I've come to realize that one can honestly acknowledge the subjectivity that goes into any evaluation. A work of art, and how we perceive it, becomes inseparable from the emotion we bring to it. That's true whether it's a recording by Miles Davis, a poem by Emily Dickinson, or a goofball comedy in which Diane Keaton places a baby on a supermarket scale. Henri Matisse's exquisite 1916 painting *The Piano Lesson*, for example, hits me on several levels. One is undoubtedly purely aesthetic. The inexplicable symmetry of the painting, its replication of triangular light shafts across a boy sitting at a piano, works on a subliminal level, and it made me rethink what I find beautiful.

At the same time, I can't help but feel a personal connection to what one might call the "narrative" of the painting: after all, I was once a young boy perched in front of a piano, with my music teacher (here evoked as a faceless phantom in the background), hovering and watching as my fingers hit all the wrong notes.

Every time I visit the Museum of Modern Art in New York I return to that painting. It always reminds me that art and taste work on levels we can only partly rationalize, but which are not distinct from emotional connections forged in childhood. Art can pull you back to an experience from your youth, but it can also beckon you into something inherent or inexplicable inside yourself. What are the hidden parts of the self that a movie can lay bare?

In the previous chapter, I felt compelled to write a bit about *Avalon*, a movie I've been for years convinced that Barry Levinson—

whom, let's be clear, I've never met—made especially for me. I feel in my ancestral bones the film's central observations, about how the loss of American cultural Jewishness is experienced as a gradual pruning away, and how time buries rather than upholds history. I am not a practicing Jew; I don't believe in God, and I haven't attended a synagogue service of any kind since I was a preteen. This is likely one of the reasons that this movie's secular representation of Jewish culture—though, rather oddly, the word *Jewish* never is uttered in the film—appealed to me. It's the sense of being untethered, a natural aspect of being part of a global diaspora, that consistently leads me back to cultural, mainly cinematic, representations of Jewishness. They bring with them the feeling of coming home.

Perhaps this is the hidden part of myself—the thing that's both *of* me and around me, which doesn't seem to define me, yet which is as pervasive as any inherited trait. Too often cultural Jewishness is boiled down to a handful of easy markers, from popular comedy icons to baked goods. Yet whether it's Mel Brooks or a bagel, signifiers of Jewish life have long been essential to mainstream American popular culture. Jewish identity goes deeper, to a place so indefinable that it enters the realm of the uncanny.

Some years back, I was watching *Crossing Delancey*, the 1988 romantic comedy directed by Joan Micklin Silver that has been a staple of my mother's movie diet since its release. Her love for *Crossing Delancey* is so great that on occasion I've heard her call it her "favorite movie." Who knows if this claim would hold up under cross-examination. Nevertheless, I grew up knowing that it held a special pride of place in her heart. And while I can't say that this movie, which concerns the cultural and professional self-actualization of an urban-dwelling Jewish woman, ever spoke to me with the same emotional pull, during this rewatch I found myself almost bodily drawn toward the screen. By the end of this light comic character study, in which the emotional stakes never seem higher than whether our heroine will choose the obviously right romantic partner, I found myself in tears. Why was I so moved? Where did the movie hit me, and why did it feel like a kind of return?

There was little question in my mind that *Crossing Delancey* would be our 1988 selection—too rich were the possibilities of watching it again, too varied were the questions about my own heritage and my mother's that I wanted answered, and too delighted would be her face upon learning we'd be watching it together. Making it even more personal was the fact that I had now been living in New York for more than twenty years, and the movie struck me as a quintessential artifact of New York in the eighties. The only other movie we had watched together for this book that took place in New York was *Baby Boom*, and that film's suits-and-sneakers Park Avenue corporate milieu was about as far from my cultural understanding as *Aliens'* uninhabitable planet, LV-426. *Crossing Delancey*, set largely on New York's historically Jewish Lower East Side, with its narrow streets, 19th-century tenement buildings, bakeries and pickle shops, was much more relatable, as was the film's central conflict between the "old" and "new" New Yorks, between tradition and progress, between independence and love, between heritage and assimilation.

The investigation and dissection of cultural Jewishness is as much a central theme of the cinema of director Joan Micklin Silver as it is for more widely known directors like Woody Allen, Mel Brooks, and Albert Brooks. Yet American moviemaking has always been ruled by men, and Silver has remained anything but a household name, despite the fact that she has made films with significant cult followings. After writing Barbara Loden's fascinating, feminist-tinged 1975 educational short *The Frontier Experience*, Silver embarked on her directorial debut, *Hester Street*. Remembered fondly by anyone who's seen it, *Hester Street* is one of the most lived-in screen portraits of the American Jewish immigrant experience at the turn of the 20th century, and it was a breakout sleeper despite being an independently financed, black-and-white, culturally specific production with no stars and mostly subtitled Yiddish dialogue. Earning newcomer Carol Kane a Best Actress Oscar nomination, *Hester Street* quietly chronicles the emotional journey of Gitl, an Eastern European woman who transforms from meek wife to strong, self-motivated individual after relocating to New York's Lower East Side and, ultimately, divorcing her husband. The film also wrestles with the question of how much one should adapt to a new world, and how much one needs to hold on to tradition, which in Gitl's case are the trappings, behaviors, and superstitions of *shtetl* life.

Released thirteen years later, *Crossing Delancey* returns to many of these themes, in breezier, if no less provocative, fashion. This adaptation of an off-Broadway play by Susan Sandler—who also wrote the screenplay—features the comfortably single Isabelle "Izzy" Grossman (Amy Irving) as its Jewish heroine. In her job at a trendy upper-Manhattan bookstore, she has the pleasure of liaising with hot authors and feeling like she's on the industry vanguard; however, she's constantly drawn back, with no small measure of hesitation, to her traditional Jewish heritage as represented by her "bubbie," Ida (Reizl Bozyk), who lives in a cramped high-rise apartment on the Lower East Side off the Delancey Street subway stop. This was, unfathomably, the supremely charming Bozyk's only movie appearance, following a legendary career in downtown Yiddish theater in both Poland and New York; she would die five years after *Crossing Delancey*'s release, at age seventy-nine.

The octogenarian Bubbie, who proudly admits to keeping five hundred dollars wadded up in her stockings, and who employs her good granddaughter to pluck her whiskers or massage her arthritic legs, represents everything the upwardly mobile Izzy is trying to leave behind. Specifically she's an obstruction to her desire to assimilate into literati circles, typified by Anton

Maes (Jeroen Krabbé), the smooth-talking best-selling author she's attracted to. So she's particularly chafed to discover that her bubbie has hired a neighborhood marriage broker, the eccentric and uncouth Hannah Mandelbaum (Sylvia Miles), to make a match between Izzy and Sam Posner (Peter Riegert), the kindly, unassuming proprietor of the local Posner Pickles. For Izzy, this is more than meddlesome—it's a connection to an outmoded cultural tradition, leftovers from an old world order. Never mind that Sam turns out to be a sweetheart: to seriously consider him as a romantic partner would be to capitulate to a past from which she has tried to divorce herself.

It's to the film's great credit that its central themes of tradition versus progress remain subtext; none of this is explicit in Sandler's sharp, clever, warm yet unsentimental script. *Crossing Delancey* was first performed at the Jewish Repertory Theater in April 1985, a five-character stage work with three distinct but narratively fluid locations: Bubbie's kitchen, the bookstore where Izzy works, and an outdoor bench in the heart of the Lower East Side. Reading the play now, I can't envision it as taking place anywhere other than within the film's on-location shooting. But the intended chamber atmosphere of *Crossing Delancey* as a theater piece also clearly expresses the central dichotomy of the work, of cleanly delineated spaces between the different ethnic and emotional factions that always war inside Izzy.

I had the pleasure of speaking with Sandler, who I was delighted to learn is a professor of screenwriting at my alma mater, NYU's Tisch School of the Arts. During the conversation, I learned just how deeply autobiographical *Crossing Delancey* was for her. "At its core, it's about this love affair between a girl and her grandmother," Sandler said, instantly recalibrating for me the parameters of what constitutes this "romantic comedy," while also painting a vivid picture of her past. "This relationship that Izzy had with her grandmother I had with my bubbie. All she cared about was my happiness. Whatever that was, it didn't have to be any measure of traditional success." In this sense, pickle-man Sam, an emissary of the world that Izzy is trying to get away from, is representative of the happiness that Bubbie believes is in the cards for her granddaughter.

The schism between uptown Izzy and downtown Izzy, between champagne-and-canapé Izzy and lox-and-cream-cheese Izzy, is also a split Sandler strongly identified with. Sandler grew up in Virginia, though she would spend her summers with her bubbie in New York. When she moved to the city as a young adult to make it as an artist, she found herself pulled between the exciting world of theater and art, and the Lower East Side apartment where, like Izzy, she would pull Bubbie's chin-hairs and relate her fears and hopes while looking out the window at the Williamsburg Bridge. (I loved when Sandler called her bubbie her *dream-spinner*.) "The trips downtown felt almost dutiful," she told me. "I felt a sense almost of guilt because I enjoyed it too much. I enjoyed the food, I enjoyed the little *pekalach* she would pack up for me, and I didn't think I was supposed to be enjoying it. I didn't understand what the pull was and why I needed it. I didn't realize it wasn't about duty, but that I needed it emotionally."

Often we don't realize that what we've chosen to do is filling an emotional need rather than a social, financial, or professional obligation. This very book, for instance, with the frequent visits home it's necessitated, has increasingly revealed itself to be more of an emotional fulcrum for my early forties than the merely analytical project I initially expected it to be. It's taken up a different space in my head, unlocking a part of the brain that functions on nourishment rather than mere intellectual engagement. Perhaps this is the beginning of answering the question of why I cry at the end of *Crossing Delancey*. Because it's not simply about the satisfaction of a rom-com resolution. Izzy doesn't only choose wisely in love, picking the sweet-souled pickle-man over the accomplished but hollow novelist. She chooses wisely in faith. And that the final scene takes place in Bubbie's apartment, where Sam has been getting drunk with her on Schnapps waiting for Izzy to show up (to *come home*), turns the resolution of a love story into a simultaneous familial return.

Crossing Delancey devotees are legion. It's not just me and my mom—there are the superfans who showed up for the thirtieth anniversary screening at Film Forum in 2017 with director and stars in attendance; there's my friend and former coworker Rachel, whose mother bestowed upon her the middle name "Delancey" based purely on her love for the film. I have no doubt that the film's special alchemy has something to do with the unusual star who holds it all together. It's difficult to imagine anyone in the lead role other than Amy Irving, who has a specific on-screen carriage like no other. One could picture an entirely different incarnation of Izzy, perhaps played by a character actress such as Mercedes Ruehl, or, if it had been made years later, Patricia Arquette or Natalie Portman, but no one who leaps to mind has the singular mixture of ethereality and inner, steel-spine strength that Irving brought to her roles. That she never became as well-known or bankable as any of the other headlining actresses discussed in this book is a shame, but also perhaps not a surprise: while an endlessly compelling performer, her subtle expressivity is more commonly utilized for supporting roles in American studio moviemaking. Her romantic-comedy leading-lady status is just another of *Crossing Delancey*'s little miracles.

Amy Irving was the daughter of a performing arts family—her father, Jules Irving, of Russian-Jewish heritage, was a playwright and director. Her mother, Priscilla Pointer, a theater and screen actor from a New York family. Amy first came to prominence in the seventies. Though she had auditioned for the part of Princess Leia in George Lucas's *Star Wars* and for Richard Dreyfuss's character's wife in Steven Spielberg's *Close Encounters of the Third Kind* (both 1977), her first film appearances would be in a pair of thrillers by Brian De Palma, a close pal of both Lucas and Spielberg. First, in *Carrie* (1976), she was the ambiguous moral compass of the high school girls who taunt and torment Sissy Spacek's telekinetic Carrie White; then, in *The Fury* (1978), she was cast as the telekinetic, tormented by governmental officials wanting to harness her powers. In both, the actress was playing teenagers, and in both she seemed wise beyond her early twenty-something years, lending the roles a similar quality of soft opacity, as though we were watching her through a gauzy curtain or the thick glass of a fish tank.

This remote yet likable quality is detectable in all her films—especially in her role as the deceptively savvy Haddass, an underestimated Jewish woman in turn-of-the-century Eastern Europe in Barbra Streisand's *Yentl* (1983). But she never had a better showcase for these qualities than *Crossing Delancey*. By the time this role came to her, Irving was likely most famous for being married to Steven Spielberg, by this point the most popular moviemaker in the western world. Spielberg and Irving had begun a four-year romantic relationship in the late seventies, after they had run into each other a few times following her audition for *Close Encounters*, yet Irving felt like his wild creative ambitions were overshadowing her own in this early stage of their careers. Irving and Spielberg had first ended their turbulent romance in 1979, and she moved to the Southwest. "Having come from a relationship with a very public man, I needed to go and find out what my life on my own was about," she would say. But after wending their own ways professionally through the early eighties, which for Irving included getting an Oscar nomination for *Yentl*, the two romantically reconnected in 1984; she gave birth to their first and only child together, Max, in June 1985; and they were married in November 1985.

Crossing Delancey is a film that's in large part about the social and cultural expectations heaped upon modern single women, and it would be the only major movie Irving would make during this period of her life, when she became a mother and a wife. It was a difficult time, as the same conflicts came roaring back, and she constantly felt as though her husband's projects were taking precedence over her own, due to his mammoth industry profile. Nevertheless, they supported one another's careers, and Joan Micklin Silver said in a 2018 interview with *Filmmaker* magazine that Spielberg was instrumental in helping *Crossing Delancey* get made. Silver says she thought Irving would be perfect for the role ever since spotting her by chance at a screening and being instantly enchanted. She flew to Spain to meet Irving and Spielberg, who was on a film shoot. Discovering over the course of the dinner that the film hadn't yet found financing, Spielberg, who'd read and adored Sandler's script, offered on the spot to take it to Warner Bros. Silver thought it a lovely gesture, but didn't perhaps realize the seriousness of the offer right away. Said the director: "We finished our meal and Amy said, 'I guess we'll make it at Warner Bros.' I said, 'Amy, we don't know that—he hasn't even said anything yet!' But she of course knew that if he wanted it to happen, it would happen."

It's a thick but unsurprising irony that a film directed by, written by, and starring women would need a studio green light from a superstar male director. Yet the cultural specificity and unlikely nature of *Crossing Delancey* clearly needed all the support and nurturing it could get in an industry that had become increasingly reliant upon male-driven summer blockbusters, and which would only grow more single-minded about testosterone-fueled franchises and sequels as the years and decades wore on. Sandler, who called Spielberg the film's "godfather," told me that the film was made outside of the usual routes, going through publicists to reach Irving and Spielberg. "Agents weren't going to handle a script so Jewish, so small, and which didn't seem to have the size and importance of a studio film," she told me. "It was made without any fingerprints... Every word from the screenplay was intact, and there were no studio notes." (In some alternate universe, Spielberg and Irving might have made a great producing team, but they would divorce in April 1989, sharing custody of Max. "I started my career as the daughter of Jules Irving," said Irving, as quoted in Joseph McBride's Spielberg autobiography. "I don't want to finish it as the wife of Spielberg or the mother of Max.")

Sandler said she had recently happened upon *Crossing Delancey* on television. She had not seen it in years, and watching it felt surreal, a transmission from the past, like the world's most accomplished home movies. After all, even the lobby of Izzy's apartment, where we see Amy Irving entering and exiting many times during the film, was literally filmed in the building where Sandler lived at the time. But *Crossing Delancey* has been such a part of my family's past that—like *Avalon*, like *Meet Me in St. Louis*, or *Home for the Holidays*, or *It's a Wonderful Life*—they might as well be home movies for us, too. Each film we watch captures moments in time that exist outside its narrative parameters. *Crossing Delancey* would take on new, unexpected significance during my visit in early March 2020.

I was visiting days before my mother was getting ready to take a plane out to visit a dear friend in Arizona, a vacation she had been looking forward to for months. Her suitcase was packed; a neighbor had already been employed to take care of the cat. Yet there was a gradual trickle of news on television about something called the coronavirus, which had made landfall in the States after laying waste to untold numbers of people in China. She was feeling apprehensive. We didn't know much about this sudden virus, which felt more like a rumor than a reality, but it seemed like no one—especially a woman in her early seventies on medication for atrial fibrillation and myeloproliferative neoplasms—should be traveling on an airplane right now.

The suitcase was unpacked, her clothes put back in her drawers. The disappointment of the moment was considerably mitigated by one unavoidable truth: that night, after beef stew, *Crossing Delancey* was going into her DVD player.

The table was like a magic trick. What looked like an unassuming, waist-high wooden cabinet, which might hold stacks of vinyl records, old magazines, or perhaps a collection of gravy boats, was actually a contraption that never failed to amaze and amuse the young brothers. After swinging open the cabinet door, their grandmother pulled out a long, accordion-like contrivance that extended the length of the small apartment's living room. On this flimsy-looking frame she then placed a series of wooden panels that had also been quietly hidden in the cabinet, creating a flat surface that she then covered with a simple, extra long tablecloth. Suddenly it was ready for the seder, with room for ten.

Michael and Jonathan didn't always get to see this spellbinding transformation take place. By the time they would arrive at Grandma Bertha's apartment—located in the Golda Meir House, a senior living community in Newton that always smelled slightly of moldy oranges—the table was usually already fully made, with dishes of gefilte fish and beet horseradish placed at each table setting, whether you liked it or not. Bertha's insistence on having appetizers waiting for everyone upon arrival flew in the face of the Passover tradition, which was to make everyone suffer through seemingly endless readings about the historical enslavement and liberation of the Jewish people, through the rituals of the maror and the matzo and the haroset, each scant bite of which tasted like the richest, most heavenly four-course meal to the family's growling stomachs.

As the years wore on, Bertha would forego the seder portion of the seder altogether and, much to the delight of everyone, jump right to the brisket, dried-fruit-and-matzo *tzimmes*, roasted chicken breasts doused in apricot sauce, asparagus spears so soft they'd turn to green soup with the slightest piercing of the fork. It was clear that the food was the showcase, not the suffering.

Michael and Jonathan didn't complain—all the better to get to dessert, which usually meant Grandma Lil's marble cake and biscotti-like cinnamon *mandel* bread. The taste, the smells, of all these foods would linger in their minds as the years wore on. Memories of the apartment would be inextricable from the rib-sticking dishes served during the holidays, the cups of tea and coffee scattered across the stained tablecloth after the meal. Finally, the last ritual: the panels came off the table one by one, revealing the wispy accordion skeleton, shoved back into the cabinet for safekeeping. The living room was suddenly a living room again. It was time for the long drive home.

"What is kishke exactly?"

We had eaten a filling meal just a couple hours ago, but when *Crossing Delancey* was over, the first thing we talked about was food. The movie is filled with the kind of culinary delights that remind me that yes, I am, indeed, undoubtedly, inextricably, gastronomically Jewish. The food is often already spread out on tables when you walk in the door. Jewish people do that. They make you a "little spread." They make sure you don't leave their house hungry.

"I'm not sure what was in it, but it was stuffed with all sorts of things that would give you a heart attack instantly," my mother replied. "It was dense and rich, a lot of butter. It would be an hors d'oeuvre during special occasions like weddings." I later looked it up and indeed it's rich—it's stuffed beef intestine. The word *kishke* actually comes from the Yiddish word for intestine. I'm not surprised that we didn't eat this in the house when I was growing up in the eighties, when American families were more cognizant of health, and when my parents still thought that margarine was a necessary fridge staple. On the other end of the spectrum, just about every recipe in the *Art of Jewish Cook-*

ing book my mother passed down to me seems to contain generous helpings of lard.

Other than kishke, I think I can recognize most of the dishes in the movie. Whenever Bubbie entertains the matchmaker Hannah Mandelbaum, she knows she has to have a little spread laid out for her. But Hannah, gargantuan in person and personality, requires more than a little. As though sating a beast, Bubbie seems to have bought out the local deli: mounds of kugel, dishes of applesauce, matzo crackers, pickled beets, crispy potato latkes, dense knishes. It's here, in the kitchen, seated in front of the spread, that Sam tells Izzy the story that gives the movie its title. One day, as his friend, lox and caviar importer Harry Shipman, was crossing Delancey Street, a gust of wind blew off his trusty cap right into the path of an oncoming truck. Leaving him no choice but to try something new, Harry ended up with a new, broad-brimmed gray felt Stetson; the very next day he got engaged. Sam intends this as a romantic parable for Izzy: "You should try a new hat sometime, Isabelle; it might look good on you."

Sam's story also speaks to the power of food, and not just because Sam tells it while they're digesting their lunch. Sam suspects Harry traded some primo nova for the Stetson. This makes perfect sense to me. My dad used to say the best smoked salmon was "like gold." I remember him humming to himself with delight and nearly dancing around the room when layering a bagel with a shmear of cream cheese and a slice of really good lox.

My happiest holiday memory, the one my mind returns to whenever I need a rejuvenating dose of warmth, is connected to the pleasure that Jewish food brought my dad. One cold winter morning a few days before Christmas 2008, I left New York for Massachusetts in a rental car at 4 a.m. in order to avoid traffic. By the time I got off the Chelmsford exit from Route 495, the sun was just coming up. The city had been dry as a bone, but my hometown was a winter wonderland, snow blanketing the common, icicles clear as crystal sparkling off tree branches in the morning light. This must be how Ebenezer Scrooge felt leaving the smog of London to revisit the rural countryside of his past, I thought.

Upon arriving at the house on Walnut Road, my parents were waiting by the door. My father was at this time fairly far along in his illness yet the memory loss hadn't yet ravaged him. I recall him uncontrollably giggling at my unexpectedly early arrival. The best was yet to come. I had precious cargo: a surprise bag of bagels, lox, cream cheese, chopped liver, and pickled herring from New York's Russ & Daughters, the Lower East Side delicatessen whose salmon, sliced right in front of your eyes to melt-in-your-mouth paper thinness, can send fish-lovers into paroxysms of pleasure. My parents' eyes lit up at seeing my sack of gold as they welcomed me in from the cold.

In my mind, I may have romanticized the moment, like it's my own personal Folgers coffee commercial—you know, the one that's been on TV during Christmastime since the eighties in which good son "Peter" creeps into the house in the wee hours of the morning and awakens his parents with the aroma of brewing coffee. When coming home to watch *Crossing Delancey* that early March, I had originally planned to surprise my mom with a Russ & Daughters smorgasbord, where I could also pick her up a pound or two of the dried apricots she loved. Perhaps some part of me wanted to re-create the memory of that Christmas past. It also seemed an apt occasion to sink our teeth into some Jewish goodies. Alas, work stresses and subway delays thwarted my plans, and I arrived in Chelmsford with nothing more than a pathetic bag of kale chips.

The gift of authentic New York Jewish food is essential to us for the way it connects to the past. I send my brother and his wife a selection of salmon every Christmas. For my mother, it's a reminder of the specialties she enjoyed growing up in the Jewish enclaves of Boston. So many of the delis and bakeries she frequented are gone. As a result she's fairly picky about the Jewish food she eats. When she had visited New York for Thanksgiving, I bought her a knish from the world-famous Katz's Deli, though her reaction wasn't the joy I expected. "That's not a knish," she begs to differ, before waxing nostalgic about the ones she grew up eating. "The meat was so delicious inside, and the outside was like phyllo dough, but it wasn't fried and it was round on top." At first I was disappointed that she was disappointed, but I can relate, because my love of Russ & Daughters' lox has nearly ruined me for all other smoked salmon. On occasion, I'll find myself humming "You Don't Know What Lox Is" to the tune of the Billie Holiday standard "You Don't Know What Love Is."

My mother can trace her cinematic Jewish pride back to 1958 when at ten years old she first saw the dark Jean Simmons melodrama *Home Before Dark* with her mother. Not only was it the first movie she had seen that dealt in any way with themes of anti-Semitism, it was also shot on location in Massachusetts, a revelation for a child who had never felt like she had seen herself on-screen. By the end of the sixties, Jewish stars were breaching Hollywood's walls in bigger ways than ever before (looking back at the era, some now call it the Jew Wave), so my mother could suddenly feel simultaneous kinship and awe with such headlining movie stars as Barbra Streisand, Dustin Hoffman, and George Segal.

Our bookshelves boasted religious philosophy books by Martin Buber, Isaac Bachevis Singer story collections, and more books about the Jewish experience in World War II–era Germany and Poland than you could hope to read in one lifetime, but the theology and belief systems of Judaism were never of much concern to my household. As I discovered after we rewatched *Crossing Delancey*, neither were they to my mother's.

"Was your family religious growing up?" I asked.

She shook her head back and forth, with a surprisingly dismissive expression that read as "feh...are you kidding?" I was somewhat surprised, as I knew she held a belief in God, but also because my guilty conscience had always led me to assume the loss of certain aspects of our heritage—of language, of ceremony, of belief in a greater power—were specific to me, as though somehow my own apathy or disinterest was to blame for this loss of knowledge; that my own lack of a bar mitzvah was the linchpin in this slow death of tradition.

Like so many Americans then and now, her family only went to religious services on holidays, and even then it was a slog. "It was *boring*," she said matter-of-factly. "And I didn't know Hebrew! I might as well have gone to a church service entirely in Latin."

When I ask her if she feels connected to her heritage, she talks with fond reminiscence about this aspect of her childhood. She summons up vivid images of past rituals, of getting dressed up for Rosh Hashanah and Yom Kippur with her parents, brother Jeff, cousin Jason, and her aunts and uncles, and walking up legendary Blue Hill Avenue through Dorchester, Mattapan, and Roxbury, the areas that had been home to much of Boston's Jewish population since the early thirties. Memories of these neighborhoods make my mother particularly wistful; they were no longer predominantly Jewish by the early seventies, when bottom-feeding real-estate companies exploited racist fears of an encroaching "Black menace," driving out Jewish residents and selling subprime mortgages to African-American families looking for affordable places to call home. Her memories fashion a story I'd like to learn more about, a perspective I'd like to take on, a narrative I'd like to one day write.

For my mother, the demographic shifts in the locales of her youth is poignant evidence of a heritage loss that is particular to the diasporic Jewish experience. "Eventually it always falls off," she says. "The problem for Jewish people is that we came here and lived in a Christian society. The Sabbath for everyone else is Sunday; for us it was Friday at sundown into Saturday, so after a while people just stop trying. Outside of tightly enclosed orthodox communities, it's impossible to maintain."

As an assimilated Jew living in a town with an extremely sparse Jewish population, I recall the oddness of having to get up in front of my elementary school classrooms every year to show-and-tell the significance of a menorah or the way to best spin a dreidel. All the while I wanted nothing more than to decorate my neighbor's Christmas tree. Never did I think such presentations were exposing anything wrong about myself, though I realized they marked me as different when, following my first-grade Hanukkah presentation, a nasty kid poked his finger into my shoulder while I was putting on my coat at the end of the day and said, "I'm a Christian, you're a Jew, you're my enemy." I was too stunned and confused to respond.

For my mother, it was the opposite. Growing up in Jewish enclaves, it was the *others* who were stigmatized as different. She told me there was a nice little girl named Kathleen, who lived across the street from their apartment in Dorchester. But Bertha didn't want her to play with Kathleen because she was Italian and Catholic. My mother still looks regretful when she talks about it.

"The Jewish girl she made me play with was an asshole," she chortles. "I really liked Kathleen. But I was stuck playing with *Barbara*." When she says the name, she looks like she has a mouth full of Lucille Ball's Vitameatavegamin. "Man, was she a spoiled brat. Her mother really thought the sun rose and set on her face."

Of course, it makes sense for communities historically targeted by bigotry and violence to stick together with almost pathological certainty and drive. Jews have been so vilified and mistreated for centuries that their distrust of other groups is a given, and for many religious communities such a closed-off, cocoon-like perception of the world persists. "If you married outside of your religion, you were considered as good as dead," my mother says, even as recently as her parents' generation.

Today, just about all my friends are in mixed marriages of one kind or another; I am at a loss to think of a single Jewish friend of mine who married another Jew, which I take as less a sign of neutralizing the faith than spreading it around. I recall worrying slightly more about my grandmothers' disappointment that Chris wasn't Jewish than that he was male.

Inspired by *Crossing Delancey*—its romance, its culture, its food—Leslie tells me she'd like to host Passover this year. It's been a few years since we've done a seder in Chelmsford, and it always feels like a special occasion, especially because growing up it was almost always at Grandma Bertha's, owner of a magical, jack-in-the-box-like table extension that could hold two entire sets of in-laws, but which was hidden away at all other times.

I was delighted by the idea of continuing this tradition in Massachusetts, but a 2020 seder in-the-flesh proved impossible. Less than a week after returning to New York, the coronavirus that had curtailed my mother's trip to Arizona had escalated into the first stages of the full-blown pandemic. I had left Massachusetts on a Tuesday; by Friday, I was quarantined for the foreseeable future in our Brooklyn apartment with Chris and Lucy. (The dog would prove delighted to have both of her daddies at home *all the time*.) Daily life was about to change drastically, and even the notion of togetherness suddenly took on a different meaning.

Passover came nearly a month into our experience of at-home isolation. Feeling like traditions were more vital than ever, we invited a group of dear friends to join us for a virtual seder. They couldn't taste my brisket, *tzimmes* with prunes and apricots, my all-day-simmering pot of chicken soup and matzo balls, or Chris's flourless citrus torte, but we could go through the motions together, reading from an online Haggadah, sharing thoughts, smiles, and words of appreciation, and reminding one another to be grateful for what we have. All seders get off to a bumbling start—especially mine—and this was no exception. Yet defenses fell, and tears welled. A few weeks of semivoluntary seclusion and a daily barrage of horrifying dispatches from the front lines of the city's overstuffed, underresourced hospitals resulted in the most emotional seder I'd ever taken part in, regardless of the fact that its participants were in five different rooms scattered about Brooklyn.

As gratifying and diverting as that Passover was, something—or someone—was missing for me. Earlier that day, while cutting up a raw chicken and covering it with water, onion, and carrots in a large pot, I was on the phone with my mother, who had been managing well in her own isolation, having had much practice as a widow of eight and a half years.

"So we're doing a Passover on Zoom," I told her. "It would be fun if you could join."

"That sounds lovely, but leave me out of it. I can't figure out the technology and I'll just get frustrated."

"But I could walk you through the steps for downloading the program, and then I could just send you the link. I could teach you. It's easy enough."

"It'll just be confusing and it won't be the same. I know everyone is doing these Skype chats or these Zoom things. I just don't have any interest."

She sounded like she was getting firmer in her refusal, but I tried one more time. After all, she recently purchased a laptop.

"It's not as hard as it seems. I could help—"

"No, Michael. I don't want anything to do with it," she said definitively. The conversation was over. "Don't worry about me. I hope you have a wonderful time with your friends."

My mother's discomfort—bordering on antipathy—toward technology was legendary. That she held her ground even in such extreme circumstances both impressed and disappointed me. Knowing that we wouldn't be able to see each other, and also that we were unlikely to complete our movie-watching project together as envisioned, made every moment of possible union seem necessary. Yet perhaps letting go of one's traditions is just as important as upholding them.

I thought about Izzy Grossman's birthday celebration in *Crossing Delancey*. When asked by her bookstore coworkers if she has anything special planned for the night, she responds proudly, "Dinner at Lutèce," referring to the famous French restaurant that would close its doors in 2004. After a cut, however, we see Izzy in line at Gray's Papaya hot dogs, a completely different kind of New York institution. "A little extra sauerkraut on hers, it's her birthday," Izzy's friend insists.

As represented in the movie, Gray's Papaya is a social leveler, teeming with people from all walks, races, and classes. The sound is wonderfully cacophonous: hip-hop from a boom box, sirens cascading in from the street, and, finally, a garishly made-up middle-aged woman in soothsayer garb serenading Izzy with Rodgers and Hammerstein's haunting "Some Enchanted Evening," a song about coming face-to-face with a stranger. The camera tracks in on the singer and on Amy Irving, who gives an impenetrable expression that reads like resentment, fear, and acquiescence all at once.

It's a scene that Susan Sandler told me she considered "Felliniesque" and it's one of my favorite moments in *Crossing Delancey*, an expression of the unexpected connections and communions we can experience every day, especially—but not exclusively—in New York. There will always be next year's seder. Until then, we will keep connecting with each other, with loved ones, with strangers, sometimes with just a glance across a crowded room.

1989: Harmony

Though I had begun taking piano lessons at age five, it wasn't until several years later that music began to open up for me. This was when my attention swerved from the maddening precision of classical music—via villainous practitioners like Brahms, Chopin, and Handel—to the wider, wonderful world of the Great American Songbook. Rather than hitting every note at the exact time as had been laid out for me by some long-dead European, I was suddenly able to improvise off chords, place my own emphasis and feeling on notes and phrases; my fingers became individuals with their own thoughts and ideas and expectations. Even if I wasn't singing the words that were written on the page, my hands were.

The music in front of me made sense now. Music itself made sense now. I loved how the lyrics played with or against the notes. I loved how a simple chord change could ascend a single word into the stratosphere. These were mostly American standards written even before my mother was born, yet they cascaded down the century, expressing for me the way that pop music becomes part of a consciousness, a means of experiencing, feeling, seeing, hearing, and remembering the world.

These songs just felt right. The emotions they imparted—of grand melancholy, of a conspiratorial, winking relationship with loneliness and abandonment—have certainly not been historically alien to the queer experience. So I cannot imagine my own incipient gay sensibility had nothing to do with my response to, say, 1959's "Ballad of the Sad Young Men." Such a song is, for lack of a better term, cinematic. You can practically see the cigarette smoke drifting through a bar bathed in chill blue and high-contrast lighting. They evoked states of being, candid psychological portraits filtered through metaphorical imagery. Rather than my eyes, though, I used my fingers to see them, to feel my way through them.

I didn't come to these songs on my own. As with movies, a love of music had been passed down to me through the generations, from my mother and her mother before her. By the time it got to me, music was very much in the family blood. This was true on both sides: my father's father was a professional musician, a clarinetist and saxophonist in the thirties and forties for a variety of big bands, including, occasionally, the world-famous Tommy Dorsey Orchestra. Tales of Papa Eddie were legendary in the house; he was never a star soloist, but the fact that he had once been adjacent to glamour—a framed photo of him and movie star Linda Darnell hung by our piano—gave off a mild thrill. Even more intriguing to me was that he had once played so many of these songs in their heyday. Surely, Papa Eddie performed "Star Dust" more than once.

"That's a good one," my mom would say about this or that, picking songs out of the piles of fake books and sheet-music singles accumulating around the piano on Walnut Road. My eyes would scan the chords and I would try them out, just hoping the song wouldn't be in the trickier keys of G-sharp or D-flat. Often I had never heard any recordings first. Years before I ever

really listened to famous renditions by the likes of Ella Fitzger-
ald, Billie Holiday, Sarah Vaughan, or Frank Sinatra, I came to
appreciate the songs by songwriter. I loved Kern the most. But
there was also Ellington and Gershwin. And Arlen and Warren. And Berlin and Porter and Rodgers and Hart. These were
songs that my mother always seemed to know intimately. How
was her knowledge of these great songs, so many of which were
before even her time, so extensive?

"My mother turned the radio on in the morning and right
through the day, all the way to dinnertime, when the evening
news came on," Leslie told me. "She also sang the songs all day,
throughout the house. I had an ear for music, I think, from the
time I was a baby. I'd hear some tune and I'd want to hear it
again."

Songs, especially from the forties, meant a lot to her, something more than just nostalgia. "I felt very close to music and
movies of that era, like it was mine," she says, although having been born in 1948 she didn't really consciously experience
the decade. "I often feel like I should have been in my parents'
generation. I would have liked to be a big-band singer, like
Doris Day."

This isn't as far-fetched a fantasy as it sounds. Gifted with a
soaring soprano, my mother showed a considerable talent early
on, and began performing at a young age, at first in the parlors
of her parents' friends and extended family members, then in
talent shows and high school musicals, including the female lead,
Nellie Forbush, in Rodgers and Hammerstein's *South Pacific* (this
is why "Some Enchanted Evening" has long had resonance for
me way beyond its appearance in *Crossing Delancey*). She continued to ply her skills during college, in community theater and
gigs at weddings and bar mitzvahs. In her early twenties, she set
performing aside to marry and start a family.

"I had never given my career enough serious thought to do
anything about it," she says. "I didn't come from a family that

understood any of that stuff. I didn't know there were oppor-
tunities. I was a complete ignoramus." Her mother pushed her
to sing locally, but there was nothing more than that, no awareness of schools where one could hone that craft, no one telling
her the importance of learning how to read music.

Nevertheless, she insists, "I don't pine for some big, fat celebrity career. I really don't."

It's May, and we're having this conversation over the phone
after viewing the final film in our time-travel project back to the
eighties: 1989's *The Fabulous Baker Boys*. It's a sunny but otherwise dismal Mother's Day. Springtime taunts from outside; the
"franken-tree" that blooms both pink and white cherry blossoms
in front of our apartment every year, and which usually hearkens
a casting off of winter gloom, has already relinquished its petals.

My mother and I hadn't seen each other in two months, and
it would likely be quite a bit longer. Stay-at-home orders in the
wake of the coronavirus pandemic made it impossible for us
to conclude our project while inhabiting the same space, and I
had no interest in defying those orders, especially after reading
a *New York Times* article in April listing atrial fibrillation—a
condition of my mother's—as one of the top COVID-19 co-
morbidities, alongside high cholesterol, asthma, and dementia.
Therefore, out of necessity, we decided to watch *The Fabulous
Baker Boys* on our respective couches, syncing up our viewings.
She pressed play on her DVD at the same time that I hit Go on
a YouTube rip of the film. It wasn't the same, but a certain intimacy remained nonetheless.

Perhaps the separation made sense for this particular selection. Out of all of the films we've rewatched in this book, it's
the one that she's always adored in a much deeper and very different way than I have. It's a movie she is drawn and feels connected to. Certainly this cannot be unrelated to the fact that its
central female character is a small-time lounge singer, and that
the film's in a constant negotiation between presenting her world

as glamorous and seedy, enviable and unpleasant. I'm struck that she says during our postmovie talk that the film "feeds into the fantasy life of a lot people—mostly women, maybe."

The Fabulous Baker Boys was released in 1989, the year my mother first began taking formal singing lessons as an adult. She was forty-one at the time, the age I'd be turning in just two months.

"I *love* Susie Diamond." It's not the first time I've heard my mother say this, in the same tone of cheerful admiration. Over the years she has consistently talked about Susie as though she's a real friend rather than a fictional character.

Michelle Pfeiffer plays Susie with her patented combination of serrated-edge toughness and eggshell-thin vulnerability. Pfeiffer's Susie is a hard-as-nails, high-priced former call girl turned Seattle lounge singer whose beauty, grit, and gumption cause serious problems for brother pianists, Jack and Frank Baker (Jeff and Beau Bridges). Jack is the loner, the tortured genius who craves artistic thrills. Frank is the family man all too happy to settle for banality and a steady paycheck. The tension between the brothers simmers and finally explodes once Susie is in the picture, and as the attraction between Susie and Jack grows. Despite the screenplay by first-time director Steve Kloves hitting all the expected notes, the fragility and unexpected nuance that the actors bring to the film lend it an emotional authenticity, enhanced by its considerable technical bona fides: the nocturnal, neon-soaked cinematography of Michael Ballhaus and the sultry, smooth, saxophone-inflected score by Dave Grusin, both nominated for Oscars. It's like the midtempo, lower-budgeted golden-age Hollywood pictures they no longer made in the eighties—and which they *really* don't make anymore.

The Fabulous Baker Boys is told from more of a male perspective than any other film in this book: the battle between the brothers—who stand for art vs. commerce, standards vs. compro-

mise, ambition vs. banality—takes center stage. Yet when Pfeiffer
shows up, fifteen minutes into the film, she slices through the
movie and the brothers' strained repartee like a freshly sharp-
ened saber. In her first, unforgettable scene, Jack and Frank have
suffered through hours of increasingly mortifying singing au-
ditions when Susie stumbles in, ninety minutes late, chewing
gum, dripping with sarcasm. "It's one of the best entrances I've
ever seen in a movie," my mom avows. After being chastised
by Frank for her lateness and lack of professionalism, she instantly turns the tables on him, looking around the sparse digs
and wrinkling up her nose: "In my mind it was a little more
glamorous." She's unafraid of instantly putting off her potential employers, and has no interest in concealing her true self to
get the job. With Jack at the ivories, she sings the 1929 chestnut "More Than You Know." She hesitantly warbles the song
but casts a spell over the brothers and us. When she finishes,
the brothers exchange a knowing glance. Susie puts her gum
back in her mouth.

Though Pfeiffer had been acting in leading roles for seven
years, starting with her striking debut in the otherwise inauspicious flop *Grease 2*, it was *The Fabulous Baker Boys* that thrust
her into the stratosphere. When the film was released in October 1989, Pfeiffer was rising in critical estimation, coming off
a Supporting Actress nomination for her role as a naive, ma-
nipulated young wife in 1988's *Dangerous Liaisons*. It would be
dishonest to deny that the manner in which a movie star pos-
sesses the screen is inextricable from that actor's looks, whether
we're discussing Vivien Leigh, John Gavin, or Lupita Nyong'o.
Yet one would be hard-pressed to find an article written about
Pfeiffer in the first decade of her stardom that didn't focus, to an
almost pathological degree, on her beauty. Roger Ebert in his
original *Chicago Sun-Times* review wrote, "This is the movie of
her flowering—not just as a beautiful woman, but as an actress
with the ability to make you care about her." The very opening

moment of her 1992 Barbara Walters interview shows her being asked, "Do you think you're beautiful?" ("Sometimes," she said, nodding in admittance, but in a way that somehow manages to come across as self-effacing.) Critic Pauline Kael said in a 1992 interview about Pfeiffer: "She's so beautiful that I think people don't want to recognize her full talent."

When one considers the inability of critics and journalists to look past the perfection of Pfeiffer's facade, it becomes rather tricky to parse her star-is-born appearance in *The Fabulous Baker Boys*. For her role as Susie Diamond, she ended up sweeping all four major Best Actress critics awards, leading to a Golden Globe win and an Oscar nomination, though ultimately losing the Academy Award to the more sentimental choice of Jessica Tandy in *Driving Miss Daisy* (the ingenue never had a chance against the legend). So much of the praise for her role was tied up in her looks, her sexiness, her brash appeal, that today it feels as though this wildly acclaimed part is somehow *under*appreciated. The most famous clip in the movie, in which Susie performs Gus Kahn and Walter Donaldson's risqué 1929 Tin Pan Alley classic "Makin' Whoopee" while slinking across a piano in a formfitting red dress and trying to make eyes with an unflappable Jack, is memorably seductive, but also somewhat uncharacteristic of the rest of the film. Shooting the scene made Pfeiffer nervous; she was fearful that it would look silly, and that she would make a fool out of herself. To say she made it work is an understatement, but she did surely in part because she remains so in control of the scene. Susie, like Pfeiffer throughout her career, refuses to succumb to objectification.

One year after *The Fabulous Baker Boys*, Pfeiffer used her rising celebrity and industry power to form her own production company. Cofounded by partner and friend Kate Guinzburg—who had worked as a production coordinator on Pfeiffer's 1987 film *Sweet Liberty*—Via Rosa Productions was specifically intended to help develop projects with strong roles for women. "No victims," Guinzburg said of Via Rosa's philosophy on character-driven movies in a *Los Angeles* magazine article about Pfeiffer from 1997. Through Via Rosa Productions, Pfeiffer ended up starring in a handful of female-headlined films throughout the nineties—the decade she became a major box-office attraction—including *Love Field, Dangerous Minds, One Fine Day, A Thousand Acres*, and *The Deep End of the Ocean*. The dissolution of Via Rosa Productions in 1999—occasioned in part by Pfeiffer's decision to spend more time at home raising her children—and the increasing scarcity of strong, mature roles for actresses in the 21st century doesn't feel like a coincidence. According to that same *Los Angeles* article, Via Rosa had two projects in development in the late nineties, neither of which would come to pass: a dramatization of a true story about a woman who went undercover for the DEA and took down a drug cartel, and an adaptation of Edith Wharton's *The Custom of the Country*. The importance of production companies formed by Hollywood players like Pfeiffer and Guinzburg—who died in September 2017 at age sixty of ovarian cancer—seems increasingly important in the rearview mirror, providing the right kind of oversight when it comes to a performer's image consciousness.

No victims. That defines Pfeiffer's post–*Baker Boys* career. Even when, on the page, her characters are literally victimized by men, as with her Selina Kyle in *Batman Returns* or her weary New York diner waitress in Garry Marshall's *Frankie and Johnny* (an elaborately altered version of Terrence McNally's play *Frankie and Johnny in the Clair de Lune*) or her hardened farmer's daughter in *A Thousand Acres*, she is the definition of resilience, overcoming past abuse to stare down life, square in its cruel face. Perhaps that's what makes seen-it-all Susie Diamond such a revelation, and such a singular creation: she may seduce an audience by stretching her body across a piano, but never do we get the sense that she's merely the recipient of that audience's look. She controls how we see her, and she gives back as good as she gets. Pfeiffer's eyes—among the most extraordinary in cinema—consistently refract our gaze. However much you think you've figured Susie Diamond out, she's probably already sized you up first.

Pfeiffer's reputation for being private and standoffish, an understandable defense mechanism in an industry that judges people based on looks, has only deepened the sense of an actor selectively and successfully cultivating her image. For someone whose name is so instantly recognizable, she's remained remarkably—and one can imagine healthily—out of the limelight. She's her own path-forger, even as a parent: in 1993, she adopted her first child, Claudia Rose, as a single working woman. She famously turned down many roles that ended up being iconic for other women, including *Pretty Woman*, *The Silence of the Lambs*, and *Thelma and Louise*, yet it's easy to speculate why the themes and images of these films might not appeal to someone so carefully sculpting a screen persona. Though she's called herself an "introvert" in interviews, Pfeiffer effortlessly conveys a confidence and strength on-screen, and never more so than in *The Fabulous Baker Boys*.

In her way, Susie is an old-fashioned, tough-talking dame, always ready with a sarcastic comeback. Once upon a time, she might have been played by the Lauren Bacall of *To Have and Have Not* or the Rita Hayworth of *Gilda*. And like those films, *The Fabulous Baker Boys* works so well because it allows the viewer to see and feel the desperation and need beneath the unflappable exterior. Kloves's film is ultimately a dark, pragmatic look at the disappointments and disillusionments of show business, set in a series of evocatively crummy city streets and threadbare apartments. None of the three main characters become stars. By the end, even after Susie has broken away from the brothers to pursue her own paychecks, they're all still creatively unfulfilled, hoofing it from one gig to the next, hoping that more money comes their way.

I ask my mother why she is so drawn to Susie Diamond. Her response takes me momentarily aback: "I love the idea that she's this wiseass broad." This takes me back to the first film of our project, *Nine to Five*, through which my mother taught me to never, ever call women broads. Now, she's wielding the word with abandon. At this moment I recall my mother's surprise upon learning, not terribly long ago, how the historically derogatory term *queer* had been recouped by LGBT people as a type of armor; similarly, as a woman, she was weaponizing *broad* in a way I hadn't heard her before.

Her adoration, even emulation, of Susie is tied not simply into her profession, but her independence and her attitude: "It's almost like a fantasy to be that much of a bigmouth."

In our postfilm telephone discussion, my mother made me realize this fantasy is more important to her than I had realized. As a child, my grandmother Bertha guided her away from friends she deemed "bigmouths," kids who didn't apply the proper amount of hands-in-lap courtesy at all times. Because of this, Leslie only became more attracted to young women who spoke their minds, and who spoke up for themselves. "I think that was the natural me, and it was suppressed," she says. "I wasn't allowed to contradict my mother. I couldn't say no, I couldn't say 'I don't want to,' and I wasn't allowed to close my bedroom door."

She still speaks with pride and astonishment when she recalls that, in the fourth grade, she yelled, "You go to hell," to a group of taunting girls in the schoolyard. "It's a good thing no teacher was around. If my mother found out I had swore, I would have been beaten, probably. But that was the real me."

Mostly acquiescent, Leslie spent her childhood doing what she was told, and this frequently included singing on command. She recalls starting at a new school in the third grade and on the first day feeling mortified when the teacher called her up in front of the room. "A little birdie tells me you have a nice voice. Would you sing for the class?" That little birdie had, of course, been her mother. Though embarrassed, she did it. "I was like a performing seal. When I was told to sing, I sang." It wasn't until she was fourteen that she first spoke up for herself, assuming enough courage to rebuff her mother amid a family gathering: "Never ask me to sing in someone's house again."

By the time she was singing semiprofessionally while attending Boston University—hired out for parties, weddings, showers, and B'nai B'rith events—she was able to start equating performing with independence. She remembers the first time that she brazenly tested boundaries was during the 1969 season she spent working as both performer and server in the cabaret of a summer stock at the famous Falmouth Playhouse in Cape Cod. Before burning down in 1994, the theater, a New England outpost for top talent from the New York theater world, had been a Massachusetts cultural institution since its opening in 1949. As with stories of Papa Eddie, I have long been fascinated by this chapter of my mother's life for how she came in contact with stars, meeting and interacting with a host of large-screen luminaries. Today, their names would be unknown to many, but to me Myrna Loy (a "sweetheart," she swears), Richard Castellano (just three years away from being immortalized as Clemenza in *The Godfather*), Constance Towers, Imogene Coca, and young Bruce Davison (future Oscar nominee for the groundbreaking AIDS drama *Longtime Companion*, which would have an impact on me so many years later), were blown up to mythic proportions.

The young performers were required to wait tables between putting together shows for the guests. She had lied about her age in order to land the gig. Mistakenly, she let the truth slip out when she announced her upcoming 21st birthday in earshot of the manager. "He started shaking. I thought he was going to hit me," she tells me. "I can't believe I actually got out of there alive."

I had never heard this anecdote before, and was suddenly

amused by the thought of my mom as a rule breaker. She seems delighted to recount the story to me over the phone. She says she was terrified in the moment, though I'm sure she would have preferred to respond with a Susie Diamond shrug and a chewing-gum pop. She might have turned to the manager and said, "So, who wants to know?" Or maybe: "Age is a state of mind, Charlie." Or perhaps: "Take a buck outta my tip jar." Who doesn't want to sneer like Stanwyck? Who doesn't want to flourish like Pfeiffer? I can't help but wonder if these fantasies—of being part of a lounge act, of being a little mouthy, of not caring what men think—are, like so many of our dreams, movie-made.

After marrying, having her first baby, and moving into the house on Walnut Road, Leslie had put her singing career, along with her full-time administrative work at the hospital, in the rearview mirror. Yet by the late seventies, she was itching to flex her vocal muscles again. Her first step was to purchase a piano, an old clunker she got for a bargain from an ailing, retired music teacher in the neighborhood. Her plan was to take lessons and finally learn how to read music. But too busy raising her kids, she gave up. The piano collected dust in the basement, an odd relic that became a kind of toy for my brother and me to bang on.

By the time I was five, she noticed that my banging was becoming a little more deliberate, a little more measured. I grew fascinated by the instrument, wanting to make pretty sounds rather than noise; by age five I was begging for lessons.

As the years wore on, and I became more invested, the piano moved upstairs into the living room. I went through phases of loathing and loving it. Like any child, I grew frustrated with getting the fingering right on Beethoven's "Für Elise" and Bach's "Well-Tempered Clavier." But the discovery of Gershwin's "Someone to Watch Over Me" was transformative. There was a wit, an earnestness, and an ease to it. One popular standard led to another: "Bewitched, Bothered, and Bewildered," "On the Street Where You Live," "My Heart Stood Still." Soon enough, my mother was joining in, and I was learning how to accompany a singer, an entirely different kind of skill, in which the playing both guides and depends upon another.

Our musical cooperative went beyond the wit and politesse of the Great American Songbook, as she passed down her love of Stevie Wonder, The Beatles, Aretha Franklin, Whitney Houston, Michael Jackson, Barbra Streisand, Joni Mitchell. In the spirit of equity, as I grew into teenagehood and began to expand my music horizons, I found myself making her mix tapes and CDs of my latest discoveries. She claimed to enjoy my onslaught of R.E.M., The Smiths, and Blur, though I've long been convinced she was being overly courteous and conciliatory. As with movies, sharing music with my mother, in the years before coming out of the closet, was a kind of unspoken testing of boundaries, a gauging of her potential interest in unfamiliar things. If she responded at all to the fey, resolutely nonmasculine stylings of bisexual artists like Morrissey or Michael Stipe, did that mean she could be eased into an acceptance—or more importantly, an understanding—of my general taste? (No matter that, in regularly playing the entire song score from *Carousel* on the piano, I had probably given myself away long ago.)

Leslie began to perform more regularly as she approached fifty, singing with local jazz bands, joining nearby theater troupes, and taking parts in revues of songs by Tom Lehrer or Rodgers and Hammerstein. She costarred as Cole Porter's wife in a musical called *Red, Hot, and Cole*, in which she had two sultry solos, including "In the Still of the Night." My father, always a content and proud audience member, would accompany her to nearly every rehearsal and performance, watching from the back of the theater with a smile permanently beaming on his face—his patience and support an eternal part of his charm. She took great pleasure in this creatively reinvigorating period, though with a full-time secretarial office job, she must have been more overextended and exhausted than I could have appreciated at the time. I recall, however, being impressed by her professionalism and skill—and intrigued by her consorting with an entirely new group of acquaintances met through the theater: extroverted, artistically inclined people so far from the types I was used to seeing. The talented actor who played Cole Porter was the first openly gay man I had ever knowingly met—he wouldn't remember me, but his tangential presence, his anomalousness, stands out in my mind like a sparkling emerald underwater. I don't remember his name.

My mother's singing renaissance had begun as the eighties came to a close, the same year as the release of *The Fabulous Baker Boys*. Entering her forties, Leslie knew she wasn't destined to be Susie Diamond. But she also hadn't really wanted to be someone like Susie Diamond. She says she felt rewarded by family life. Before the nineties were up, however, my brother and I would both have graduated high school and would be out of the house, and by the first year of the new century, my father would begin falling, quite suddenly and unexpectedly, into the deep depression that was the first sign of the illness that would stretch over the entire next decade. Throughout all this, music was an enormous release for her, a source of catharsis and pride.

In one of the more poignant memories for me during this period, Chris and I were in from New York for a weekend one summer. We drove with my parents up to York, a charming beach town in southern Maine where my mother had a gig. My husband, my father, and I, along with a small but welcoming crowd of weekend pleasure-seekers, sat on folding chairs on the grass, watching my mother sing a set of standards, including, if fuzzy memory serves, "My Funny Valentine." She was standing on a gazebo, surrounded by the traveling Chelmsford jazz band, mic in hand; down the stretch of beach you could see the buzz and clamor of distant ice cream shops and arcades. The weather could not have been more perfect, with a slight breeze coming off the water, cooling the backs of our necks as the sun began to set. I remember my father's broad smile as he gazed up at his wife performing, a look of complete contentment.

The pleasure of the moment lingers even now, but that day would prove fleeting. That night, on the lengthy drive home, my father grew panicky. The car was low on fuel, he was a little confused, and we got momentarily lost. What was the right exit? Could we find a gas station open this late? Where would this unfamiliar back road take us? My parents, who just a couple hours ago had been lost in magic-hour musical bliss, devolved into nervous bickering on the pitch-black highway. A fantasy life, immediately followed by the actual one, and an unsettling development for the traveling salesman who knew every New England road like the back of his hand. It was the first time I had seen the increasing alterations in him that my mother had been living with, a harbinger of the changes to come.

I'm an audience member. I watch. I can never truly get in the head of the performer, can never understand where that adrenaline comes from. The thought of the crowd stretching out before me, seeing viewers' expectant faces rather than the backs of their heads, instills a kind of primal terror in me. Having to give film lectures, introductions, and Q&As has been a source of recurring panic. My most frequent nightmare over the years has been of performing Shakespeare before a full house and forgetting every line. My mother's fearlessness on a stage has always underlined the most essential difference between us. It's something I aspire to. Her fantasy of embodying Susie Diamond's brazenness isn't too far a leap from who she already is; for me it seems outside the realm of possibility.

The summer I turned forty, I decided to start taking singing lessons of my own. Thanks to stints in karaoke party rooms, I found I could carry a tune, but I had no finesse, no mastery, and singing made me tired. I had kept this from my mother until

Chris and I, and a handful of friends, took her out for her first karaoke trip during a New York visit for her seventieth birthday. Never having sung in front of my mother, and more than a bit mortified to do so, I got up the courage to belt out Stevie Wonder's "Lately," a rather depressing breakup song but a strong showcase ballad. Her calm, measured, and immediate response, paired with a knowing smile, was: "You should take lessons." I received her words as compliment, insult, and challenge all at once.

It would be more than a year, but eventually I took her up on that challenge. Her singing teacher back in Massachusetts, an associate professor of voice at the Boston Conservatory, recommended a former student working as a private tutor in Brooklyn. Never have I felt less confident in my singing abilities than when I strained my way through some sample tunes in front of the clearly patient, compassionate teacher, Annie. And never had I more acutely felt my forty years than during the months of lessons I took, during which I tried to strengthen and project my voice, and would feel so exhausted at the end of a session that I would nearly faint. I was taken by surprise at the physical and emotional exertion, and how many different parts of my body would have to be incorporated: my back, my legs, my feet, my neck, my chin. I had to find a way to sing *out* but also *down*, to plant my feet firmly on solid ground while letting my voice rise up. All contradictions, it seemed to me, and so much to keep in my head when it felt like I should be letting go.

I really could never tell whether or not I was getting the hang of singing, but I was sufficiently thrilled by the novelty of doing something out of the ordinary as I entered my fifth decade on Earth. About nine months along in my lessons, I was feeling comfortable enough that I began planning to do the heretofore unthinkable: allowing my mother to hear the fruits of my vocal labors. Perhaps I'd sing one of the pieces I had been practicing with my teacher: Giacomo Carissimi's "Vittoria, mio core!" or

Giuseppe Giordani's "Caro mio ben," 17th- and 18th-century Italian arias, respectively, the words of which I was learning phonetically.

Of all the personality traits that remind me of how different I am from my mother, this is the one that creates the biggest gulf. I could never really be a performer. I could never be a brassy broad. I could never get out of my own head long enough to even fantasize about being a Susie Diamond. Imagine if I got up the courage to sing for my mother. Imagine if I could let go of my self-consciousness, even for the length of a short Italian aria. Imagine if I could stop myself from being embarrassed for once. Better to stay at the piano bench, keep my mouth shut, and hide behind my fingers.

I could think of no better time to head into this unknown realm than the weekend I was going to come home for *The Fabulous Baker Boys*. Perhaps I could create a grand climactic performance for this book, a showstopping denouement, a reminder of all the ways we connect, a loving tribute to how movies, music, art bring us together despite the essential realities that keep us apart. I don't think I decided to learn how to sing for anyone other than my mother. I could picture how it would play out: I would sing, nervously at first, but I would get into the rhythm. I'd be sweating buckets, as I always do when I'm the center of attention, whether reciting, performing, lecturing, or talking in a business meeting. She would applaud, and encourage me to continue my lessons, but she'd also be practical, reassuring me that I had a long way to go.

You know how the story ends: life snuck up on us. On everybody. Since we weren't together for the movie, I didn't sing. Just as I hadn't brought the bag of bagels and lox for *Crossing Delancey*. Of all the havoc wreaked by the coronavirus, the inability of a mother and son to watch a movie together is *extraordinarily* low on the list of indignities. Still, as I sat here in early May 2020, thinking back on all the films and conversations we had had over the past sixteen months while trying to finish our little project, rewatching movies that meant so much to me, or to her, or to us, and allowing them to kindle conversations, re-alizations, and revelations that we never had, I began to feel ir-retrievably sad.

We had rightfully taken on the act of "social distancing," but we hadn't mastered the art of it. Since our lives had largely been confined to our apartments, viewing movies together-but-apart had become a challenge to conquer among various groups of friends. There was Netflix Party Tuesdays, which, considering the minimal selection of classics on the streaming service, de-volved, rather entertainingly, into "garbage movie night." Then there was Midnight Movie Fridays, with a separate, even more sarcastic roundelay of pals live-chatting movies on WhatsApp, digging our talons into selections from our childhoods that held up about as well as a bridge made of toothpicks. (Woe to the unfortunate soul who tries to wade through the mind-boggling racism and homophobia of *Crocodile Dundee* in 2020.)

With my mother, it was different. I hadn't *seen* my techno-phobic mother, even through a screen, during these months of quarantine and separation. Unlike seemingly everyone else I know, she cannot and will not be contained in a computer frame. So our process of watching our final movie couldn't be any more complicated than "press Play, talk after." At the same time, it felt somehow right that our final movie conversation for this project be conducted over a technology not consider-ably more advanced than the phone, which brought together Aurora and Emma in *Terms of Endearment*. (It seemed like we watched that a lifetime ago.)

As *Terms* attests, though we may make up our own lives far from home, we're never fully detached. In our apartment in Brooklyn sits an electric Yamaha piano, a gift as cherished as any I've ever received, a surprise from my husband. It's a token of our love, and it is ours to share, but it also hums with the reverberation of every Ellington or Rodgers song I ever played on the piano at Walnut Road. Our home is scattered with mementos and reminders that, like all of us, I am made up of my parents' leftover parts.

When I look at my prized, beautifully illustrated hardcover book on the making of *Fantasia*, I wonder if I would have been as obsessed with the film if my mother hadn't instilled in five-year-old me the excitement *she* felt when she first saw it as a college kid in the late sixties. I wonder *when* I would have come to *2001: A Space Odyssey* or *Citizen Kane* or *Vertigo* if she hadn't shown them to me first. Would they have been stodgy, studied texts from a cinema studies class rather than part of an expansive education right there on my couch? I wonder how much my love for the rhythms and cascades of a song inspire and cross-pollinate with my obsession with the structure and sway of cinema. I wonder how much of my emotional and aesthetic needs and desires came from nurturing, and how much they were naturally part of me.

These are mysteries, never to be solved. Just as my queerness— a term I use beyond sexual preference—feels both implanted in me from a young age and made up of a series of ever-developing social determinants, taste is clearly formed both within and without. Many of the filmmakers who would influence me as a "grown-up" searching for his identity—artists like Chantal Akerman, Terence Davies, and Tsai Ming-liang—may remain enigmas to Leslie. Nevertheless the aesthetic sensibilities they cast off contain similar properties as movies that she showed me, movies that unlocked passageways into thinking about how seeing and being were one and the same, movies that taught me about the moral contours of the world without ever devolving into moralization.

Leslie didn't have a career on the stage or screen, but her life has nevertheless been shaped by music and by movies, and my life, as a result, has been created around that shaping. Neither of us will ever be famous, neither of us will ever be in the movies, but we've had a life in pictures nevertheless. This is hardly unique. I would love to learn about how everyone I know is also a mosaic of all they've seen and heard, all they've given and taken and shared.

When I was growing up, our family didn't own a camcorder. But my father rented one, just for the weekend of my fifth birthday: July 1984. The casual, prosaic images he captured would become the only document of my childhood, immortalized on one precious VHS tape.

I remember the contents of the videocassette like narrative movements in a scripted drama. There's the incriminating camera-test prologue, in which I'm nattering and squirming, screaming at my mother off-screen that I *don't* want watermelon, and hyperactively performing for the camera while my brother tries to deliver a quiet monologue he never gets to finish. Then there's the next day's birthday party, in which I'm surrounded by a group of other five-year-olds in paper birthday hats out on the deck my dad built. He's forty-one, the age I am now, and looks incredibly young as he takes burger and hot dog orders for the barbecue. Then there's the entirety of the professionally staged puppet show in the basement playroom, featuring a fabric, wide-grinned hostess named "Pat-a-Cake," an elaborate surprise never to be repeated. Then, after a bit of fuzz, there's the next day's family gathering, an extraordinary image of grandparents and great-aunts and -uncles resurrected, milling about the backyard, nonchalantly eating potato chips and talking about the hot weather.

A couple of days in our lives, the only ones ever commemorated in moving images: nothing monumental happens, yet everything in it feels monumental. It's our only movie, the only moments of which we have moving visual evidence. Sometimes it feels like this was the only real day of my youth. It's here, it's tactile, it's recorded. Every other memory is faulty, given to the whims of the fragile mind—impossible dreams of some other kid's youth.

Today—when kids the same age I was when I first saw *Nine to Five* are wielding cameras more sophisticated than the one my dad rented—I think of this video as though it's some sort of skeleton key. But what does it really unlock? It shows the way we moved, the way we interacted, talked, and squealed and joked. It provides proof that we were once together, there, in that house. More than that it makes us the momentary shining stars of our own narrative. It's a significant movie, one of the great movies of the eighties, if you ask anyone in my household, even if it never won any Oscars and even if the cinematography is a bit lacking.

What's most surprising is how little my mother is in it. She appears briefly at the beginning, mugging at my dad's insistence, inhabiting some invented character named "Blanche," wearing an unattractive rain hat. She quickly exits stage left, as she has work to attend to in the kitchen. Later, at the party, she's seen wandering around the deck, but again she is too busy going in and out of the house tending to all of us kids to really make any kind of visual impact on-screen.

A casual viewer of this one portrait of our lives might wonder why my mother is so invisible, so sidelined. After all, she's central to everything, the one who held it all together. She clearly was the mastermind behind that party: sending out the invitations, hiring the puppet master, ordering the cake, buying the hot dogs, wrapping the presents. Stardom is elusive here as ever, but she's clearly the star of this show. Just like she was the real motivating force—the star—behind all of the movies we watched, each of which tells her story as much as its own. It's impossible for me to think of Aurora Greenway, Violet Newstead, Jewell Ivy, Izzy Grossman, or Susie Diamond without thinking of my mother. Her experiences elucidate theirs; their dramas clarify hers.

Near the end of the second decade of the weird 21ˢᵗ century, it was reassuring to reenter the matriarchal utopia of the films my mother and I watched in the eighties. Had *Terms of Endearment* or *The Color Purple* prepared me for an eventual reckoning with mortality? Did *Come Back to the Five and Dime, Jimmy Dean, Jimmy Dean* lay any groundwork for my seeking out questions of identity? Did *Country* open up for me a sense of the importance—and precariousness—of home, and did *Crossing Delancey* encourage me to question my own cultural identity once I was out of that home? Movies don't have to "help" us to be worthwhile; they should not have to be "good for you"— they have the ability to hold too many complex, contradictory emotions to be seen in such prescriptive terms. At the same time, to be human is to seek answers, and art can enrich the search.

You know those days when everything feels grim and pointless? Of course you do. Maybe it's because your father died. Maybe it's because your mother is sick. Maybe it's because you've always felt a little different, like you don't know who you are. Because you were born into a world that's always defined itself by political and social rules that you never agreed to in the first place. Because a leader has failed us, or a friend has disappointed. Maybe a pandemic has made touching a loved one impossible. Or maybe you just woke up that morning and had a hard time seeing the light at the end of the tunnel. But then you watched or heard something you loved, or that challenged or inspired you. Maybe you didn't feel better, but you saw something else, and momentarily felt outside of your own body and mind.

This is how it is, and this is how we are, and while movies— despite so often being called "escapist"—cannot truly provide an escape from our darkest thoughts, they can allow us to better define the world we live in, and thus the world we choose to create around us. I don't believe in bromides that movies can "change the world." I do believe that movies can instill desire, define love, enhance vision, and give us the sense that, if we look at them with generous eyes, we become part of the grand narrative, and that the watcher is as essential as the watched.

Epilogue

Barbra Streisand has come up a lot this weekend. This is hardly unusual in the Koresky household, as would presumably be the case for any American family parented by Jewish Baby Boomers. For members of the tribe, especially those born during or soon after World War II, the Brooklyn-born *meeskite* turned mainstream music titan and movie star, who conquered the recording and film industries and won every imaginable award—a Tony and Emmy here, an Oscar and a Grammy there—is not merely an extraordinary talent but a symbol of promise, possibility, and then-unheard-of upward mobility. As her star rose in the sixties, her "ethnic" looks became an armor rather than a hindrance, a representation of shifting American beauty standards, and an implicit suggestion that Jewish women could break through if given the chance.

Streisand was everywhere in my house: on record album covers, on books and VHS cassettes and CD box sets, on taped television concert specials. My father adored her as much as my mother did. So while today my continued love of Streisand might seem pro forma for any red-blooded gay American, my respect for this diva extends from a time when I was unaware of her worshipped status in the queer community. She's simply an icon, a given—not a singer, but *the* singer—and nothing could allow her to relinquish her grip on our cultural or personal narrative. After all, *Funny Girl* was the movie my parents saw on their first date.

It's early September, a few days before Labor Day; following a sweltering summer spent mostly indoors, the air carries with it the promise of fall. There's so much to talk about, and we do—a world turned upside down by a pandemic, a country rocked by renewed fights for racial equality, an upcoming election that feels unimaginable, nearly paralyzing in its importance. But there's also Barbra. I become acutely aware at one point that our recurring conversations about her are there as distraction. The state of things has us tentatively grasping at hope, tainted by despair and overall fatigue.

Chris and I have traveled to Chelmsford in a rented car for a brief visit, Lucy in tow. The world has become so small, an encroaching gloom of gathering shadows. For us this can be momentarily alleviated by getting out of the city, being within the expanse of suburban neighborhoods that offer such exotic features as backyards and distanced houses, feeling the grass beneath our feet, looking up at swaying oaks that are blissfully unaware of things like presidential elections and that won't be felled by human disease.

It's the first time we've seen my mother since the beginning of the coronavirus crisis. Since I haven't set eyes on her virtually, I'm only just getting acquainted with her new hair, which she's letting grow out for the first time in years. The extra layers provide a blanket for the gray, giving her a more youthful appearance. We've decided to keep it safe: Chris and I are staying in a nearby hotel and only visiting her on the porch—a part of the house I've never been more thankful for. If my father hadn't built this outdoor space in the eighties, where would we be sitting, I wonder.

At one point, I look up and notice something surprising. Although summer is not over, only one of my mother's wind chimes is hanging, tinkling in the warm breeze that has made this outdoor visit so pleasant. I inquire as to the whereabouts of the wind chimes, which usually glissando and clang in breezy symphony, and which customarily stay up through October.

"They all broke," she tells me, a melancholy admission. They had frayed to the breaking point or rusted to dissonance.

"*All* of them?"

"All but this one." She points to the survivor, a gift Chris and I had purchased in a little shop in Wellfleet on Cape Cod some years ago, bedecked with translucent pieces of flat cobalt. As keepsakes, the wind chimes have limited sentimental value and are eminently replaceable, but in my heightened mood of nostalgia brought about by the pandemic, the absence of their calming tinkling in the breeze strikes me as strangely sad.

The death of the wind chimes is only the most delicate of all the ruptures experienced that weekend. More upending is the realization that safely distancing outside means we'll be unable to watch a movie together. It's a gaping hole at the center of the visit. We're not complaining, but its lack is palpable. She even asks if maybe, just maybe…*if we sit on the couch with enough space between us…if we're "good…"*

"That wouldn't be the smart thing to do," I sigh, practical and positive, even if all I really want to do is grab a mug of tea and watch *Crimes of the Heart* or *Hannah and Her Sisters* or *Working Girl* or one of the other, many eighties movies we never got to revisit over the past sixteen months. With just one film per year, our personal movie club of two was hardly exhaustive, and it feels as though it's only just begun.

Movies aren't on any screens, but they're in the air. They come up in conversation, like promises, expectations of a better time.

Not being able to watch movies on Walnut Road is like adding insult to injury, in light of the fact that movie theaters have been shuttered since early March. It's a development that's been downright harrowing for the cinephile community; by April, my movie-loving kin were already reminiscing about movie-going on social media as though remembering some long-lost civilization. With autumn creeping in, it began to feel downright cruel, the inability to experience movies together in dark rooms, to be able to surrender to the screen for a couple fleeting hours, just one more indignity in an era in which even hugs had grown scarce. For those of us who really love movies, who breathe and see through them and make them part of our daily discourse, who use them to make sense of the nonsense around us, this isn't a mere inconvenience—it's a dramatic shift in living. All movies right now are home movies.

Movies are beginning to seem like a thing of the past—the clock has sped up on something insidious that had already been in process. The theatrical experience of cinema had been notably in decline in the age of streaming, and the transition to home viewing only required a pandemic to cement its domination over the culture. Raised on VHS and cable, I understand the appeal—the safety, the choice, the comfort—of movie-watching at home; after all, every chapter of this book is centered around a movie my mother first showed me on videotape. Yet I firmly believe that the primal power and pull that the cinema has had over me was born in a movie theater, and I know this is especially the case for my mother, and her mother before her. Watching a movie at home is like reaching toward some impossible memory, the outline of a past experience, the sketch of a lost dream. Movies were invented to be light projected onto a dark wall; they're meant to arrest us in time, to envelop us in longing, or fear, or laughter.

Movies are also a business. The health of the American film industry is reliant on the health of the public and its willingness to show up. There had been innumerable articles written that summer about whether Hollywood can weather this storm, whether people will come back to the movies when and if they widely reopen. Christopher Nolan's would-be summer blockbuster *Tenet* had become the linchpin of the query: Is it worth potentially risking one's life to venture to a functioning multiplex to see it? And if enough people think it is, would *Tenet* be able to "save" Hollywood? My imagination hasn't been captured by these questions. Perhaps it's because I'm indifferent to übermasculine movie spectacles, even and maybe especially during a pandemic.

If mainstream American moviemaking goes back to business as usual, we'll continue to see goofy animated franchises with supplemental merchandising, endless streams of superhero spinoffs and sequels, and big-budget products whose reasons for being stem from "Intellectual Property" ownership rather than artistic ambition. What will we continue to *not* see? The kinds of movies that my mother showed me growing up, the films we revisited in this book—movies fronted by women, by adults, movies about the negotiations of life, the heartaches, movies about togetherness and love and identity that don't have to signal their virtues as such but just reflect who we are and why that's important as a matter of human course.

Hollywood's gradual move away from films about and starring women has been a process concurrent with its moving away from movies about human beings. When did Hollywood's producers start thinking we'd stop caring about other people's stories? In the nineties, there remained traces: my mother and I would admire the neurotic command of Gen X-er Winona Ryder in *Reality Bites*, the undaunted strength of Angela Bassett in *What's Love Got to Do With It* and *Waiting to Exhale*, the deceptively folksy brilliance of Frances McDormand in *Fargo*. The new millennium has been a different story, an evolution—or a degradation, depending on one's perspective—of Hollywood into a group of mutually devouring conglomerates that make decisions based purely on profit motive in the hopes of eventually monopolizing the industry. The 21st-century renaissance of eighties queen Meryl Streep—my mother's generational peer, born less than one year later—as a bona fide middle-aged female movie star, for instance, has been endlessly gratifying, although her dominance has been as reliant on her box-office track record as any positive or sentimental feelings about her. As has always been the case in Hollywood, hers is a rare and precarious perch, and anyone is a flop away from being cast out of the kingdom. Today, that kingdom seems beleaguered, withered, and relinquished of its domination.

My mother and I are debating the relative merits of *Hello, Dolly!* which Chris and I had both managed not to watch until a few weeks earlier. I'm making the point that while the movie adaptation of the toe-tapping Broadway musical is often turgid and overblown, Streisand is the best thing about it despite being miscast at age twenty-six as seen-it-all matchmaker Dolly Levi—she's usually played onstage by a middle-aged diva. My mom has not been able to get past this casting since the film came out in 1969. Later, my mom tells me she had streamed Streisand's most recent concert on Netflix, and goes off on a contemplative aside about how much her mezzo-soprano has changed as she's aged into her mid- to late seventies. Streisand's voice is now deeper, smokier, more strained, but still beautiful and full of character. It carries a lifetime of experience, joy, disappointment, and power, even if it is no longer the thrilling instrument it was when she burst out of the gate singing "A Sleepin' Bee" on *Tonight Starring Jack Paar* in 1961. My mother remembers Grandma Bertha proclaiming at the breakfast table the next morning: "I've never heard a voice like this in my life. She was so *ugly*. But if you closed your eyes and didn't look at her, it was the most beautiful thing." She must have thought that was the ultimate compliment.

Barbra comes up yet again. We've picked up our trays for lunch at a local outdoor restaurant with picnic tables—a lobster roll and a pulled pork sandwich—and after we've removed our masks, it doesn't take long for us to get into one of our extensive movie chats, prompted by nothing more than habit and enthusiasm. We've been talking about the historical lack of female directors in Hollywood, and how we've for too long taken the industry's patriarchal dominance as an unquestioned given. My mother asks me a pointed question: "Well, when *did* women start making movies in America?"

As she so often does, her phrasing and directness makes me feel like I'm being treated as though I have all the answers about movies, when in fact I'm sometimes at a loss. I tell her about the historical exceptions that have long proved the rule: Dorothy Arzner, the legendary lesbian director, who was half welcomed into the boys' club of Hollywood in the twenties and thirties, before her career unceremoniously ended in the early forties and she left town; Ida Lupino, the movie star turned filmmaker, who directed smart, tough, economical dramas and genre films under her own independent production company in the forties and fifties; Shirley Clarke, whose low-budget experiments in the sixties, movies about marginalized people that skirt the line between documentary and fiction, are among the jazziest, most daring American movies ever made.

If we're talking about mainstream contemporary Hollywood, however, one must tip one's hat to Streisand, whose eighties directorial debut *Yentl* was a significant box office hit despite being an ultra-Jewish, pretty queer, feminist period musical set in Eastern Europe. The film confirmed her as a movie mogul and established her as an accomplished filmmaker, but even one of the world's biggest stars had to "audition" as a filmmaker for her studio, sending in proof-of-concept footage; was forced to work at scale; and was refused final cut by the studio—impossible to imagine for such male actors turned directors of the day as Robert Redford and Warren Beatty.

Yentl has begun to strike me as an essential addendum for a book featuring ninety percent films directed by men as it's a cornerstone eighties movie. But I don't think we have watched it together since I was very young—many years before I began giving it more serious consideration as a bold expression of an iconoclastic woman forging untrendy paths in a male-dominated industry. Perhaps when we start watching movies together again, we can go back through the decade, with all new alternative selections. We can start over again.

As we sat on the porch, the neighborhood quiet, the late-summer sun casting shadows across the lawn, I asked her, "How does it feel to be the subject of a book?"

I wasn't sure she fully knows just yet the extent to which she's central to each chapter, which I've only recently started to let her read. Finally sharing these words with her has provoked not a little bit of anxiety in me.

She quickly responds, "I'm not embarrassed about anything. I'm out there. I'm definitely a Leo."

"But do you find your life interesting enough to be in a book?"

She stops and considers. I hear the single wind chime swaying in the breeze. She answers, "Everybody, every single human being in the world, has a story. They're all interesting stories."

It has always annoyed me when someone tells me I talk about movies too much. My response is that talking about movies is talking about life.

Time has a way of settling things. For all the fears that had sprung up over the course of the last year, my mother's health seems fine. After some tough starts, her medications are working, and despite living alone as a widow during the most socially isolating moment in our country's recent history, she seems to be in good spirits.

There is clearly so much left to uncover, so many questions these films didn't allow, indulge, or impress me to ask over the course of the project. I never asked her what the experience was like living in the house alone after my father was gone, or about the experience of going to therapy for the first time after his death. We never talked specifically about her status as an older sister and her relationship with her younger brother, an essential part of her personality. We never went in-depth about what it was like growing up in the tumultuous sixties, echoes and embers of which are everywhere in today's America. I never asked her how it really felt to lose one friend to suicide, and another to ovarian cancer. I never asked her what it was like to fall in love.

I imagine there are movies that will one day give me the courage to do so.

★ ★ ★ ★ ★

Acknowledgments

Writing any book is terrifying, but the anxiety and self-doubt can be exponentially greater when the nature of the project is so personal. It's much easier for us critics to disconnect ourselves from our subject, to do everything we can to turn the gaze outward. So it's with unspeakable heapings of gratitude that I acknowledge those who helped guide and encourage this book along its wending way, convincing me of the concept's worth. None of these guiding lights burned brighter than my brilliant and beautiful husband, Chris, whose love and support are about as central to my life at this point as air and water.

It's not remotely an exaggeration to say that *Films of Endearment* wouldn't exist without the wisdom, support, and tenacity of Farley Chase, who peered through what surely must have seemed like a pile of preliminary thoughts—a mere incantation for a book rather than coherent narrative—and saw something that gave off enough of a shimmer to make it worth excavating; and John Glynn, whose emotional acuity, warmth, and editorial discernment have made the book immeasurably better. Both of them continually pushed me to go deeper, and the results undoubtedly reflect their spirited engagement. Without the vivid memories of Farley's and John's faces separately lighting up at the idea of the book, I never would have had the fortitude to continue. Further thanks to Peter Joseph and the rest of the amazing team at Hanover Square Press—Rachel Bressler, Eden Church, Laura Gianino, and Linette Kim—for their unflagging support and enriching enthusiasm for this odd personal project.

I have to pinch myself sometimes because so many writers who have been personal inspirations for me have also been kind enough to help see this book through to its final stages. My deepest and somewhat amazed thanks go out to Mark Harris, Durga Chew-Bose, and Wesley Morris, and to Molly Haskell, whose writing on women in American cinema basically set the template and the historical record for all future generations; we're just dancing in her shadow.

My sincerest thanks to the wildly accomplished Susan Sandler and Patricia Resnick for their time, their candor, and for writing two of the movies that partly defined my childhood and also likely helped shape how I see the world.

Writing may be a solitary endeavor, but none of us writes alone, so important are the voices and minds of the writers and artists who are constantly floating around us, helping to clarify and justify all that we do. Some of us are lucky enough to have such writers and artists as friends. So I wouldn't be honest if I didn't thank Melissa Anderson, Ari Aster, Andrew Chan, Ashley Clark, David Connelly, Julien Allen, Shonni Enelow, Neal Block, Dan Fetherston, Michael Garofalo, Bronwyn Cunningham, Eric Hynes, Tim Lightell, Aliza Ma, Danielle McCarthy, Stacy Meichtry, Roberta Mercuri, Adam Nayman, Asha Phelps, Nick Pinkerton, Nicolas Rapold, Suzanne Scott, Andrew Tracy, Genevieve Yue, and Farihah Zaman for always supporting my work and for pushing me to be better, either explicitly or by example—and of course to Jeff Reichert for always and eternally being a phone call or a Zoom away at my best or worst moments.

Apologies to Jonathan, Lisa, Uncles Jeff and Ric, and Karen and Sam—you're family or at least the closest thing to family, and you may be minor characters in the book, but there isn't a chapter that isn't fully imbued with at least one of you. You're all dearer to me than you know. And speaking of relatives, thank you, Jason, for making the time to tell me a little more about our gnarled family tree.

Finally, if you've made it this far, you'll understand why it seems almost ridiculous to mention my mother here, since you know and she knows that this is all for, about, and in a certain sense, by her. So I'll leave this spot for my dad. He may actually have read this book, not necessarily because I wrote it but because it was about his favorite subject: Leslie, who brought a smile to his face and put a song in his heart every day, even in the darkest times.

—October 31, 2020

Sources and References

Introduction

Haskell, Molly. *From Reverence to Rape: The Treatment of Women in the Movies*. New English Library; University of Chicago Press [second edition]. 1974.

1980: Work

"Classic Interview: Dolly Parton for *9 to 5* 1980." Interview with Dolly Parton [video]. *The Bobbie Wygant Archive*. http://bobbiewygant.blogspot. com/2012/06/classic-interview-dolly-parton-for-9-to.html.

"Lily Tomlin Explains Why She Turned Down Coming Out on Time Magazine." Interview with Lily Tomlin and Jane Fonda [video]. *The Ellen DeGeneres Show*. January 15, 2019. YouTube. https://www.youtube. com/watch?v=QjmApP4i8ZM.

Neary, Lynn. "A Cup of Ambition and Endurance: *9 to 5* Unites Workers Across Decades." NPR. July 11, 2019. https://www.npr. org/2019/07/11/738587297/a-cup-of-ambition-and-endurance-9-to-5-unites-workers-across-decades.

"Nine @ 25." Interview with Dolly Parton, Jane Fonda, and Lily Tomlin. *Nine to Five*, DVD. Twentieth Century Fox Home Entertainment. 2005.

Rapkin, Mickey. "The One and Only Jane Fonda." *Du Jour* magazine. Spring 2015 issue. https://dujour.com/news/jane-fonda-interview-pictures/2/.

Shabecoff, Philip. "March of the Nine-to-Five Woman." *New York Times*. March 29, 1981. https://www.nytimes.com/1981/03/29/business/march-of-the-nine-to-five-woman.html.

Syme, Rachel. "The Original Six: The Story of Hollywood's Forgotten Feminist Crusaders." *Pacific Standard*. February 26, 2016. https://psmag.com/social-justice/the-original-six-and-history-hollywood-sexism.

Vilanch, Bruce. "The Entertainer Lily Tomlin." *The Advocate*. November 10, 2009. https://www.advocate.com/comedy/2009/11/10/entertainer-lily-tomlin.

1981: Mommie

Alda, Rutanya. *The Mommie Dearest Diary: Carol Ann Tells All*. Self-published, CreateSpace. 2015.

Brandt, Harry. "Box Office Poison." *Independent Film Journal*. May 1938.

Colman, David. "To 'Mommie Dearest,' a Twisted Mother's Day." *New York Times*. May 10, 1998. https://www.nytimes.com/1998/05/10/style/to-mommie-dearest-a-twisted-mother-s-day.html.

Crawford, Christina. *Mommie Dearest*. William Morrow. 1978.

Dunaway, Faye. *Looking for Gatsby*. Gallery Books. 1998.

Lester, Peter. "Dunaway Does Crawford." *People*. October 5, 1981.

Newquist, Roy. *Conversations with Joan Crawford*. The Citadel Press. 1980.

Riedel, Michael. "Faye Dunaway Fired from Broadway-bound *Tea at Five* for Slapping Crew Member." *New York Post*. July 24, 2019. https://nypost.com/2019/07/24/faye-dunaway-fired-from-broadway-bound-tea-at-five/.

Sontag, Susan. "Notes on 'Camp.'" *Partisan Review*. Fall 1964.

Spoto, Donald. *Possessed: The Life of Joan Crawford*. William Morrow. 2010.

"The Revival of Joan." Interview with Frank Yablans. *Mommie Dearest*, DVD. Paramount Home Entertainment. 2006.

1982: Found

Gardner, Caden Mark. "Body Talk with Willow Maclay: Conversations on Transgender Cinema Part VIII." Interview with Willow Maclay. *Daffy Duck in Hollywood*. September 22, 2018. https://daffyduckinhollywood.wordpress.com/2018/09/22/body-talk-with-willow-maclay-conversations-on-transgender-cinema-part-viii/.

Sterritt, David [ed.]. *Robert Altman: Interviews*. University Press of Mississippi. 2000.

Thompson, David [ed.]. *Altman on Altman*. Farrar, Strauss and Giroux. 2006.

1983: Lost

Brooks, James L., Penney Finkelman Cox, and Polly Platt. Audio commentary. *Terms of Endearment*, DVD. Paramount Home Entertainment. 2019.

Farber, Stephen. "Where There's Smoke, There's a Fiery Actress Named Debra Winger." *New York Times*. July 6, 1986. https://www.nytimes.com/1986/07/06/movies/where-there-s-smoke-there-s-a-fiery-actress-named-debra-winger.html.

MacLaine, Shirley. *My Lucky Stars: A Hollywood Memoir*. Bantam. 1995.

McMurtry, Larry. *Terms of Endearment*. Simon and Schuster. 1975.

1984: Home

Canby, Vincent. "Screen: *Country*, with Jessica Lange." *New York Times*. September 28, 1984. https://www.nytimes.com/1984/09/28/arts/screen-country-with-jessica-lange.html.

Drinkard, Jim. "House Democrats to Hear from Three Actresses on Plight of Farmers." Associated Press. May 2, 1985. https://apnews.com/article/ed7e2db6bb85cfc01879876687a7d248.

"Interview with Jessica Lange" [video]. KOLN/KGIN-TV (Lincoln, Nebraska). October 1984. YouTube. https://www.youtube.com/watch?v=mLDGtMHFujA.

Jones, Chuck. "Amid Trump Tariffs, Farm Bankruptcies and Suicides Rise." *Forbes*. August 30, 2019. https://www.forbes.com/sites/chuckjones/2019/08/30/amid-trump-tariffs-farm-bankruptcies-and-suicides-rise/?sh=469083462bc8.

O'Kane, Caitlin. "'Your Life Matters': Suicide Prevention Hotline Number Carved into Family Farm's Corn Maze." CBSNews.com. https://www.cbsnews.com/news/your-life-matters-suicide-prevention-hotline-number-carved-into-family-farms-corn-maze/.

"Task Force on Agriculture." Jane Fonda, Jessica Lange, Sissy Spacek testimony before Congress [video]. C-SPAN. May 6, 1985. https://www.c-span.org/video/?125430-1/task-force-agriculture.

1985: Garden

Breznican, Anthony. "Steven Spielberg: The EW Interview." *Entertainment Weekly*. December 2, 2011. https://ew.com/article/2011/12/02/steven-spielberg-ew-interview/.

Ebert, Roger. "Whoopi Goldberg: *The Color Purple*." Interview with Whoopi Goldberg. *Chicago Sun-Times*. December 15, 1985. https://www.rogerebert.com/interviews/whoopi-goldberg-the-color-purple.

"How Whoopi Goldberg Landed the Lead in *The Color Purple*." Interview with Whoopi Goldberg [video]. *Oprah's Master Class*. Season

4, episode 402. June 1, 2014. http://www.oprah.com/own-master-class/how-whoopi-goldberg-landed-her-role-in-the-color-purple-video.

Madison III, Ira. "Elizabeth Banks Gets Dragged Over *The Color Purple*." *The Daily Beast*. June 16, 2017. https://www.thedailybeast.com/why-elizabeth-banks-diversity-plea-failed-so-miserably.

"Oprah Winfrey on Breakout Role in *[The] Color Purple*." Interview with Oprah Winfrey and Thandie Newton [video]. *Variety*. June 6, 2017. https://variety.com/video/oprah-winfrey-color-purple-thandie-newton/.

"Oprah Winfrey Part 2." Interview with Oprah Winfrey [video]. *Oprah's Master Class*. Season 1, episode 110. April 3, 2011. http://www.oprah.com/own-master-class/oprah-winfrey-part-2.

Walker, Alice. *The Color Purple*. Harcourt Brace Jovanovich. 1982.

1986: Monsters

Carroll, Noël. *The Philosophy of Horror: Or, Paradoxes of the Heart*. Routledge, Chapman and Hall, Inc. 1990.

Superior Firepower: The Making of "Aliens," featuring interview with Sigourney Weaver and dir. Charles de Lauzirika [video]. Twentieth Century Fox Home Entertainment. 2003.

1987: Kids

Faludi, Susan. *Backlash: The Undeclared War Against American Women*. Crown Publishing Group. 1991.

Jermyn, Deborah. *Nancy Meyers: The Bloomsbury Companions to Contemporary Filmmakers*. Bloomsbury Academic. 2017.

Keaton, Diane. *Brother and Sister: A Memoir*. Knopf. 2020.

Love, Heather. *Feeling Backward: Loss and the Politics of Queer History*. Harvard University Press. 2009.

Nelson, Maggie. *The Argonauts*. Graywolf Press. 2015.

Russell, Candice. "Bringing Up 'Baby Boom[…].'" *Sun-Sentinel*. November 8, 1987. https://www.sun-sentinel.com/news/fl-xpm-1987-11-08-8702040515-story.html.

1988: Lox

Carter, Graham. "Joan Micklin Silver on Casting *Crossing Delancey*[…]." *Filmmaker Magazine*. July 17, 2018. https://filmmakermagazine.com/105642-joan-micklin-silver-on-casting-crossing-delancey-and-steven-spielbergs-role-in-getting-the-film-made.

Friedman, Lester D. and Brent Notbohm [eds.]. *Steven Spielberg: Interviews*. University Press of Mississippi. 2000.

McBride, Joseph. *Steven Spielberg: A Biography*. Simon and Schuster. 1997.

White, Edmund. *The Beautiful Room Is Empty*. Knopf. 1988.

1989: Harmony

Brantley, Will [ed.]. *Conversations with Pauline Kael*. University Press of Mississippi. 1996.

Dougherty, Margot. "Michelle's Odyssey." *Los Angeles Magazine*. September 1997.

Ebert, Roger. "*The Fabulous Baker Boys*," review. *Chicago Sun-Times*. October 13, 1989. https://www.rogerebert.com/reviews/the-fabulous-baker-boys-1989.

The Barbara Walters Special with Michelle Pfeiffer [video]. ABC-TV. March 1992.